The Resilient Enterprise

The Resilient Enterprise

Overcoming Vulnerability for Competitive Advantage

Yossi Sheffi

The MIT Press
Cambridge, Massachusetts
London, England

To Anat

Additional material can be found at www.theresiliententerprise.com

First MIT Press paperback edition, 2007

MIT Press books may be purchased at special quantity discounts for business or sales promotional use. For information, please email special_sales@mitpress.mit.edu or write to Special Sales Department, The MIT Press, 55 Hayward Street, Cambridge, MA 02142.

This book was set in Sabon by SNP Best-set Typesetter Ltd., Hong Kong
Printed and bound in the United States of America.

Library of Congress Cataloging-in-Publication Data

Sheffi, Yosef, 1948–
    The resilient enterprise : overcoming vulnerability for competitive advantage / Yossi Sheffi.
        p. cm.
    Includes bibliographical references and index.
    ISBN 978-0-262-19537-9 (alk. paper)—978-0-262-69349-3 (pb.: alk. paper)
    1. Business logistics—Management. 2. Strategic planning. 3. Competition. I. Title.

    HD38.5.S547 2005
    658.7—dc22

                                                    2005040875

10 9 8 7 6 5

Contents

Preface to the Paperback Edition

This book arrived in stores shortly after August 2005, when Hurricane Katrina hit the U.S. Gulf Coast. The aftermath of Katrina accentuated many of the lessons in the book, particularly those which discuss organizational culture.

In many cases it takes a while for organizations to detect that a significant disruption may be in the works, even when they are warned about it in advance. While the 9/11 Commission demonstrated the failure of U.S. intelligence agencies to "connect the dots," there was ample warning about Katrina. Seasoned forecasters warned of the impending disaster days ahead of it. Yet New Orleans did not order evacuation on time, Louisiana did not call the National Guard or the U.S. military, and the Federal Emergency Management Agency (FEMA) was late and ineffective in its response. On the other hand, organizations like Wal-Mart, Home Depot, Procter & Gamble, and Mississippi Power performed superbly and effectively.

Some argue that this performance disparity demonstrates the superiority of the private sector, which is subject to competitive forces. But one of the organizations mentioned is a utility, which is not subject to normal market forces. Furthermore, not all public sector agencies or even all agencies of the Department of Homeland Security faltered. The U.S. Coast Guard (USCG) performed heroically and quickly. In fact, during a normal year the USCG saves about 4,000 people across the U.S., while during the first few days following Katrina's landfall, the USCG saved over 33,000 people.

To understand why the USCG was so successful, it is enough to look at their principles of operations. High among them are on-scene initiative and flexibility, characteristics that explain their "can-do" attitude and success in saving so many lives on the Gulf Coast.

Mississippi Power restored power to 195,000 customers in just 12 days, and provided their own security, food, and shelter to the 11,000 workers they brought in from the rest of the U.S. and Canada to assist the local contingency of 1250 employees. While FEMA was still struggling to organize a bus convoy from New Orleans, all customers in Mississippi Power's service area were up and running. A "can-do" attitude, smart improvisation, and decentralized decision-making were the keys to restoring the power.

These same principles helped Procter & Gamble salvage the largest coffee plant in the world—the Folgers plant in New Orleans. The plant lost its electric supply, water supply, port of entry, rail and trucking distribution links, and workers' homes. Yet within less than six weeks the plant started production and was fully operational a little over two months after Katrina hit.

Many of Katrina's lessons are rooted in organizational culture, which is difficult to define. Chapter 15 offers several characteristics of resilient organizations' cultures, including communications, empowerment, and passion for the work. Resilient companies communicate obsessively. This is particularly important considering that they let decision-making take place at the lowest level of their organizations, with employees who are facing the disruption directly. Most importantly, a resilient organization has a strong value system and employees who really believe in it, and thus are passionate about the organization's mission.

Such organizations, whether public or private, can overcome disruptions for competitive advantage—and for the public good. With this paperback, I hope that even more readers will learn how—when things go wrong—the resilient enterprise can respond, help, and prosper.

Preface

This book examines the ways in which companies can recover from high-impact disruptions. The focus is on the actions they should take to lower their vulnerability and increase their resilience. A notion borrowed from the materials sciences, resilience represents the ability of a material to recover its original shape following a deformation. For companies, it measures their ability to, and the speed at which they can, return to their normal performance level following a high-impact/low-probability disruption.

After 9/11, governments around the world elevated the fight against terrorism to the top of their agendas. The U.S. government reorganized its defense and intelligence agencies and adjusted its foreign policy for that mission. In contrast, the private sector quickly went back to business. The daily pressures to perform—worrying about yields, supplier performance, machine up-time, customer requirements, product launches and market response—quickly overtook most terror worries.

Yet in the United States, and increasingly in Europe, most of the economic infrastructure, such as transportation, energy, retail, manufacturing, and finance, is in the hands of the private sector. In early 2002, a group of researchers and several corporate members of MIT's Supply Chain Exchange program began a series of discussions to address the rising concerns about terrorist disruptions. It quickly became apparent that there are no clear management guidelines, models, or theories for corporate security and resilience. These discussions spawned a three-year research effort that culminated in this book.

As the research progressed, it became clear that the study needed to expand to include different kinds of disruptions. Many random phenomena, such as earthquakes, floods, and accidents, have just as much impact on a company as a terrorist action. Furthermore, the high frequency of general disruptions provided more data for the research.

Questions raised as part of this research effort include the following:

- How should companies define and prioritize threats?

- What are the common characteristics of all high-impact disruptions?

- Can companies prepare without knowing the type of disruptions they may face?

- How should companies maintain lean operations, which aim to reduce redundancy, without increasing vulnerability?

- Are intentional disruptions fundamentally different from accidents and random phenomena?

- How can disruptions be detected when so many simultaneous events are taking place in the normal course of commerce?

- How can a company build in flexibility so that it can be resilient?

- Should companies always prefer multiple suppliers to single-sourcing?

- What new risks and rewards affect collaboration in this new world?

- What is the role of corporate culture in resilience?

- How can security investments support the main mission of the enterprise? Can they be cost-justified?

This book sheds light on all these questions and more. It is a call for action based on the experience of many companies—those who did well in the face of disruptions and those who faltered. Furthermore, a company is typically a citizen of its supply chain. Thus, the book answers many of these questions with emphasis on the extended enterprise—the web of suppliers, manufacturers, distributors, retailers, transportation carriers, and the other participants in the process of bringing products to markets.

Acknowledgments

This book is a product of a research project conducted between 2002 and 2005 at the Center for Transportation and Logistics (CTL) at the Massachusetts Institute of Technology (MIT). The project was funded, in part, by the U.K. government through the Cambridge-MIT Institute (CMI) to study the impacts of disruptions on supply chain operations. In addition, the following companies have contributed funds through the Integrated Supply Chain Management Program at the CTL: Avaya, Helix, Intel, Lucent, Monsanto, Proctor & Gamble, and Texas Instruments.

The project was directed by Jim Rice of the CTL. Jim contributed with leadership, vision, and able day-to-day management of the project. He also managed the interviews and the interaction with the many of the companies and executives who contributed to the research effort and to the book. In addition, he edited, commented and pushed. Without him this book would not have been written.

Dan Dolgin offered ideas, comments and editing throughout the project. Andrea and Dana Meyer organized the material, added many examples, and put on paper many of the early drafts. Scott Campbell edited various versions of the text and made invaluable suggestions. Nicole Blizek collected and checked references. Yali, my brother, was very generous with his time, providing unique access to senior Israeli executives.

Many students participated in the project and the fruits of their labor show up in many parts of the book. They include Abby Benson of the 2005 class of the Master of Engineering in Logistics (MLOG) at MIT, Deena Disraelly (MLOG 2004), Chris Picket

(MLOG 2003), Reshma Lensing (MLOG 2003), Chris Hamel (MLOG 2003), Sophi Pochard of the 2004 Technology and Policy Program at MIT, and David Opolon of Ecole Nationale Supérieure des Mines de Paris and Federico Caniato of the Politecnico di Milano, who were visiting students at MIT at the time.

The interactions with Dr. Helen Peck and Professor Martin Christopher of Cranfield University were informative and useful.

Several of my colleagues at MIT participated in the various conferences conducted as part of this study. They include Professors Richard DeNeufville, John Deutch, Dan Hastings, Dan Roos, Joe Sussman, and Steve van Evera.

Many corporate executives have contributed significant time and ideas to the research effort. In particular, Steve Lund of Intel, Dr. Debra Elkins of General Motors and Phil Spayd of the U.S. Customs and Border Protection were actively involved in various stages of the project. Additionally, many members of the UPS organization shared their experience with the research team generously and willingly.

Other executives, researchers and government officials devoted time and provided insights. They include Dave Grubb and Mike Princi of Accenture, Bob Scholtz of Agilent Technologies, Steve Anderson of Anderson Risk Analysis, Earl Agron and Chris Corrado of APL, Dean Harper of Avaya, Paul Tagliamonte of Bose, Phil Licari of Boston Scientific, Tim Boden, Ian Hamilton, Dennis Luckett, and Frank Stone of BT, Robert Gecielewski of C. H. Robinson Worldwide, Jamie MacIntosh of the Civil Contingencies Secretariat in the U.K. Cabinet Office, David Lacey of Consignia, Steve Potter of CSX, Con O'Sullivan of Cummins, Bruce Riggs, and Stuart Smith of Dell, Ofer Lichevski of Egged, Nissim Malki of El Al Airlines, Shlomo Sherf of Electra, Dave Hempen of Energizer, Douglas Witt of FedEx, Mark Everson of Ford Motor, John Dinsmore of GE Aircraft Engines, Rick Dufour, and Datta Kulkarni of General Motors, Tom Cummings, Jim Hutton and Don Patch of Gillette, Rob Fantini of Hasbro, Charles Chappel and Janet Rosa of Helix Technology, Tony Gentilucci, Patrick Scholler and Fred Smith of Hewlett Packard, Glen Gracia of Hill and Knowlton, Bob Byrne of IBM, Jay Hopman, Jim

Kellso, Mary Murphy-Hoye, and Dan Purtell of Intel, Mike DiLorenzo of Jabil Circuit, Peter Gartman of Limited Brands, Vince Freeman of the London Metropolitan Police, Joe Belle-feuille, Kapil Bansal, Rob Draver, Dan Fischer, Hector Lozano, Sita Nathan, and Steve Sherman of Lucent Technologies, Tim Cracknell of Marsh McLennan, Cleo Pointer of Masterfoods, Steve Wooley of Nike, Mike Wolfe of North River Consulting Group, Rich Widup of Pfizer, Larry Curran of Pinkerton Consulting and Investigations, Bill Castle of Procter and Gamble, Joe DeLuca and Rob Shepard of Reebok, Scott Dedic of Seagate Technology, Mike Lech of Shaw's Supermarkets, Alan Fletcher and Bill Tenney of Target Stores, Amit Wohl of Taro Pharmaceutical Industries, Keith Hodnett, Ann Lister, Rod McPherson and Tom Shields of Texas Instruments, Bob Bergman, Jordan Colletta, Tom Flynn, Daniel Franz, Dick Germer, Chris Holt, Joe Liana, Dan McMackin, Debbie Meisel, Dan Silva, Dan Silvernale, Marty Stamps, Ken Sternad and Albert Wright of United Parcel Service, Vice Admiral Vivien S. Crea of the U.S. Coast Guard, Charlie McCarthy of Volpe National Transportation Center (U.S. Department of Transportation), and Dee Biggs of Welch's.

While I was writing this book, my colleagues and the staff at the MIT Center for Transportation and Logistics held the fort ably, demonstrating that the best assets of any organization are its good people. Thanks go to Chris Caplice, Joe Coughlin, Ken Cottrill, Jarrod Goentzel, Larry Lapide, and David Riquier. I am particularly grateful to the capable administrative staff at CTL, led by the resourceful Mary Gibson with Lisa Emmerich, Will Garre, Kim Mann, Paula Magliozzi, Nancy Martin, Becky Schneck-Allen, and Karen van Nederpelt.

My wife, Anat, provided encouragement, editorial comments, daily shipments of coffee from Dunkin' Donuts, and loving support throughout.

My sincere thanks to them all.

Naturally, all information provided and views expressed here are my sole responsibility.

I

When Things Go Wrong: Disruptions and Vulnerability

1

Big Lessons from Small Disruptions

On Friday night, March 17, 2000, a line of thunderstorms rolled through the desert city of Albuquerque, New Mexico. When lightning lit up the desert sky, one bolt struck an industrial building that housed a distant outpost of Philips NV, the Dutch electronics conglomerate. The furnace in Fabricator No. 22 caught fire. Immediately, alarms sounded inside the Philips plant and at the local fire station. Sprinklers went off and Philips-trained staffers rushed into action. In less than 10 minutes, the fire was out.

By the time the firefighters from Albuquerque Fire Station 15 arrived, they had nothing to do. "All we did was walk in and check it out," said firefighter Ray Deloa. "It was fully extinguished by their staff."[1] After the standard safety check, local firefighters agreed that the situation was under control. So the firefighters filled out their paperwork and left the scene.

A routine investigation showed that the fire had been minor. Nobody was hurt and the damage seemed superficial. The blaze did not make headlines in Europe, did not appear on CNN, and did not even appear in the Albuquerque newspapers. The fire had been extinguished, but the real drama was yet to begin; few would have imagined that it would affect the future of two Scandinavian companies.

The Spreading Impact of an Extinguished Fire

To the firefighters' experienced eyes, the damage seemed minor. Compared to the devastation created by a full-scale fire, this small blaze was hardly worth the firefighters' trip to the plant. What the firefighters did not realize, however, was that the blaze's location had once been one of the cleanest places on earth.

Philips's plant, a semiconductor fabrication plant, or fab, tolerates no dirt. "Every surface has to be completely clean," said Paul Morrison, spokesman for Philips.[2] The smallest spec of dandruff, lint, hair, or soot can ruin the delicate microscopic circuits that dominate the insides of modern electronics. Specialized air filters, cleanroom coveralls, and painstaking procedures ensure that no particle larger than half a micron[3] gets either inside the cleanroom or into the delicate machinery or silicon wafers.

But on the night of the 17th, the fire resulted in very different cleanrooms. Inside the damaged furnace, eight trays of wafers were immediately ruined. With hundreds of chips per eight-inch diameter wafer, each tray of wafers represented thousands of cellphones worth of production.

Worse, the effects weren't confined to Fabricator No. 22. Smoke had spread throughout the facility—further than Philips realized. As staffers rushed to deal with the blaze and as firefighters tramped through the facility on their inspection, their shoes tracked in dirt. The smoke, the soot, and the tramping of staffers and firefighters left the cleanroom facilities anything but clean. The contamination ruined wafers in almost every stage of production, destroying millions of cellphones' worth of chips in those few minutes.

Even worse than the loss of valuable chips was the damage to the cleanrooms themselves. "It's as if the devil were playing with us," said one senior Philips manager who was involved in the clean-up. "Between the sprinklers and the smoke, everything that could go wrong did."[4] Two of Philips's four fabricators in Albuquerque were contaminated that night. "Water and smoke creates about as messy an environment as you can imagine. Everything has to be completely sanitized," said Philips spokesperson Paul Morrison.[5]

Returning the cleanrooms to their prior pristine state quickly would be a big job. Nervous executives in Amsterdam joked about showing up in Albuquerque with toothbrushes to help scrub the fabricator themselves. "We thought we would be back up after a week," said Ralph Tuckwell, a spokesman for Philips semiconductors.[6]

The first order of business was to communicate with the plant's 30-some customers, and in particular its two most important ones—the Scandinavian cellphone giants Nokia and LM Ericsson AB—which accounted for 40 percent of the affected orders at the Albuquerque plant.

Nokia Responds to Potential Disruption

Meanwhile, 5,300 miles away in Espoo, Finland, some puzzling numbers were appearing on the computer screens at Nokia's headquarters. Shipments of some Philips chips seemed delayed.[7] On Monday, March 20, Philips called Tapio Markki, Nokia's chief component-purchasing manager, to explain the delay.[8] The Philips account representative explained the evolving situation, the fire, the lost wafers, and the expected one-week delay.

Mr. Markki was not overly concerned after that first call on the Monday after the fire. One-week delays happen in all global supply chains. Downed machinery, material shortages, production schedule errors, quality issues, shipping delays, and minor industrial accidents (like the Philips fire) can all create short delays. Such events require prompt actions, but manufacturers usually keep safety stock—inventory of parts and finished goods—so that production schedules and customer service are not disrupted. Consequently, such routine disruptions create only faint numerical burbles in the smooth global flow of goods, but they don't usually cause shortages for customers. Nokia could easily cover a short delay with existing parts inventory and shipments from other suppliers.

Although he did not see it as a major issue, Mr. Markki communicated the news to others inside Nokia, including Pertti Korhonen, Nokia's top troubleshooter. "We encourage bad news to travel fast," said Mr. Korhonen, who has worked at Nokia for 15 years. "We don't want to hide problems."[9] Mr. Korhonen decided that the situation needed closer scrutiny, even though it was not yet perceived to be a crisis. He placed the affected parts on a "special watch" list. Five types of chips from the

Albuquerque plant would receive more intensive scrutiny. Nokia would make daily calls to Philips to check the status of the evolving situation.

Mr. Korhonen also initiated a process of collaborating with Philips on recovery efforts. He suggested that two Nokia engineers in Dallas, Texas, could hop over to Albuquerque to help Philips. Philips feared that the outsiders would only add to the confusion in the disrupted plant and declined Nokia's offer.

Nokia's fears were justified when Philips called Mr. Markki two weeks after the fire to explain the full scope of the disruption. Philips now realized that it would take weeks to restore the cleanrooms and restart production. All told, it might take months to catch up on the production schedule.

At that juncture, Mr. Korhonen realized that the disrupted supplies would prevent the production of some four million handsets. Nokia was about to roll out a new generation of cellphones that depended on the chips from the infirm Philips fab. More than 5 percent of the company's annual production might be disrupted during a time of booming cellphone sales. Messrs. Korhonen and Markki quickly assembled a team of supply chain managers, chip designers, and senior managers from across Nokia to attack the problem. In all, 30 Nokia officials fanned out over Europe, Asia, and the United States to patch together a solution.[10]

The team quickly ascertained the availability of alternative sources for the parts. Three of the five parts could be purchased elsewhere. Japanese and American suppliers each could provide a million chips. Because Nokia was already an important customer of these two suppliers, the suppliers agreed to the additional orders with only five days' lead time. Expedited deliveries would help Nokia maintain production.

But two of the parts came only from Philips or a Philips subcontractor. "This was a big, big problem," Mr. Korhonen remembered realizing.[11] Nokia held meetings at the highest levels with Philips to convey the importance of the issue. When Messrs. Korhonen and Markki went to visit Philips headquarters, Mr. Jorma Ollila, Nokia's chairman and chief executive, diverted his return flight home from the United States to drop in on the meeting.

They spoke directly with Philips's CEO, Cor Boonstra, and the head of the company's semiconductor division, Arthur van der Poel.

Nokia was "incredibly demanding," according to Mr. Korhonen.[12] They demanded to know details about other Philips plants. Mr. Korhonen said that they told Philips "We can't accept the current status. It's absolutely essential we turn over every stone looking for a solution."[13]

The Nokia team dug into the capacity of all Philips factories and insisted on rerouting that capacity. "The goal was simple: For a little period of time, Philips and Nokia would operate as one company regarding these components."[14] The Finns' earnestness got results.

A Philips factory in Eindhoven, the Netherlands, would provide 10 million chips to Nokia. A Philips factory in Shanghai worked to free up more capacity for Nokia's needs. Nokia engineers developed new ways to boost production at the Albuquerque plant, creating an additional two million chips when that plant came back on line.

Through its extraordinary efforts and intensive collaboration with its suppliers, Nokia was able to avoid disrupting *its* customers. Handsets ultimately kept rolling off Nokia's assembly lines, onto store shelves, and into the hands of consumers.

Ericsson Waits for Parts
Across the Baltic Sea, Nokia's arch rival, Ericsson, also bought a sizable number of Philips's chips for its cellphones. The two companies have a long-time rivalry. Not only do Ericsson and Nokia compete in building cellphones and cellular networks, Ericsson and Nokia are each a source of national pride for Sweden and Finland, respectively. Because Sweden controlled Finland from the early sixteenth to the early nineteenth century, the two countries have an intense, ongoing rivalry.

As a major customer of Philips, Ericsson received the same phone call that Nokia did on the Monday after the fire. Yet Ericsson's reaction was very different. It reflected the more consensual and laid-back nature of Swedish culture, while Nokia had the more individualistic, aggressive culture of the Finns. "Ericsson is more passive. Friendlier, too, but not as fast," said one official who dealt with both companies in the fire's aftermath.[15]

Ericsson treated the call from Philips on March 20 as "one technician talking to another," according to Roland Klein, head of investor relations for the company.[16] Ericsson was content to allow the one-week delay to take its course. The company assumed that Philips would ship the chips after a short delay, that the fire was minor, and that everything would work out. Lower-level staffers at Ericsson neither bothered their bosses with news of this minor glitch nor delved further into the magnitude of the disruption.[17] Even when it was clear that the much-needed chips were significantly delayed, lower-level employees at Ericsson still did not communicate the news to their bosses. The head of the consumer electronics division (which oversaw mobile phone production), Jan Wareby, did not learn of the problem until several weeks after the fire. "It was hard to assess what was going on," he said. "We found out only slowly."[18]

By the time Ericsson realized the magnitude of the problem, it was too late. When it finally asked Philips for help, Philips couldn't provide it because Nokia had already commandeered all of Philips's spare capacity. Ericsson then turned to other chip makers for parts. But, unlike Nokia, the company didn't have alternative suppliers available for the chips that had come from the stricken Albuquerque plant.[19] With semiconductor sales running hot in the spring of 2000 and Nokia's lock on all spare capacity, Ericsson failed to obtain needed parts from other sources. "We did not have a Plan B," conceded Jan Ahrenbring, Ericsson's marketing director for consumer goods.[20]

End Result

Philips's lost sales of the high-margin, high-tech chips resulting from the fire were on the order of US$40 million.[21] Lost sales amounted to the majority of the financial hit that Philips took from the blaze. Direct damage to the plant was offset by a 39 million Euro insurance settlement.[22]

For that reason, the direct impact to Philips was relatively minor. The lost sales amounted to less than 0.6 percent of the US$6.8 billion in semiconductors made by Philips in 2000. And, more important, the impact to Philips was minuscule compared to the impact on Philips's customers.

Ericsson bore the brunt of the disruption because it was unable to obtain secondary supplies of the disrupted parts. "These were pretty necessary components," said Kathy Egan of Ericsson.[23] In the end, Ericsson came up millions of chips short of what it needed for a key new generation of cellphone products.[24] That shortage of millions of chips meant a shortage of millions of high-end handsets. Without the high-end handsets, Ericsson had the wrong product mix for the fast-moving cellphone market. At the end of the first disruption-affected quarter, Ericsson reported losses of between three and four billion Swedish Kroner (between US$430 and US$570 million) before taxes owing to a lack of parts.[25] This immediate loss, by itself, exceeded Philips's losses by a factor of more than ten.

The after-effects of the disruption lingered for two more quarters beyond March 2000, including the critical (summer production) holiday 2000 quarter, which is ordinarily a time of high production and profitability. "That's definitely some market share that they're missing out on," said Mary Olsson, principal analyst with Dataquest.[26]

The total impact of the shutdown of the Philips plant took more than nine months to resolve. At the end of 2000, Ericsson announced a staggering 16.2 billion kronor (US$2.34 billion) loss in the company's mobile phone division. The company blamed the loss on a slew of component shortages (including the Philips parts disruption), an incorrect product mix, and marketing problems.[27]

The disruption was more than just a temporary hit to Ericsson's financial growth curves. About a year after the fire, the fallout from the New Mexico fire and other problems (with components, marketing, and design) reached a climax for Ericsson, when the company announced plans to retreat from the phone handset production market. In April 2001, Ericsson signed a deal with Sony to create a joint venture to design, manufacture, and market handsets. Sony-Ericsson would be owned 50-50 by the two companies.[28]

The fire's impact on Nokia was very different. Ericsson's inability to ship quantities of its high-end models removed one of Nokia's major competitors from the marketplace. Within six months of the fire Nokia's year-over-year share of handset market increased from 27 to 30 percent, while Ericsson's dropped from 12 to 9 percent.[29]

Although both Ericsson and Nokia were hit by the same disruption, one recovered while the other exited significant parts of the business. This example illustrates many of the concepts that are the focus of this book. The fortunes of Nokia and Ericsson were set well before the fire hit the cleanrooms in Albuquerque. Ericsson sat idle while Nokia acted. Nokia's culture encouraged dissemination of bad news; immediate action to monitor the supply of critical parts continuously helped it detect the problem early; deep relationships with its core suppliers helped rally them to fast action; knowledge of supply markets allowed it to procure elsewhere; and modular engineering design enabled the use of chips made by other manufacturers in some of its products.

The Challenge Ahead

Today's supply chains span the globe and involve many suppliers, contract manufacturers, distributors, logistics providers, original equipment manufacturers (OEM), wholesalers, and retailers. This web of participating players creates complexities, making it difficult to realize where vulnerabilities may lie. It also creates interdependencies that exacerbate these difficulties.

Consider, for example, the globe-trotting involved in manufacturing an Intel Pentium processor that powers a Dell computer.

The process starts in Japan, where a single crystal is grown into a large ingot of silicon by Toshiba Ceramics. The silicon ingot is then sliced by suppliers, like Toshiba Ceramics or others, into thin wafers that are flown across the Pacific to one of Intel's semiconductor fabs in either Arizona or Oregon. At the fabs, hundreds of integrated circuits are etched and layered on each wafer, forming individual dies on the wafers. Finished wafers are packaged and then flown back across the Pacific to Intel's Assembly and Test Operations in Malaysia. The wafers are treated and cut into die, and the dies are finished into sealed ceramic "packages." The packages are then placed in substrate trays that are put into Intel boxes and then packed again in blank boxes (to conceal that they are Intel products) for shipment back across the Pacific to Intel warehouses in Arizona. Having traveled across the Pacific three times already, the chips are then shipped to Dell factories in Texas, Tennessee, Ireland, Brazil, Malaysia, and China, or one of its contract manufacturers in Taiwan, to be used as components in Dell computers. The journey ends when the product ships from Dell to the customer's home or office anywhere in the world, amounting to a fantastic and complex global voyage.

Neither Intel nor Dell is alone in its reliance on a global supply chain. Most modern manufacturers are part of global, interwoven networks of companies involved in getting goods to markets. Responding to cost and efficiency pressures, such networks have achieved unprecedented levels of efficiency in moving information, products, and cash around the globe. Even smaller, less-known manufacturers are employing global supply chains. For example, Griffin Manufacturing of Bedford, Massachusetts, buys the fabric for its patented sports bras in Taiwan, moves the fabric to its Massachusetts plant, cuts the fabric to the required sizes on modern computer-controlled machines, ships the cut fabric pieces to Honduras for sewing, and then ships the final products to a Vermont distribution center to be tagged and distributed as Champion jogging bras to retailers across the United States.

Although responsible for high levels of customer service and low costs, modern supply chains also bear the seeds of vulnerability to high-impact/low-probability events.

The very complexity of global supply networks means that, in most cases, it is difficult to assess a priori vulnerabilities. For example, Ericsson's vulnerability to the disruption in the Philips plant was not only the result of relying on a single supplier; it was also the result of having another major industry player rely on the same supplier. When Nokia moved fast to secure all of Philips's capacity as well as the capacity of other global chip suppliers for the needed chips, Ericsson was stuck.

The vulnerability of the connected world to disruption is not limited to supply chain operations; it affects any business that depends on a reliable global communications network. On March 21, 2000, for example, a contractor laying a fiber-optic cable for McLeod Communications in Iowa mistakenly severed a U.S. West Communications cable carrying Internet traffic for Northwest Airlines. Without use of the lines, the airline was grounded—it lost booking and baggage information, along with systems that calculate the amount of weight and fuel-use of each flight and all its web operations.[30] Because Northwest Airlines also handled traffic for its code-sharing partner, KLM Royal Dutch Airlines, KLM flights in Singapore and elsewhere could not take off. Very few employees of KLM imagined that their airline operations were subject to the care with which a ditch-digging contractor in Iowa ran its business.

Another factor that increases the vulnerability of many firms is the tougher competitive environment they are in. As developing nations join the world of global commerce—and given the speed with which knowledge moves around the world—it is difficult to maintain a competitive edge based on technology or know-how. Consequently, many products are sold like commodities; because these products have many similar characteristics, buyers base their purchase mainly on the lowest prices. This leads to continuously lower prices as sellers try to capture market share by reducing their prices below the competition. For example, from 1999 to 2004 the average prices of sporting goods were down 4 percent, appliances were down 8 percent, and apparel was down 13 percent.[31]

Tough competition means not only that consumers have better choices, and that firms must work harder, but also that when an enterprise fails for any reason, others are waiting to take its place. Thus, firms have to be more resilient than their competitors. They have to invest in the ability to recover quickly from any disruption and make sure that their customers are only minimally affected.

In response to the need to provide high levels of service at low costs, many firms have attacked their idle inventory with a vengeance. Following the lead of Toyota Motor Corporation in the 1980s, they have introduced just-in-time lean operations that have brought both higher quality of goods and much lower costs.

The resulting tight operational environment, however, carries with it a price tag that is not always apparent. For example, Ford Motor Company had to idle several of its assembly lines intermittently following the 9/11 attack as component-laden trucks were delayed at the Canadian and Mexican borders. This led to a 13 percent reduction in Ford's output in the fourth quarter of 2001 compared to its production plan.[32]

At the same time, Toyota came within hours of halting production at its Sequoia SUV plant in Indiana, because a supplier was waiting for steering sensors shipped by air from Germany that were stalled because air traffic was shut down.[33] Ford, Toyota, Chrysler, and other manufacturers were vulnerable to transportation disruptions because they operated tight supply chains with little safety stock, keeping material on hand for only a few days and sometimes only a few hours of operation.

Why This Book

As supply chains are becoming more brittle and the world is growing uncertain, concerns are increasing about low-probability/high-impact events that can bring about major earning shortfalls or even unplanned exits from the business. This book is based on a research project at the MIT Center for Transportation and Logistics involving dozens of companies. It presents revealing case studies dissecting disruptive events that have affected the operations of the companies involved.

The events of 9/11 have brought home for many U.S. executives the dangers of a terror-based disruption, but accidents and random events such as severe weather or earthquakes can also cause significant disruptions. Intentional attacks are more worrisome, though, since the threat is *adaptive*—that is, increasing defenses or resilience in one part of the system will increase the likelihood of an attack elsewhere. (And intentional attacks are not limited to terrorism; on a different scale, they also include sabotage, computer hacking, and labor actions.)

The number of possible disruptions to a global supply chain is endless. Manufacturing can be disrupted directly because of a problem in a plant, a disruption at a supplier's plant, a glitch in the transportation system, a disruption to the communication and information system, or a snag with a customer. It can also be disrupted indirectly because some other disruption takes capacity out of the supply chain. Several high-technology equipment makers were shut out of chips supply during the time that Philips directed all its manufacturing to Nokia and other suppliers were trying to help Nokia as well.

When thinking about reducing a company's vulnerability to disruption, executives need to look at increasing both security (thus reducing the likelihood of a disruption) and resilience (thus building in capabilities for bouncing back quickly). Increasing security is based on the creation of layered defenses, tracking and responding to "near misses," increasing the participation of all employees in security efforts, and collaborating with government agencies, trading partners, and even competitors.

When thinking about resilience, it may not be productive to think about the underlying reason for the disruption—the kind of random, accidental, or malicious act that may cause a disruption. Instead, the focus should be on the damage to the network and how the network can rebound quickly. When focusing on resilience, then, one can look at existing supply chain designs in industries that are disrupted frequently. Such supply chains exist mostly in the high-technology and fashion industries. These industries are subject to particularly uncertain demand and thus have to develop the capabilities to respond quickly to large changes in the demand pattern. The essence of most disruptions is a reduction in capacity and therefore inability to meet demand. The situation is not dissimilar to large supply/demand imbalances resulting from an unanticipated demand spike.

To respond quickly to supply/demand imbalances companies should build in redundancy without increasing costs; they have to develop supply chains in which products are not customized to the users' requirements until the last possible point, allowing the movement of products from surplus areas to areas where there is an unmet need; they should develop part and platform commonality and modular product designs, so that the same part can be used in several products; they should increase their use of standard rather than special parts; and they should be tied to their suppliers in flexible contracts allowing for changing quantities and delivery times.

Many of these actions characterize leading supply chains in consumer electronics, computers, or fashion industries. Companies like Dell, the personal computer manufacturer, and Zara, the Spanish retailer and manufacturer of apparel, are faced with demand disruptions continuously. Because these companies and others have developed supply chains that can cope with changes, it is instructive to look at them for relevant lessons.

Robust supply chain designs, however, are not enough. Resilience is also dependent on a set of collaborative relationships with trading partners, since each enterprise is only as resilient as the weakest link in its supply chain. Suppliers whose relationship with a customer is strong, and who identify with that customer, are likely to do more to help in case of a need.

Finally, the right corporate culture—a shared passion to be successful—is a crucial ingredient in creating resilient enterprises. Such different cultures were on display during the 2002 West Coast port lockout; several transportation and logistics companies considered the lockout as a "force majeure" and did not understand that customers like Dell and Procter & Gamble (P&G) did not expect excuses but rather expected their suppliers to find solutions. The result was that Dell, P&G, and others changed several of their transportation and logistics suppliers once they found their suppliers' attitudes incompatible with their own urgent and passionate mind-set.

Disruptions can take place in numerous ways and affect companies in unanticipated manners, and at any time. To get a handle on the challenge, chapter 2 explores a framework for identifying and prioritizing vulnerabilities. The framework can be applied to determine the relative vulnerability of various firms to a specific type of disruption, or the relative vulnerability of a specific firm to various possible disruptions.

2

Understanding Vulnerability

In an average year, 134 strong earthquakes (magnitude of 6.0 to 6.9 on the Richter scale) and 17 major or great earthquakes (magnitude of 7.0 or greater) take place around the world.[1] Although many strike remote and less-developed sections, some hit major centers of economic activity. When they hit, they expose the vulnerability of global supply chains.

Living on Shaky Ground

In the predawn hours of a chilly winter morning—on January 17, 1995, at 5:46 am—the five and a half million residents of the bustling port city of Kobe, Japan, awoke in terror as the ground shifted violently beneath them. A major fault deep under an island in the Kobe Bay ruptured, shifting some seven to nine feet upward and laterally in 20 seconds of intense shaking. Older buildings with heavy tiled roofs collapsed, often damaging newer structures that had been built to modern earthquake-resistance standards.

Even before the shaking in Kobe stopped, more than 150 fires started. Ruptured gas lines, broken electrical lines, and overturned equipment started blazes in many parts of the city. Rubble-strewn roads, collapsed expressways, and damaged bridges stymied firefighters' attempts to reach many of the burning buildings. When firefighters did reach the scene, they often found the fire hydrants dry; the quake had shattered Kobe's network of water mains in 2,000 places. Had the winds been stronger that day, the entire city would have burned in a fire storm.

In all, the quake destroyed more than 88,000 buildings, injured at least 30,000 people, and killed almost 6,000. A million people lost electricity, 850,000 lost gas supplies, and 70 percent of Kobe's water and sewer systems were destroyed.[2] Even nine days after the quake, some 367,000 households and 190 factories had no water.[3] Because of the thousands of broken pipes, it took months to restore water and gas to the affected areas.

The Kobe earthquake was measured at 7.2 on the Richter scale[4]—in the range of a "major" earthquake but short of the highest magnitudes recorded[5] (such as Sumatra's 9.0 on December 26, 2004,[6] San Francisco's 8.0 on April 18, 1906,[7] and Alaska's 9.2 on March 27, 1964[8]). The full impact of the Kobe quake, however, would not be felt until days, weeks, even years afterward.

The earthquake damaged all the transportation links in and around Kobe. In particular, the world's sixth-largest shipping port was virtually destroyed on that January morning, halting one-fifth of Japan's export and import activities. The quake damaged all 22 of the massive loading cranes used to load and unload 2.7 million containers each year from transoceanic freighters,[9] and along Kobe's sprawling waterfront, only four of its 239 berths survived the morning unscathed.[10]

The port of Kobe took many months to recover, losing two-thirds of its shipping volume in 1995. Even after two years, the port was still below its pre-quake levels of activity.[11]

Vulnerability of Lean Operations

Large-scale disruptions like earthquakes illustrate companies' dependencies on a web of infrastructure connections. Phone lines, power lines, water lines, gas lines, rail lines, highways, and ports connect companies to critical services, suppliers, and customers. Damaged commuter rail systems, blocked roads, and personal needs brought high employee absenteeism in the days and weeks following the quake. Many employees just could not get to work or had to devote time to securing food, medical care, and housing for their families.

Japan's leading companies rose to industrial prominence, in part, through reliance on their vaunted lean manufacturing systems—processes that produced high-quality products with a just-in-time flow of goods from suppliers to assemblers. Japanese companies, especially leading carmakers, minimized the inventory of parts stored in their plants by synchronizing their supply chains so that parts could be delivered just in time for them to be installed in the vehicles moving down the assembly lines. But the Kobe earthquake of January 17, 1995, exposed a vulnerability of this manufacturing paradigm.

Although the Osaka plant for Sumitomo Metal Industries wasn't damaged by the quake, it lost gas and water supplies. This factory was the sole source for most of the brake shoes used by Toyota Manufacturing Company in all of its domestic cars. Because Toyota relied on lean manufacturing, it had no inventories of the parts. Lack of brake shoes halted production at most of Toyota's car manufacturing plants all over Japan as these plants quickly exhausted their supplies. Toyota lost production of an estimated 20,000 cars (representing approximately $200 million of lost revenue) as a result of parts shortages. Other Japanese car makers—Honda, Mazda, Daihatsu, Mitsubishi, and Nissan—faced similar problems with suppliers or factories in the Kobe region. These other makers lost about 16,000 cars as a result of delayed and disrupted parts supplies.[12] Even where the factories were intact, it took time to re-route truck and rail shipments around the area's shattered infrastructure.[13]

The Kobe earthquake also demonstrated the connectivity of global industry. The Japanese economy is the third largest in the world and virtually all of the world's global companies have operations there, many of them in Kobe. The quake directly affected companies such as Eli Lilly, Caterpillar, Texas Instruments, and IBM.[14] Procter & Gamble suffered damage to its local headquarters and had to shut down and evacuate its factory after gas leaked at a neighboring company's plant.

Because many suppliers to multinational companies were affected, even U.S. companies without a Kobe outpost felt the impact. For example, Apple had to slow down its production of

PowerBook computers as a result of interrupted production of display monitors in Kobe,[15] and Chrysler nearly had to shut down some U.S. production because of parts shortages.

What Is Vulnerability?

A firm's "vulnerability" to a disruptive event can be viewed as a combination of the *likelihood* of a disruption and its potential *severity*. Companies assess their vulnerabilities by answering three basic questions:

1. What can go wrong?
2. What is the likelihood of that happening?
3. What are the consequences if it does happen?

Figure 2.1 provides a way of thinking about the confluence of probability and consequences of events (the second and third questions above), such as the Kobe earthquake or the fire at the Philips plant. The vertical axis is the probability of the disruptive event and the horizontal axis represents the magnitude of the consequences.

Vulnerabilities are too varied and too nuanced, and the tools for measuring the factors are too blunt, to distill these factors easily into a single "expected vulnerability" metric. Such a metric would be the product of probability and consequences. Thus, each

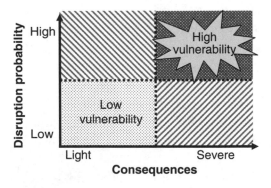

Figure 2.1
Dimensions of Vulnerability

of the four quadrants of figure 2.1 has a specific meaning. Vulnerability is highest when both the likelihood and the impact are high. Similarly, rare low-consequence events represent the lowest levels of vulnerability.

But what might appear to be a set of modest vulnerabilities may have little in common for business planning purposes. These include disruptions that combine low probability and large consequences, on the one hand, and those characterized by high probability but low impact, on the other. High-probability/low-impact events are part of the scope of daily management operations, tending to the relatively small random variations in demand, unexpected low productivity, quality problems, absenteeism, or other such relatively common events that are part of the "cost of doing business." Low-probability/high-impact events, on the other hand, call for planning and a response that is outside the realm of daily activity.

Enterprise Vulnerability to Terrorism

Different companies face different levels of vulnerability to each type of disruption. Consider, for example, a specific type of disruption, such as an anti-American sabotage or terrorist attack causing significant damage to a corporate asset. The likelihood of such an attack may be based, in part, on the extent to which the company is associated with the United States. The consequences of the attack are a function of the company's resilience and depend on the company's ability to insulate its customers from the disruption.

Using the two-axis framework, figure 2.2 depicts a hypothetical example of how different firms would have varying vulnerability to this type of attack.

As an airline with "America" in its name and flights to dozens of international destinations, American Airlines faces a relatively high likelihood of terrorist attack. In fact, two of its planes were hijacked on 9/11 and Richard Reid (the December 2001 "shoe bomber") chose to try to down an American Airlines plane.

Any airline would face a severe impact from a terrorist attack. Although the loss of a single of its several hundred aircrafts may

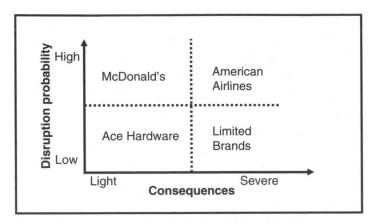

Figure 2.2
Vulnerability to a Terror Attack on Corporate Assets

not be material to the assets of the company taken as a whole, the loss of life and the consequential impact on confidence among its customers can be devastating. The attacked airline could be perceived as a favorite target of terrorists, leading to a marked decline in the demand for its services, loss of support of financial markets, and possible bankruptcy.

McDonald's also has an extremely prominent public profile as the global leader selling American-style fast-food around the world and is closely identified with the United States. Indeed, McDonald's is a very popular target for those disaffected by America's policies or concerned by the encroachment of American culture. Attacks and protests in places ranging from France and Canada to Indonesia and Turkey suggest that McDonald's faces a higher probability of attack than firms less identified with the spread of "Americanism."

But the consequences of an attack on a single (or even several) McDonald's assets are not likely to be as severe as an attack on American Airlines because of the highly distributed structure of McDonald's sprawling chain. The temporary loss of a single restaurant is not a serious blow to a company with over 30,000 outlets. Terrorists cannot even create a global food poisoning scare because each McDonald's buys food from local sources. At worst, a food tampering attack would harm the company only in a small geographic region. Thus, an attack on one McDonald's neither prevents the company from selling billions of burgers at tens of thousands of other locations nor is it likely to invoke fears by other customers that their neighborhood McDonald's might be the target of a terrorist attack.

Clothing retailer Limited Brands exemplifies a business with a relatively low risk of occurrence but possibly highly adverse consequences. Limited Brands (which owns brands such as The Limited, Victoria's Secret, and Henri Bendel) imports clothes from many countries and at one point in time used to distribute them through a single distribution center to its 4,000 retail outlets throughout the United States. Although it is difficult to imagine that terrorists would take pride in disrupting the flow of women's apparel (hence the low probability), an attack on Limited Brand's central distribution center would have disrupted the company's operations and, consequently, could have caused significant losses.[16]

Because of the structure and nature of its business, Ace Hardware faces both a low likelihood of terrorism and minimal consequences from an attack. Disrupting the local supply of nails and batteries does not have any symbolic value and the chain itself does not seem to generate anti-U.S. sensitivities. Even though it operates 500 of its stores in 70 foreign countries including Kuwait, Saudi Arabia, and the United Arab Emirates, Ace Hardware is a dealers' buying cooperative with a low profile. Like McDonald's, Ace is highly decentralized. The network's 5,100 retail outlets and dozens of distribution centers and cross-dock facilities are not vulnerable to a disruption in a single choke point. Thus, Ace is both highly unlikely to be attacked and, if an attack did take place, the consequences are not likely to be severe.

Enterprise Vulnerability

Figure 2.2 depicts the vulnerability of various firms to a terrorist attack. Clearly, different firms are vulnerable to different disruptions. For example, McDonald's may be vulnerable to a Mad Cow disease outbreak that would infect the public's attitudes toward hamburgers, but it is not vulnerable to industrial actions (such as strikes and slowdowns), because it uses franchisees rather than employees. Naturally, any firm employing union workers will be more susceptible to a labor action than a nonunion enterprise. Many large U.S. shippers (manufacturers, distributors, and retailers) routinely hedge their transportation procurement by including a nonunion, less-than-truckload motor carrier, such as Overnite Express, in the portfolio of their transportation carriers, in addition to companies such as Yellow Freight and ABF, whose workers belong to the Teamsters union. Shippers do this despite the fact that it is usually more economical to have a single less-than-truckload carrier serving any given territory, rather than split the business among two or more carriers.

Thus, different companies will occupy different quadrants of the vulnerability map, depending on the type of disruption. When a company considers the low-probability/high-impact events to which it is exposed, there are several ways to classify the risk in order to start prioritizing what managers should focus on.

Catalog of Catastrophes

At General Motors, the largest automaker in the world, 360,000 employees build over 8.5 million vehicles each year. The company's global operations span 53 countries and include vehicle sales in about 200 countries. With thousands of precision-engineered parts and electronic components in every car, and dozens of makes and models, GM procures parts through a deep, multi-tiered network from a myriad of suppliers. Managing such a large operation has put GM at the forefront of understanding the vulnerabilities of global supply chain operations. The responsibility for this process lies with GM's Enterprise Risk Management Team.

To help categorize these disruptions, GM constructed a four-quadrant map of vulnerabilities, as shown in figure 2.3.[17] The four categories include financial vulnerabilities, strategic vulnerabilities, hazard vulnerabilities, and operations vulnerabilities. The diagram also arranges the vulnerabilities on a radial, internal-to-external dimension; vulnerabilities listed toward the center of the circle tend to come from within the organization, while those

Figure 2.3
Concentric Vulnerability Map

located at the periphery of the circle tend to arise from outside the company.

GM's supply chain managers are most concerned with managing the lower two sectors: hazard vulnerabilities and operations vulnerabilities. *Operations vulnerabilities* include everything from supplier business disruptions to theft by employees. These are mainly disruptions to the means of production. *Hazard vulnerabilities* include both random disruptions (resulting from severe weather, earthquake, or accidents) and malicious disruptions, such as international terrorism and product tampering. *Financial vulnerabilities* include a wide range of macro-economic and internal financial troubles, from currency exchange fluctuations to credit rating downgrades to irregularities in the financial statements. (Naturally, every one of the disruptions in this map is likely to have a negative financial impact as well, but the emphasis here is on disruptions caused by the market, the economy, or GM's own financial mismanagement.) *Strategic vulnerabilities* include everything from new foreign competitors to external public boycotts to internal ethics violations. The focus here is on disruptions that are possibly preventable with the right strategy. In all, GM documented more than 100 types of vulnerabilities scattered across the four sectors.

GM is planning to use such vulnerability maps to construct scenarios for training managers in crisis response. According to Debra Elkins, senior research engineer in manufacturing systems research at GM: "Hopefully, we'll get to the point where we'll be able to play things off-line and do scenario envisioning rather than having to deal with the real event."[18]

The High Frequency of Rare Events

After cataloging and categorizing the different vulnerabilities, the Enterprise Risk Management team showed GM managers the list of these types of "rare events" and asked the managers how many of these types of events actually happened in the past 12 months. Virtually every one of these events had affected GM in the past year. "We went through the list and checked off, 'Yeah, we've had that one' and 'Yeah, we've had that one, too,'" said GM's Elkins. A GM plant was even struck by a tornado in Oklahoma.

While the likelihood for any one event that would have an impact on any one facility or supplier is small, the collective chance that some part of the supply chain will face some type of disruption is high. Collecting the information across the vastness of GM gave the firm a picture of its vulnerabilities.

GM's experience illustrates both why low-probability disruptions seem rare and why they are actually rather commonplace. "What we're learning is that risk is part of our daily business and we need to be good at managing it," said Elkins. Collecting the data from across the organization is the first step toward understanding how to recover and what types of plans are effective in which situation.

Learning from disruptions elsewhere does not need to be confined to disruptions within one's own organization. The same idea is the heart of the chemical industry's Safety Management Process. This process, developed in the aftermath of Union Carbide's 1984 disaster in Bhopal, India, records accidents in chemical plants across the United States. The database allows individual companies and plants to learn from the experience of all plants across the industry. A similar method is used in "near miss" analyses conducted by air forces and airlines around the world.

How Supply Chain Structures Create Vulnerability

Bad luck did not cause GM's litany of misfortunes. The inevitability of disruptions, at GM and other companies, arises from these companies' size, scope, and structure—the extent to which they are connected to the world and are therefore vulnerable to events throughout it.

Consider just one small part inside a GM automobile: the fine copper wire in the small electric power window motor inside the driver's door of the vehicle. The wire starts as copper ore, then is smelted into pure copper, alloyed to create the right physical properties, cast into an ingot, formed into a bar, drawn into wire, coated in insulating varnish, wound inside the motor, combined into a door assembly, and mounted onto the car.

With copper mines in Chile, wire makers in China, motor makers in Japan, car door makers in Canada, and final assembly in the United States, each one of these steps involves different companies in different countries. After assembly into a vehicle, the car, with the wire in that little motor in the door, is shipped to one of GM's worldwide network of 7,500 dealers for sale to the public. In all, the materials might travel tens of thousands of miles before the customer buys the car.

A disruption can strike any link in the chain—either a participant's factory; the web of transportation services that move materials and parts from source to plants and products from plants to distribution centers and to retailers; or the network of computer and communication systems that support modern supply chain operations. For any company involved in this supply chain—be it GM, the electric motor maker, or the copper smelter—the chain has three main sections:

- The *inbound* or supply side of the chain includes all the processes and suppliers responsible for furnishing the company with materials and parts.

- The internal processes, or *conversion* part, include all the activities and manufacturing steps performed inside the company's facilities.

- The *outbound* or customer-facing side of the chain includes all the distribution processes and customers of the company.

Disruptions can occur at any section of this inbound-conversion-outbound chain of companies and processes that connect raw materials sources to the ultimate end-user of the finished product.

Disruption in Supply

On the supply side, GM endured the consequences of disruptions not only to its suppliers but also to its suppliers' suppliers deep inside the semiconductor industry when a chemical spill at a chip plant contaminated a clean room and shut down production. The disrupted chip company made the little chips that go inside automobile keyless entry systems. Without the chips, the next company in the supply chain could not make the little black key fobs for GM cars. Without the keys, GM couldn't sell the cars.

Supply disruptions do not result only from disasters, however. In industries that grow very fast, capacity can be tight because of the time it takes to build new plants and bring new capacity on line. In 2000, for example, a shortage of the metal tantalum led to a three-fold price increase and a shortage of tantalum capacitors. Prized by electronics makers for their high capacity and compact size, tantalum capacitors are the capacitors of choice for cellphone and computer makers. The shortage hit these manufacturers at a time of booming demand. Lead-times of over one year meant that product makers could not get the parts they needed.

Similarly, Nissan, Japan's second biggest car maker had to suspend operations in three of its four Japanese plants at the end of 2004 because of a shortage of steel. This shortage was caused mainly by the huge demands created by the over-heated Chinese economy. Again, the shortage hit at a time of booming demand for Nissan cars following the introduction of six new automobile lines.[19]

The power blackouts of 2003 in the United States, Europe, and the U.K. illustrated the fragility of the power infrastructure. GM discovered that although the phone lines worked during the Midwest blackout of August 2003, because telephone companies had their own independent power supplies, GM's office phones—like so many modern multifunctional office phones—required electricity to function and therefore could not be used.

Disruptions in Internal Operations

Internal disruptions have a special dimension because in many cases they involve company personnel who are in harm's way. For example, a powerful tornado hit the General Motors assembly plant in Oklahoma City, Oklahoma, on Thursday, May 8, 2003. The three-million-square-foot plant suffered extensive damage, leading to GM's second quarter charges of $140 to $200 million related to lost production and facility repairs.

Internal disruptions also extend to the loss of people themselves. Akamai lost its cofounder and chief technology officer, who was on board one of the 9/11 planes. The bond trading company Cantor Fitzgerald experienced a disruption of a different magnitude when it lost 658 people in the collapse of the World Trade Center. In addition to the human toll, such tragedy involves the loss of the relationships with employees, customers, and suppliers that can be crucial to recovery efforts.

The increasing use of information technology creates vulnerability to computer viruses, software problems, and other technology outages. For example, SQL Slammer was a computer worm that spread directly to vulnerable computers on the Internet in January 2003.[20] Needing no human intervention, Slammer infected 90 percent of vulnerable hosts within only 10 minutes of its first appearance. Hardest hit were Internet service providers in

Asia. Slammer downed Seattle's 911 call center, American Express's customer service, and Continental Airlines's computerized reservation system. It also disabled almost 13,000 automated teller machines at Bank of America. In all, Slammer did an estimated $750 million to $1.2 billion in damage. Of course, information systems disruptions are not only internal; they affect companies' communications with their suppliers and customers, as well.

Disruptions in Demand

Demand disruptions typically include massive, unexpected declines in the demand for a company's products or services. These disruptions can be caused by technological changes, new competitors, disruptions to a major customer, or the sudden loss of customer confidence. In 1982, Johnson & Johnson (J&J) enjoyed a 37 percent share of the nonprescription market with its popular pain reliever, Tylenol. Then, in late September, seven people died when someone placed bottles of cyanide-laced Tylenol capsules on store shelves. Although the poisonings were confined to the Chicago metropolitan area, the company took no chances, pulling all 31 million bottles of Tylenol off the market. The news of the poisonings and the withdrawal of the capsule version of the product caused J&J's share of the market to drop to 8 percent and its stock market capitalization to drop by 7 percent. Many analysts and advertising experts proclaimed that Tylenol would never sell again under that much-tainted brand name.

J&J kept the product off the market for more than a month—using the time to redesign the packaging to prevent tampering. This included switching from powder-filled capsules (that can be easily disassembled and refilled with a foreign substance) to solid caplets. The company also redesigned the bottles to add three tamper-evident layers of protection.[21]

By the end of the second quarter of 1983, within a few months of the reintroduction and with heavy promotions, Tylenol had regained its original market share.[22] Nonetheless, J&J lost hundreds of millions of dollars because of forgone sales and added costs.[23]

A sudden, massive loss of customer confidence in a company's products can, of course, be devastating. J&J countered this with its decisive response. By contrast, Firestone and Ford took months to acknowledge the problem with the Firestone tires on Ford Explorers in 2000, resulting in tarnished reputations and lost business for both companies (see chapter 3).[24]

Naturally, demand imbalances can also include unexpected spikes in demand, leading to lost sales, bad service, and even lost customers. Such disruptions, however, are rarely catastrophic for a company.

Prioritizing Vulnerabilities

Given their complexity, modern supply chains can be disrupted in many ways. Each individual link in the chain is not likely to suffer a particular rare event, but the chances are that the chain as a whole will be disrupted somehow.

The challenge for managers is to understand and communicate this vulnerability to their colleagues and senior executives. Various graphic presentations can help managers visualize their company's vulnerability. Each provides a different view onto vulnerability in terms of how much, where, and to whom.

Figure 2.2 used a two-axis framework of likelihood vs. impact to compare the vulnerability of various companies to specific disruptions. Similar, yet differently focused, *enterprise vulnerability* maps can be used to categorize and prioritize different possible disruptions for a given company. Although it may be quite difficult for any enterprise to estimate accurately the likelihood and consequences of each disruption, such maps serve to highlight the relative vulnerability along these two dimensions, leading companies to focus on the disruptions to which they may be most vulnerable. Figure 2.4 depicts such a map for a hypothetical manufacturing enterprise.

Multinational companies realize that many disruptions are tied to geography; floods, earthquakes, political upheaval, fluctuating exchange rates, and other potential causes of disruption are

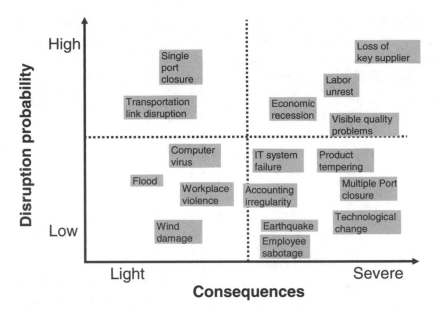

Figure 2.4
Enterprise Vulnerability Map

focused on certain geographical locations. GM is tracking the geographic content of parts to help understand the total enterprise risk of disruptions in particular parts of the world. To this end, GM follows the *bill of material*, which is a list of all the parts and quantities used in the manufacturing of each product (see chapter 5). Aggregating these data at the enterprise level helps paint the total exposure of the enterprise to countries and regions. At a minimum, a geographic vulnerability simply depicts which suppliers of what parts are located in each area of the world. Such a map can focus the company's planning efforts on sensitive regions and help it spot a problem area at a glance and respond quickly. What most companies do not have is a complete vulnerability picture that includes their suppliers' vulnerabilities.

A more advanced version of the geographic vulnerability map focuses on the connectedness of the supply chain to help understand interdependencies. Such a supply chain map highlights the flow of parts out of given regions, depicting who is involved and the plants in other parts of the world that are dependent on them.

Such a map can become a tool for understanding the extent to which a flood in Brazil will affect production in Singapore or sales in Germany.

GM uses such supply chain vulnerability maps to simulate the impact of disruptions and the efficacy of proposed mitigation efforts. The data for these simulation models are taken from the *bill of material* for all GM products. But the data also include process maps depicting the dependency between various processes across the enterprise.

GM's work on risk management offers benefits beyond dealing with disruption. Studying how the company is interconnected and how different processes affect each other helps the company improve day-to-day operations. "We've learned a lot about the enterprise as we've been working on this," Elkins says.[25] In particular, supply chain mapping can lead to identification of redundant processes, opportunities for consolidations (for example, when several divisions are buying parts from the same supplier and can aggregate their volume to achieve better procurement terms), coordination of logistics activities across plants and divisions (for example, using back-and-forth trucking services rather than one way), and many others.

What Next?

The three questions posed in this chapter regarding low probability/high-impact disruptions are:

1. What can go wrong?
2. What is the likelihood it will take place?
3. How severe will it be?

The operating consequences of these questions are:

1. What should managers focus on?
2. What can be done to reduce the probability of a disruption?
3. What can be done to reduce the impact of a disruption?

There are two ways to look at what managers should focus on. The first is to list and prioritize events (such as earthquake, hurricane, strike, and sabotage) that can lead to disruptions. The second is to list disruptions (for example, reduced production capacity, shortage of a critical part, or a severed transportation link) and analyze their causes (and consequences). The first is more useful when thinking about reducing the probability of a disruption, since the relevant actions involve treating the source of the problem. The second is more useful when considering how to recover from a disruption, since the cause may be less relevant than the consequences and their severity at that point.

What is particularly important to realize is that high-impact disruptions are not as rare as they appear. Only when focusing on a single type of disruption, like an earthquake in a particular place, are the chances low. Taken as a whole, however, it is likely that some kind of disruption will hit somewhere almost routinely at a firm that depends on a global, large, and complex supply chain. As a result, companies should focus on supply chain designs, processes, and corporate cultures that are generally resilient, in addition to assessing the likelihood and the consequences of various disruptions, and investing in security.

3

Anticipating Disruptions and Assessing Their Likelihood

One of the bedrock characteristics of disruptions is that they are almost never the result of a single failure. A large-scale disruption is usually the result of a confluence of several factors. Furthermore, there are typically many signs that a disruption is about to take place. Like the tremors that precede a volcanic eruption, these telltale signs point to an impending catastrophe. Such signs are often missed or ignored by managers. But when the conditions for a disruption are present and not addressed, the likelihood of a disruption—even a low-probability one—is not very low anymore. When the telltale signs start to appear, a disruption may be imminent even though its timing, place, and exact form may be unknown.

The Confluence of Causes

On the night between December 2 and December 3, 1984, about 500 liters of water inadvertently entered Methyl-Isocyanate (MIC)[1] storage tank #610 in the Union Carbide plant in Bhopal, India. MIC is one of many "intermediates" used in pesticide production and is a dangerous chemical. Lighter than water but twice as heavy as air in its gas form, when it escapes into the atmosphere it remains close to the ground.[2]

The water leakage resulted in a runaway chemical reaction in the tank, with a rapid rise in temperature and pressure. The heat generated by the reaction, and the presence of an iron catalyst (produced by the corrosion of the stainless steel tank wall) resulted in a reaction of such momentum that the gases that formed could not be contained by safety systems. As a result, 40 tons of MIC poured out of the tank for nearly two hours and escaped into the air, spreading as far as eight kilometers downwind, over a city of nearly 900,000.[3]

The effect on the people living next to the plant—just over the fence—was immediate and devastating. Many died in their sleep, others fled in terror from their homes, blinded and choking, only to die in the street. Many others died days and weeks later.

Most people who inhaled a large amount of MIC suffocated when their lungs clogged with fluids and their bronchial tubes constricted. The human toll has been estimated at 4,000 deaths and 500,000 lingering injuries.

The Bhopal disaster, which is often referred to as the worst industrial accident in history, did not take place in a perfectly maintained plant with a faultless safety record and well-rehearsed emergency notification and response systems. Several factors, including deteriorating safety standards, poor maintenance, and lack of training, contributed to the deadly environment at the plant. In retrospect, it was easy to see it coming:[4]

- Gauges measuring temperature and pressure in the various parts of the plant showed signs of trouble, but those gauges, including those in the MIC storage tanks, were so notoriously unreliable that workers ignored them.

- The refrigeration unit for keeping MIC chilled (intended to prevent overheating and expansion) had been shut off for some time.

- The gas scrubber, designed to neutralize any escaping MIC, had been shut off for maintenance. Even if it had been operative, post-disaster inquiries revealed that it could have handled only one quarter of the actual pressure reached in the accident.

- The flare tower, designed to burn off MIC escaping from the scrubber, was also turned off, waiting for replacement of a corroded piece of pipe. The tower was also inadequately designed for its task, being capable of handling only a quarter of the volume of the gas actually released.

- The water curtain, designed to neutralize any remaining gas, was too short to reach the top of the flare tower, from which the MIC was billowing.

- The alarm on the storage tank failed to signal the increase in temperature on the night of the disaster.[5]

- MIC storage tank #610 was filled beyond recommended capacity.

- A storage tank that was supposed to be held in reserve for excess MIC already contained MIC.

It is likely that any one of these factors, had it not failed, could have forestalled or mitigated the disaster. It took the confluence of all of them to create the environment in which the tragedy was just waiting to happen. In addition, the lack of trained doctors and the efforts of the Indian government to distance itself from any responsibility exacerbated the impact of the accident.

It's Not the Only Case

Large-scale disasters grab media headlines. In many cases, they are investigated thoroughly, revealing the various conditions and unheeded warning signs that led to the catastrophe. In other cases, the resulting lawsuits bring the story into the public eye. These investigations and court cases show how management failures to identify and remedy unsafe, insecure, or otherwise dangerous conditions are likely to foreshadow disaster.[6] Examples include the following:

1. *The Challenger Explosion*   On January 28, 1986, the space shuttle Challenger exploded in midair less than two minutes after takeoff from Cape Kennedy in Florida. The investigation blamed failed rubber "O-rings," designed to seal the joints between sections of the shuttle's solid rocket boosters. Engineers had identified and reported degraded O-ring seals on previous missions dating back to 1982, with degradation increasing as ambient lift-off temperature fell below 53°F (12°C). The night before the accident, two engineers from Morton Thiokol, the firm responsible for making the solid-fuel rocket booster, recommended against the launch and went home, convinced that the launch would be canceled. Under pressure from NASA, Morton Thiokol management overruled the engineers. The temperature during liftoff was 36°F (2°C).[7]

Most of the factors contributing to the ill-fated launch had nothing to do with technology. In 1986, NASA was under pressure to launch a large number of missions; Morton Thiokol was due an incentive pay for each successful flight; the Challenger featured the heavily publicized "teacher in space"; and the mission had been canceled the night before. All of these factors added to the pressure on NASA management and contributed to its decision to overrule the engineers' warnings and proceed with the launch. Interestingly, the Columbia Accident Investigation Board that probed the 2003 Columbia shuttle crash 17 years later concluded that "cultural traits and organizational practices detrimental to safety were allowed to develop [in NASA]."[8]

2. *The Paddington Train Crash*   On October 5, 1999, a train passed a red signal, number 109, in the midst of the morning rush hour outside Paddington Station in West London and continued for some 700 meters into the path of a high speed train. As a result of the collision and the subsequent fires, 31 people died and 227 were hospitalized.[9]

Between 1993 and 1999, eight near-misses, or "signals passed at danger" (SPADs), had occurred at the location (Signal 109) where the eventual collision and explosion occurred. At the time of the crash, number 109 was one of the 22 signals with the greatest number of SPADs.[10] In addition, the train engineer had been on the job for less than two weeks, with no special training on navigating the complicated route outside Paddington Station.

3. *The Morton Explosion*   On the evening of April 8, 1998, a nine-foot-tall chemical reaction tank ("kettle") containing 2,000 gallons of chemicals in Morton International's plant in Patterson, New Jersey, exploded. A fiery stream of gas and liquid erupted through the roof of the kettle's building, raining chemicals into the rest of the plant and the surrounding community. The explosion was the result of a runaway reaction inside the kettle, which was set to produce a run of Yellow 96, a dye used in tinting petroleum fuel products. Nine people were injured, two seriously.

The subsequent investigation revealed a series of failures. In two assessments conducted in 1990 and 1995, Morton did not consider runaway chemical reaction. As a result, workers were not prepared or trained to face a runway reaction in the production of Yellow 96; they did not know, for example, that at 380°F (193°C) the chemicals inside the kettle begin to decompose, initiating an even more violent runaway reaction. In addition, the kettle was not provided with sufficient cooling capacity. Furthermore, because a runaway reaction was not considered a possibility, raw materials were introduced to the kettle in bulk rather than in small batches, step by step. Finally, in 1996 the kettle size had been increased, making it harder to control.

But there were also telltale signs that pointed to an impending disruption. There were eight prior instances in which the process temperature in the kettle exceeded the normal range. None was investigated, even though the process and design changes resulting from any one of these investigations could have prevented the 1998 explosion.[11]

4. *The Firestone Tire/Ford Explorer Rollovers*   In August 2000, Firestone recalled 6.5 million tires and Ford recalled another 13 million Firestone tires the following year. The recall was the result of 148 U.S. deaths and 525 injuries related to tread separations, blowouts, and other problems with Firestone tires on Ford Explorer vehicles.[12] The companies spent more than $3 billion dollars on the recall.[13] Ford sales dropped 11 percent in the following year and Firestone tire sales dropped even further. (Ford lost almost a full percent of market share despite generous incentives to buyers.) A century-long relationship between the two companies ended in acrimony.

Several contributing factors have been cited as causes. The Firestone plant in Decatur, Illinois, where most of the failed tires were made, used a unique pelletized rubber process that led to lower tread adhesion.[14] In addition, the shoulder pocket[15] design of the tires could have led to cracking, creating a starting point for a tire failure. But Ford also contributed to the problem. The high center of gravity of the Ford Explorer aggravated tire separation accidents by increasing the likelihood of vehicle rollovers after a tire blow-out at highway speed. In addition, Ford recommended under-inflating the Explorer tires (30 psi instead of the Firestone's recommended 36 psi) for improved ride quality, resulting in excess wear and heat build-up inside the tires, reducing the margin of safety on tire performance.

Some of the damages to Ford and Firestone stemmed from how long it took the companies to realize that they had a problem. Each month of delay and finger-pointing between the two companies added more tires to the recall and fatalities to the toll. This issue of detection, discussed in chapter 9, focuses on how companies discover and internalize ongoing disruptive events in order to start recovery processes.

5. *The Chernobyl Nuclear Accident*   On April 25, 1986, reactor number 4 at the Chernobyl nuclear power plant blew up during a routine test of the facility, as a chain reaction went out of control, releasing 30 to 40 times the radioactivity of the atomic bombs dropped on Hiroshima and Nagasaki.[16] Over 30 people were killed immediately but tens of thousands of others were affected with radiation illness. Cities and villages around the plant had to be evacuated and 200,000 people resettled.[17] Cancer rates at Belarus and even the Ukraine are abnormally high almost 20 years after the accident.

Many factors contributed to the disaster. The RBMK[18] reactor used in Chernobyl had many design flaws: It lacked a contamination shell; it used a carbon moderator rather than water (the carbon caught fire during the explosion); and the design included a "positive void coefficient" that caused reactions to speed up rather than slow down (as in other designs) when the water in the reactor boiled. More important, the reactor safety systems were disabled prior to the test and, contrary to the requirement to use 30 rods to retain a controlled environment during the test, the operators used only eight rods. These were indications of the fundamental lack of safety culture at the plant.[19]

Interestingly, Iuri Andorpov, then chairman of the KGB, enumerated several construction and safety weaknesses at the Chernobyl Nuclear Plant seven years before the accident. In a 1979 letter, he informed the leadership of the KGB of the problems, letting them know that the Ukrainian KGB had notified the secretariat of the Central Committee of the Soviet Union's Communist Party, not only about the design flaws, but about a series of problem that caused 170 workers to suffer injuries at the plant during the first three quarters of 1978.[20]

As these examples illustrate, failure to use precursor data to identify and remedy systemic flaws can lead to a catastrophe. Even the 9/11 terrorist attacks were preceded by numerous other attacks on the United States, as well as a declaration of war by Osama Bin Laden, but none of those indicators was given the proper weight, and no official was able to "connect the dots." Each of these "dots" represented an unheeded warning sign. Confucius is quoted as saying, "the common man marvels at the uncommon thing. The uncommon man marvels at the common thing." Highly disruptive, uncommon events can often be tamed by those who make a policy of noticing the common danger signs.

It is typical to have an escalating series of failures that lead to an eventual disaster. To reduce the likelihood of future high impact disruptions, many industries have developed a management reporting and analysis system based on "near miss analysis."

Near Miss Analysis

On March 24, 2004, Prince Charles of Britain and members of his staff took off from the Northolt RAF base in west London on their way to attend the funeral services for the Madrid terrorist bombing victims. At 08:30 A.M. at 11,500 feet above Newberry in Berkshire, the military HS146 of the Queen's Flight came within less than 900 vertical feet and three horizontal miles of an Airbus A321, which was heading to Heathrow airport, coming from Cork in the Republic of Ireland, carrying 186 passengers. Both pilots and air traffic controllers recognized the potential conflict and acted immediately to avoid a midair collision. The incident was reported as a "near miss" by both pilots, as well as the air traffic controllers, to the British Civil Aviation Authority.

The aviation industry has long recognized the wisdom of learning from a mistake even when it does not cause an accident. It has established the Aviation Safety Reporting System (ASRS), which is used to collect and analyze confidential aviation incident reports that are submitted voluntarily. The purpose is to identify systemic or latent errors and hazards and to alert the industry about them. The ASRS receives more than 30,000 reports annually and issues alerts to the industry on a regular and as-needed basis. Most

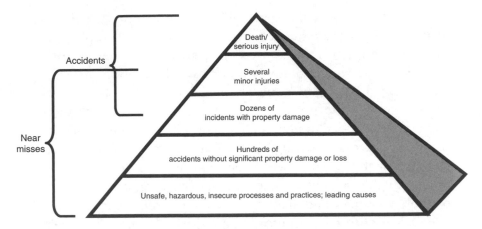

Figure 3.1
The Near Miss Pyramid

aviation experts agree that these efforts have resulted in an ever-increasing level of civilian airline safety.

A similar system of reporting and investigating near misses is used by the U.S. military and by almost every other air force in the world. The U.S. military requires pilots to report "any circumstance in flight where the degree of separation between two aircraft is considered by either pilot to have constituted a hazardous situation involving potential risk of collision."[21]

Figure 3.1[22] depicts the notion that numerous unsafe conditions and insecure processes can lead to hundreds of minor incidents or close calls. When these are not addressed, the result is likely to be dozens of incidents involving some property damage, leading to several major incidents involving large property damage and minor injuries. And, if nothing is done to address these increasingly serious losses, it is likely that a major incident involving serious injuries and loss of life will follow at some point in time.

Researchers at the University of Pennsylvania[23] have outlined a seven-step near miss management process that uses data from near misses to prevent large disruptions. The steps include

(i)   identification of an incident,

(ii) disclosure and filing,

(iii) distribution of incident data,

(iv) root cause analysis,

(v)   solution/improvement recommendation,

(vi) dissemination, and

(vii) follow-up.

Naturally, different industries will have different rules as to what incidents should be identified as near misses and reported. Airline pilots report near-midair collisions by judging the distance and trajectories of the aircrafts involved. Hospital operating room personnel may report a near miss when a sponge is detected after an unresolved count or when the wrong limb is prepped for surgery or when the wrong patient is transferred to the operating room. Process industry managers may report incidents when reaction temperatures are too high or when harmless gasses are emitted inadvertently.

Reporting an incident is the step that starts the formal process. Naturally, managers of any near miss system should not look for a reduction in the number of reports over time as clear evidence of increased safety. To encourage reporting, managers may institute a system of anonymous communications.

Distribution of incident data serves to alert people to the likelihood of a hazard even before it is investigated. It also serves to solicit broader information that can help in the subsequent analysis. The root cause analysis then focuses on both the direct and underlying factors that led to the incident. The next step is to develop mitigation measures and contingency plans.

Once the results of the analysis and its recommended set of actions are distributed, management at every enterprise obtaining the report has a business decision to make. The implicit essence of most near miss reports is an estimate of the likelihood of a major disruption. In fact, management may decide not to act when the chances of major disruption are judged too small and the cost of the mitigation too high.

Only a Fool Learns from Experience

As the saying goes, the wise person learns from *other* people's experience. There are several types of experiences from which organizations can learn. These include near misses that happen to them, accidents that happen to them, near misses that happen to others, and accidents that happen to others.

Many organizations learn from large disruptions that happen to them. (Sadly, as the Columbia accident proved, this is not always the case.) Frequently, organizations also institute internal systems of near miss tracking, analysis, and correction. Many chemical plants, transportation companies, mine operators, and other organizations that are involved in dangerous work stress such systems as part of their safety culture, and some of these systems operate industry-wide. In many industries, accident data are reported and collected by government or industry bodies that investigate and then disseminate the data and the conclusions to industry members.

The U.S. National Transportation Safety Board (NTSB) is an independent federal agency whose mission is to investigate accidents in the aviation, highway, marine, railroad, and pipeline modes of transportation. As of 2004, its aviation accident database covered 140,000 aviation accidents, with details on each one.[24] The NTSB also publishes many studies with the results of its investigations and data analysis as well as recommended improvements to infrastructure, rolling stock, and practices.

In the same way, the U.S. Chemical Safety Board (CSB) is an independent federal agency whose mission is to prevent industrial chemical accidents. It investigates chemical incidents, determines root causes, and issues safety recommendations.[25] The U.S. Environmental Protection Agency also requires the operators of more than 15,000 sites containing certain toxic and flammable substances to report their existence and each site accident under rule 112(r) promulgated under the Clean Air Act.[26]

All the CSB and EPA reports are publicly available. Similarly, the European Union Directive 96/82/EC (known as the Seveso II Directive) specifies the processes for reporting major accident hazards involving dangerous substances. Also, the Agency for

Toxic Substances and Disease Registry (ATSDR), an agency of the U.S. Department of Health and Human Services, manages an incident reporting system. This system specifically includes not only occupational injuries and illnesses but also near misses.

Studying accidents and near misses gives managers an idea of the likelihood of major disruptions to their own operations and conditions the organization to recognize dangerous situations as they develop. Examples include unusual weather, an incomplete complement of workers, tight schedules, small slip-ups, and other conditions that in the past were associated with accidents.

Disruption Likelihood

Disruptions can be divided into three categories to facilitate estimating their likelihood: natural disasters, accidents, and intentional attacks. These categories differ in the relative roles that human beings and random factors play in their cause. Consequently, the methods of estimating their likelihood also differ.

Natural Disasters

Because many natural disasters are frequent, statistical models can be used to estimate the likelihood of their occurrence and their magnitude. Insurance companies have well-developed models of the likelihood of earthquakes, floods, or lightning strikes for various areas of the United States as well as for other countries. Insurance premiums can even serve as a proxy for the likelihood of the relevant risk.

The U.S. Geological Survey (USGS) estimates that the areas most susceptible to earthquakes in the United States include the western United States, the New Madrid zone in Missouri, and a few isolated locations on the United States East Coast. The USGS publishes maps, such as figure 3.2, depicting the occurrence of earthquakes over time, which can be used to gauge their likelihood. The USGS also publishes detailed data of earthquake frequency for each state in the United States and other regions of the world.

The U.S. National Oceanic and Atmospheric Administration (NOAA) publishes statistics about severe weather. For example,

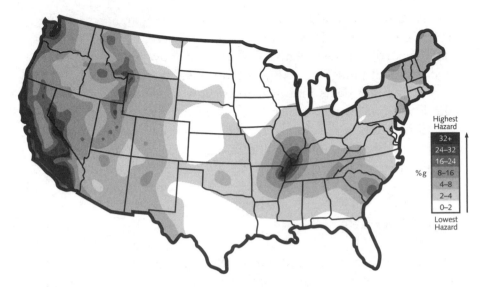

Highest
Hazard

| 32+ |
| 24–32 |
| 16–24 |
| 8–16 |
| 4–8 |
| 2–4 |
| 0–2 |

%g

Lowest
Hazard

Figure 3.2
Earthquake Frequencies

the frequency of tornadoes in Oklahoma City is shown in figure 3.3.[27] Companies located in Oklahoma City can use such figures to plan and time severe weather evacuation drills for February, just before the peak season of March through June.[28]

Figure 3.4 depicts the time of day of tornadoes in Oklahoma City, indicating that they take place mostly in the afternoon and early evening hours.[29] Again, by knowing the increased likelihood of tornadoes at these times, organizations can train the right work shift at a plant in emergency evacuation.

Such preparations proved life-saving when a tornado hit the GM plant in Oklahoma on May 8, 2003, at 5:30 P.M. None of the more than 1,000 employees who were at the plant was hurt because they all took shelter at the plant's fortified safe room when the tornado sirens sounded at 5:00 P.M. The tornado hit during the most likely month and at the most likely time of day.

Climatological models define likely rainfall patterns, suggesting the probability of floods in wetter-than-expected regions or wildfires in drier-than-expected regions. A NOAA map of precipitation outlook is depicted in figure 3.5. Such data can guide

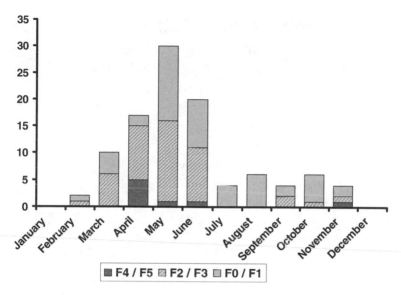

Figure 3.3
Tornado Timing

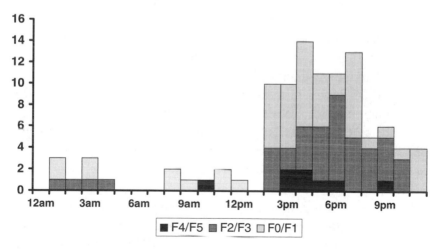

Figure 3.4
Oklahoma Tornados

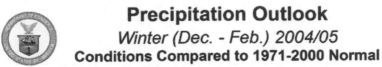

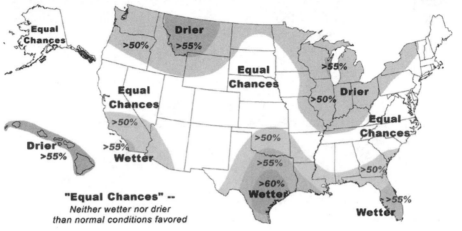

Figure 3.5
Precipitation Forecast

long-term site selection decisions, hazard insurance coverage strategies, or employee training.

The frequency and size of near misses or small disruptions can actually help predict the chance of a bigger natural disaster. Many natural (and man-made) phenomena follow statistical rank-size laws (called Power Law distributions) that relate the size of the phenomenon to the frequency of the disruption. For example, the Gutenberg-Richter Law stipulates that for each 100 earthquakes of size 3 on the Richter scale, one can expect approximately 10 earthquakes of size 4 (which are 10 times stronger than size 3 quakes) and one earthquake of size 5.

Power Law distributions are a mathematical version of the well-known 80/20 rule, the intuitive notion that 20 percent (or in general a small fraction) of the events cause 80 percent (or, in general, most) of the impact. Financial losses caused by earthquakes, hurricanes, floods, and even stock market crashes follow a Power Law distribution, as do forest fires, electricity blackouts, industrial accidents, and insurance claims. The size of cities, the popularity of weblog sites, and other socio-economic activities are also distributed according to similar rules.[30]

In the context of assessing the likelihood of low-probability/ high-impact events, one can assess the odds of such large infrequent disruptions based on the observed large number of smaller events. Such relationships are not precise enough to estimate either the timing or the magnitude of a future disruption but they can be used to estimate the probability that it will happen during a future interval and the relative likelihood compared to other potential disruptions. Such statistical distributions are responsible for statements like "we are due for a big one" regarding earthquakes in California.

Accidents

Although most safety literature is concerned with prevention, the first step in any safety process should be an assessment of the likelihood of an accident. Most analyses aimed at assessing such likelihood are based on variations of the near miss framework presented in the previous section.

One study[31] suggested that for every 300 accidents with no injury, one can expect approximately 30 accidents involving minor injury and one major accident involving serious injury or lost life. Based on 1.7 million accidents reported by 297 cooperating organizations, another study[32] suggested that for every 600 accidents with no damage or injury there are likely to be 30 property damage accidents, 10 accidents with minor injuries, and one serious or disabling injury. None of these studies separates out accidents in organizations that instituted formal processes of learning from near misses, but the consistent pattern of many small accidents foreshadowing larger ones suggests an approximate way to assess the likelihood of large accidents.

To attack safety problems at their root, companies dealing with hazardous conditions have been working to reduce the number of incidents, which should reduce the accident rate and eliminate severe accidents. These companies have implemented process safety management (PSM)[33] systems, including audit programs that verify compliance and implementation of safe procedures.

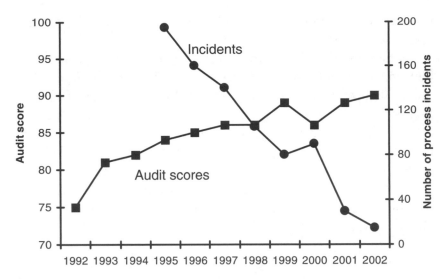

Figure 3.6
PSM Audit Scores and PSM Incidents

Such processes have been successful in many cases in reducing dramatically the number of incidents. For example, figure 3.6 depicts the marked reduction of incidents at DuPont as a function of the audit effectiveness that was part of its PSM.[34]

Intentional Disruptions
Whereas natural disasters follow statistical Power Law curves and the likelihood of large accidents can be estimated from small mishaps, intentional disruptions follow a different logic. Intentional disruptions constitute *adaptable threats* in which the perpetrators seek both to ensure the success of the attack and to maximize the damage. Consequently, "hardening" one potential target against a given mode of attack may increase the likelihood that another target will be attacked or there will be a different type of attack. It also means that such attacks are likely to take place at the worst time and in the worst place—when the organization is most unprepared and vulnerable.

Because of their high frequency, labor strikes provide many examples in which a smart adversary will inflict damage using methods and timing that the company may not anticipate or that are designed to inflict maximum economic damage. In the summer of 2002, for example, the Longshore and Warehouse Union (ILWU) staged a work slowdown in the pacific coast ports. To maximize the effect of its actions, the union timed it to October, planning to choke the ports just as the volume of shipments from Southeast Asia increased before the holiday shopping season in the United States.

Taking a page from the same book, Britain's Transport and General Workers' Union started making preparations in August 2004 for a strike against the country's biggest ports group, Associated British Ports.[35] The plan was to cripple the ports in late September and October, just as the run-up to Christmas begins.

The Canadian Customs Excise Union also chose its timing carefully. In 2004, it planned for its customs agents in Quebec to begin checking all vehicles driving into the United States as a protest in a four-year salary dispute. The act was aimed to double wait times for travelers, since vehicles are typically inspected only once, by American customs. To maximize effectiveness, the union chose July 31 to start the practice—on Canada's Civic Holiday long weekend. Many travelers were expected to visit the United States, ensuring particularly long lines and maximum disruption.

When Chapter 1199 of the International Service employees union planned to exert pressure on the Women and Infants Hospital in Rhode Island, it did not simply plan a strike. Knowing that the hospital was well prepared to use replacement workers and management personnel, it adjusted its tactics. In a September 1998 strike notice to its members, the union leadership said it was their intention to strike for one day. Chapter 1199 and other unions had used a series of one-day strikes elsewhere. "It is a crippling kind of tactic, because you can gear up for a strike, but it is hard to gear up, and step down, and gear up, and step down," explained May Kernan, vice president of the hospital's Marketing Communications.[36]

In 2003, Greenpeace wanted to torpedo efforts to test genetically modified wheat in the Eastern German state of Thuringia. Greenpeace did not, however, resort to demonstrations or other activities that Syngenta International AG, the Swiss agribusiness company, was expecting. Instead, Greenpeace sabotaged the site by sowing organic wheat throughout the test field, ruining trials because it would be impossible to tell the difference between genetically modified and conventional wheat.[37]

On November 28, 1995, French workers participated in their second nationwide strike in five days to protest austerity measures proposed by the government of Prime Minister Alain Juppe. In Paris, 85 bus drivers employed by the Parisian transportation authority, RATP, decided to create a disruption in support of the general strike. They knew exactly what to do. The 85 buses blocked the main RATP garage and within hours the entire bus and subway system ground to a halt throughout Paris.[38]

After the United States imposed tariffs on steel imports in March 2002, the World Trade Organization ruled that the tariffs were a violation of international trade rules. The WTO decision gave the European Union and several other countries the right to impose retaliatory tariffs on billions of dollars worth of American exports. Rather than retaliate by imposing steel tariffs, the EU decided to hit the Bush administration where the tariffs would hurt the most. It published a list of products targeted for tariffs that included citrus fruit, textiles, motorcycles, farm machinery, shoes, and other products. The common denominator for these products was that they were all made primarily in political "battleground states" that the Bush administration would need to win in the November 2004 U.S. presidential elections.[39]

All of these examples demonstrate the non-random, adaptive nature of purposeful disruptions. But terrorism, of course, is the ultimate form of intentional attack. The Madrid bombers did not blow up an airliner or attack an airport because after 9/11, airports around the world had enhanced security measures. The Madrid bombers struck an undefended target instead—trains in the heart of Madrid. The March 2004 attack took place at the height of the rush hour when the packed trains ensured maximum carnage. Clearly, labor actions and political maneuvering have nothing to do with terrorism; managers have only to remember that intentional disruptions will strike at the least defended place at the most inconvenient time, and they have to be ready for this.

Vulnerabilities of the Information System   As supply chains interconnect across the globe, companies are becoming increasingly dependent on reliable information and communications. Design specifications and modifications, material orders and change orders, shipping notices and deviation alerts, and payments and rebates all move electronically across the globe at the speed of light. Furthermore, as companies automate the control of many physical processes, they become more vulnerable to computer hackers and saboteurs.[40]

Sophos Plc., a British computer security company, finds more than 1,000 new computer virus variants each month using a global network of monitoring stations. Many of these viruses are harmless, but not all are. Some viruses are designed to cripple a network by flooding the attacked web server with messages. So-called "distributed denial of service" attacks spread from computer to computer by sending messages to random web addresses or via e-mail, using each computer's e-mail address book to send the virus as an attachment to other computers. Particularly destructive past viruses include the 1999 Melissa, the 2000 Love Bug, the 2001 Code Red and Code Red II, and the 2003 Slammer worm.

Although many of these attacks are not targeted at a single company, modern connected and automated systems create new vulnerabilities, as the following example illustrates.

Vitek Boden of Brisbane, Australia, was unhappy at the beginning of 2000. His application for employment with the council managing the water system for the small town of Maroochy Shire was declined. Using a two-way radio, a basic telemetry system, and a laptop computer, Boden hacked into the council's control system. On March 2000, he released close to one million liters of raw sewage into local streets, waterways, rivers, parks, and a Hyatt Regency tourist center. The cleanup took more than a week. The stench and the environmental damage lingered long afterward. While not a life-threatening attack, Boden's assault demonstrated the vulnerability of automated systems to cyber-intrusions.

Assessing Intentional Threats   Historical data are of limited use when trying to forecast the nature of a new intentional threat, because of its adaptive nature. For example, although it strengthened its airport security after the 9/11 attack, the United States is still unprepared for other types of attacks that may be more likely because of the increased security at airports.

To help assess the type of attack envisioned by intentional threats and estimate their likelihood, organizations ranging from Intel Corporation to the U.S. Navy to airport managers use "Red Team" exercises to refine and advance their understanding of intentional threats. In such exercises, a group of experts is tasked with thinking like an enemy, exploring the vulnerability of an organization, and simulating various attacks.

For example, in November 2000, the U.S. Department of Energy and the Utah Olympic Public Safety Command conducted "Black Ice," a simulation designed to understand the vulnerabilities of crucial infrastructure components when a loss of infrastructure is compounded by a cyber attack. The exercise began with a fictitious ice storm damaging power and transmission lines, degrading the ability to generate and deliver power in the region. This was then exacerbated by a simulated cyber attack on the Supervisory Control Data Acquisition system, which controls the power grid in the area. The simulation exposed the vulnerability of Salt Lake City even to partial performance degradation of natural gas, water, and communications systems.

Similarly, in July 2002, Gartner Research and the U.S. Naval War College conducted "Digital Pearl Harbor," a simulation designed to explore the potential of a cyber attack on critical infrastructure components. The experiment exposed the need for a central coordination role by government in the event of such an attack. It also discovered that isolated infrastructures proved much more difficult to breach.[41] Such "Red Team" simulations help the defending ("blue") team to assess its vulnerability and discover unforeseen dependencies. The simulation also "socializes" organizations that use it to think in terms of uncertainty, flexible response, responsibilities, and lines of authority, thus creating a more adaptive and resilient culture.

Summing the Likelihoods

Large-scale disruptions rarely take place without any warning. The likelihood of random disruptions can be assessed from actual, commonly available data regarding frequency of earthquakes, floods, hurricanes, or lightning strikes. In addition, such phenomena seem to follow statistical laws that allow inference of the likelihood of low-probability/high-impact disruptions from the occurrence of frequent small events.

Although accidents involve human factors, they also seem to follow similar relationships. A large number of small incidents may foreshadow more significant accidents. This is the basis for the near miss analysis. Learning from the small incidents can help organizations correct the conditions that lead to accidents, thereby lowering the likelihood of large disruptions.

The likelihood of intentional threats is more difficult to assess because these attacks adapt to defensive measures. To estimate modes of attack and likelihood, managers have to "think like the enemy," using other organizations' incident experience and simulated "red team" attacks.

Recognizing that many components have to fail for a system to experience a large disruption is the rationale behind the concept of layered defense described in chapter 8. The basic concept is that if one element of the system is breached, the system would not fail because other elements are capable of deterring an attack or avoiding an accident.

Estimating the probability of failure of various supply chain elements requires information that is rarely available to managers. But as investigation boards and legal proceedings have revealed, in many cases relevant data are on the record but not funneled into a useful place or not analyzed to bring out the information in the data. Thoughtful and carefully designed continuous collection of common data, feeding a frequent process of review and analysis, can point to impending disruptions and enhance the process of estimating disruption likelihoods.

As things generally are today, many companies do not have a formal process for anticipating disruptions and estimating their likelihood and those who do rely on managers' subjective estimates. Such estimates are usually relative—ranking possible disruptions in terms of their likelihood vis-à-vis other potential disruptions. Such ranking is useful in constructing vulnerability maps (such as figure 3.2) to help prioritize management's attention. They cannot, however, replace a rigorous process of threat likelihood analysis.

The limited ability to estimate the likelihood of specific disruptions means that significant management attention should be focused on general redundancy and flexibility measures. Such capabilities can help a company to recover from many potential disruptions, even those that cannot be imagined specifically.

4

Effects of Disruptions

Most companies can estimate the range of consequences of high-frequency disruptions based on their own or their industry's experience. Low-probability/high-impact events, in contrast, generate magnified outcomes, and their rarity means a lack of experience in estimating both their likelihood and their consequences. In many cases, such disruptions are accompanied by public fear that exacerbates the impact of the initial disruption. Government reactions may even aggravate the disruption further. Moreover, high-impact disruptions often have many additional indirect effects, upsetting enterprises more deeply than one may realize.

While it may be difficult to estimate the exact likelihood and impact of such disruptions, it is enough to estimate the *relative* likelihoods and potential damage in order to prioritize vulnerabilities and planning. Once the relative likelihood and consequences of each potential disruption are estimated, they can be placed on a vulnerability map such as the one dicussed in chapter 2 (figure 2.4), which can be used, in turn, to prioritize planning.

Saving the Farm, Losing the Tourists

A routine inspection of a slaughterhouse in Essex England on February 19, 2001, detected foot and mouth disease (FMD) in 28 pigs. This highly contagious disease afflicts a wide range of livestock, including cows, pigs, sheep, and goats. Although it rarely infects humans, it does kill 60 percent of young farm animals. While many affected animals (especially adults) can recover, the disease leaves them debilitated, thereby ruining the production of milk and meat. Moreover, the virus lingers in adult animals that can then infect other animals the following year.

In response to the Essex inspection, the European Commission quickly banned all exports of British meat, milk, and livestock products. The United States, Ireland, and South Korea followed suit by banning imports of British meat. The British government ordered the slaughter and disposal of the 300 animals at the afflicted abattoir and set up an exclusion zone around the area. "If we can get on top of this and get back to a disease-free status quickly, then hopefully the damage can be minimized," said Agriculture Secretary Nick Brown.[1]

Less than two weeks after the first detected case, however, the disease had spread to scattered locations across Britain. "I am absolutely determined to do everything possible to extinguish the disease," said Secretary Brown.[2]

On March 15, 2001, British officials took decisive actions, virtually closing the British countryside. Travel in afflicted regions was discouraged as officials closed parks and country footpaths. They also canceled local events to minimize traffic; the Cheltenham National Hunt, for example, which draws 200,000 people every year, was called off. Checkpoint stations used disinfectant on the tires and shoes of those traveling from quarantined areas. In addition, officials ordered the slaughter and burning of all susceptible livestock within 3 kilometers of any infected animal.

The battle to contain the disease took seven months and covered the entire length and breadth of the country. Even though officials found only 2,000 infected animals, 6.5 million cows, pigs, and sheep were slaughtered. The total cost to the agricultural sector approached £2.4 billion.[3]

With graphic TV footage of high mounds of burning carcasses and the restrictions on movements throughout the country, large numbers of potential tourists avoided Britain. Spending by foreign tourists dropped 17 percent during the depths of the crisis.[4] The tourists who did travel to Britain, and Britons on holiday, avoided Britain's scenic countryside, leading some 1,000 small rural lodges and bed-and-breakfast establishments to close in the wake of the FMD.[5]

The total impact of the FMD on tourism during the seven months of the crisis reached £3.3 billion.[6] The long-term, five-year, impact on tourism was estimated to exceed £4.5 billion.[7] It is difficult to know whether the closure of many rural areas slowed the spread of the disease, because the infection followed cattle trade patterns, which had little to do with tourist movement patterns. It certainly dealt, however, a severe blow to the tourism industry.

It seems that the government's mindset still stressed the importance of agriculture when, in fact, tourism had become a more vital part of Britain's economy. Consequently, the government's cancellations and closures caused more economic damage to tourism than the FMD caused to agriculture.

Magnified Disruptions

The British government has no monopoly on over-reaction during crises. The risk-averse culture of politics and the legitimate need to instill public confidence breed a strong predilection toward being visibly "in control" during disruptions.

Following the 9/11 terrorist attack, the U.S. government tightened security at U.S. borders and shut down all flights in and around the United States. The intermittent plant closing by Chrysler in the weeks that followed and the 13 percent reduction of output at Ford Motor Company during the fourth quarter of 2001 were not the direct result of the terrorist attack; they were the result of the shutdown of the Canadian and Mexican borders for truck movements and the resulting delays because of tighter border security. The U.S. government's reactions disrupted numerous just-in-time manufacturing systems that depended on reliable international shipping.

When the 1995 Kobe quake injured 30,000 people, many made their way to Kobe's hospitals. Yet 85 percent of these hospitals suffered damage from the earthquake and sustained a combined loss of one billion dollars.[8] Moreover, the lack of running water, gas, and electricity hampered medical care even at the health-care facilities that were not directly damaged by the quake. Naturally, the Japanese government rushed to aid injured people. In order to fill the massive health-care gap, the government established free health clinics to cover the needs of the homeless and injured. Ironically, this aid giving proved too successful by staying operational for too long—it almost bankrupted most of the area's private hospitals, which couldn't compete with free care. Again, a well-intentioned strong government intervention caused unintended secondary damage.

It is easy to criticize government actions surrounding the U.K. FMD outbreak, 9/11 in the United States, or the Kobe earthquake, after the fact. During a crisis, however, the need to instill public confidence and alleviate fears—demonstrating that the government is responding and "in control"—may outweigh the economic damage from what can be seen as an overreaction. Demonstrating that the British government was actively preserving the future of Britain's food supply, ensuring that no more immediate attacks on the United States were forthcoming, and demonstrating that government cared by providing massive and immediate health support in a time of crisis in Kobe were all important and worthwhile. The unknown consequences of not reacting decisively, even without enough data and time for careful analysis, may well have been worse.

Thus, businesses should assume that governments are likely to "overreact" and take strong measures in case of high-profile public disruptions, such as another terrorist attack, the 2003 Severe Acute Respiratory Syndrome (SARS) epidemic, or other anxiety-producing disruptions.

Anticipating the reaction of governments, however, may still not give companies the complete picture of what high-impact disruptions may entail. Second- and third-order impacts on their businesses may include problems with customers and suppliers who are not directly disrupted, as well as unexpected shifts in demand patterns.

Public reaction to rare, unfamiliar disruptions can significantly affect demand patterns. For example, when British truckers blockaded the entrance to refineries and fuel depots in a 2000 protest against high fuel taxes, consumers hoarded fuel, topping off their tanks at every opportunity. This consumer reaction, which was identical to that of American drivers during the fuel shortages in the 1970s and 1980s, exacerbated the shortages by shifting the limited inventories of fuel from filling stations into automobiles' gas tanks.

As one may have expected, the 9/11 attacks caused a significant reduction in air travel. What was less expected is that the events of 9/11 brought a sharp increase in the demand for home entertainment systems in the United States, as people opted to stay home rather than travel. October 2001 also saw a boom in new American car sales stimulated by patriotism. And while the FMD virtually shut down rural tourism in the U.K., urban tourism flourished as many Britons chose to visit the cities instead of taking rural holidays.

Lingering Effects of Disruptions—The West Coast Port Lockout of 2002

The summer of 2002 witnessed increasingly acrimonious contract negotiations between the International Longshore and Warehouse Union (ILWU) and the Pacific Maritime Association (PMA), who represents the ports' users in labor negotiations.[9] In September, the union staged a work slowdown at all West Coast ports. In response, the PMA locked the ports on the evening of September 27. The lockout ended 10 days later on October 8, when President George W. Bush intervened, invoking the Taft-Hartley Act of 1947 to force open the ports and push the parties back to the negotiating table.[10]

The lockout halted the gargantuan flow of containers through the 29 West Coast ports, which are responsible for $320 billion in imports and exports each year. With the ports processing about 30 containers per minute, every hour, 24 hours a day, seven days a week, any disruption was bound to create costly chaos.

Facing frozen port operations, the massive ocean-going freight vessels serving the West Coast had little choice but to wait off the coast. And wait and wait. Canadian and Mexican ports could not handle these huge container ships, and they were too big to pass through the Panama Canal to the East Coast. So the ships created a logjam up and down the West Coast, placing a growing inventory of materials and products within sight but not within reach.

For Wal-Mart, Costco, JCPenney, The Limited, and other retailers, the timing of this labor dispute looked like the perfect storm. With shipments streaming across the Pacific for the 2002 holiday season, the retailers knew that a shutdown of West Coast ports would cripple the holiday sales that make or break a retailer's year. As a result, these retailers took aggressive steps to minimize the impact of the potential port disruption.

"Back in June, we began to plan ahead and talked to vendors about getting early shipments. On products like Christmas lighting, we had them send our full order, or as much as they could get to us, by September," said Costco executive vice president Richard Galanti.[11] Wal-Mart made similar preparations: "We were able to clear port on most of our Christmas items before the shutdown began," said Wal-Mart spokesman Tom Williams. "We had a contingency plan and it worked."[12]

Despite forewarning, preparations, and the relatively short duration of the disruption, many of the same retailers were forced to announce reduced sales expectations in the aftermath of the lockout. Mattel executives complained that even three weeks after the lockout ended, the company had merchandise worth about $75 million to $100 million at wholesale value stuck on the water.[13] The toy manufacturer worried that retailers might cancel orders if goods didn't arrive on time, and it began to ship certain toys by air, significantly increasing its costs. Mattel and others suffered from the lingering effect of the disruption; even after the lockout was over, it took months for the ports to work through the logjam of incoming traffic and clear all the queues.

Manufacturing plants dependent on parts from Asia recognized that they were vulnerable to the lockout. New United Motor Manufacturing Inc. (NUMMI), the joint venture between Toyota and GM, knew that it was at risk since it used just-in-time inventory management. With only four to six hours' worth of parts on hand at any given time, a lengthy disruption of material flow would halt production very quickly.

Just before the lockout, NUMMI took some precautions. "We did pull more parts as a contingency, but five-to-seven days is the maximum you're going to be able to pull," said the spokesman at the beginning of the strike.[14]

Four days into the lockout, the Fremont, California, plant had to shut down and idle its 5,500 workers. Seven days into the lockout and with no end in sight, NUMMI chartered several Boeing 747s to bring parts from Japan, increasing the cost of every car produced with air-freighted parts by $300 to $600.

In the aftermath, NUMMI was able to increase its output and offset the lost production caused by the delays; it ended up making a record number of cars in 2002. Its costs, however, increased substantially during that period, because of the expensive airfreight, added storage and handling costs, and substantial worker overtime.

Whereas manufacturers and retailers could arrange for early shipment of needed goods, farmers have less control over when their agricultural goods are ready for shipment, which makes them especially susceptible to disruptions. The September 29 lockout hit during the peak of the table grape harvest, with nearly $400 million in grapes ready to ship out through West Coast ports.[15] The perishable nature of these goods meant high levels of spoilage for fruits and vegetables stuck in hot dock-side containers around the stricken ports.[16]

The delay in unloading ships even affected the World Series.[17] As part of a "Memorable Moments" promotion, MasterCard had planned to hand out 57,000 disposable cameras to fans at Game Four in San Francisco on October 23. The cameras, shipped from Hong Kong, were in a container on a ship that arrived at the Port of Los Angeles on October 15. Because of the backlog after the lockout, the small company that ordered the cameras was told the ship wouldn't be unloaded until November 1, long after the fans had come and gone.

For service businesses such as airlines, restaurants, or movie theaters, the lost business may be gone forever. Service businesses have no mechanism for creating inventory of their product to be used later or to "catch up" after the fact; if a seat on the 5:00 P.M.

flight to Detroit flies empty, there is no opportunity to resell it at a later date.

Indirect Effects Lead to Slow Recovery

The lockout affected more than just the businesses whose goods sat at the port. Across the nation, U.S. railroads ran into problems as freight cars loaded with goods were locked in at the port. Union Pacific, for example, had 23,000 containers stacked up at the California ports of Los Angeles and Long Beach alone.[18] Westbound rail traffic backed up as coastal rail-yards filled to capacity, spreading the clog eastward.

On the other side of the Pacific, ocean freight vessel operators in Shanghai faced the opposite problem: Too many ships and containers were stuck stateside. Shanghai ceased all shipments to the United States until after the lockout was over and ships and containers could start coming back to China.

After the lockout ended, shippers and carriers faced a very slow return to normalcy. Continued labor tensions at the port, clogged docks and rail yards, and a shortage of containers and freight cars all stymied a quick recovery.

Even a full month after the lockout ended, operations had only started to return to normal. Although the ports had cleared much of the backlog, 140 ships still awaited unloading. Delays of seven to nine days meant that incoming ships still queued in the waters off the West Coast. Some analysts predicted that it would take nearly three months to recover fully from the effects of the 10-day lockout.

Because of the expanding effects of events from the port disruption, the impact on the U.S. economy grew with each passing day.[19] In the early days, the disruption cost $1 billion per day in damages to the U.S economy. But as the disruption extended into its second week, the impact grew to $2 billion per day.[20] If the disruption had gone past two weeks, estimates were that the damage from lost economic activity in the United States would have reached $3 billion per day—nearly 10 percent of the U.S. GDP. The longer the disruption, the more goods spoil or become dated, and more retail sales are lost, leading to cost cutting and layoffs by retailers and their products' suppliers. In addition, more factories shut down for lack of parts, idling parts and material suppliers, laying off workers, and hurting all the services that depend on them. Overall, this labor dispute involving 10,500 longshoremen imperiled the jobs of some 4 million U.S. workers[21]

Profile of a Disruption

Disruptions go through several characteristic stages, even though their severity and duration vary from case to case.

Figure 4.1 illustrates the profile of a hypothetical disruption. It depicts the performance of a company (which can be sales, production level, profits, customer service, or another relevant metric) plotted over time. The nature of the disruption and the dynamics of the company's response can be characterized by the following eight phases.

1. *Preparation* In some cases, a company can foresee and prepare for disruption to minimize its effects. Such warnings range from the 30-minute tornado alert GM had in Oklahoma to the several months of watching the deteriorating labor negotiations at the West Coast ports. In other cases, such as the 9/11 attack or the Philips fire, there is little or no immediate warning.

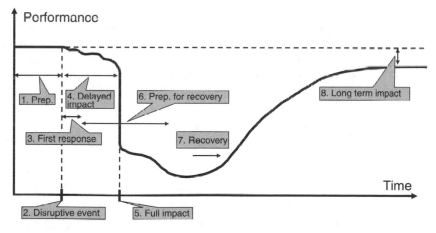

Figure 4.1
Disruption Profile

2. *The Disruptive Event*   This is the time when the tornado hits, the accident occurs, the bomb explodes, a supplier goes out of business, the union goes on a wildcat strike, or any other high-impact/low-probability disruption takes place.

3. *First Response*   Once the disruptive event takes place, the first period in the case of physical disruption is the domain of first responders (police, firefighters, first aid workers) who have to attend to an initial damage, if any. The duration of this period is anywhere from the time required to put out a fire to the months it took to dismantle and clean "Ground Zero" at the World Trade Center. Corporate resources can also participate in the first response, as Philips did when it put out its own fire or when security personnel in the World Trade Center led evacuation efforts on 9/11.

   In cases of other disruptions, such as job actions or information technology disruptions, the first response is aimed at avoiding physical damage and bodily injuries. This may involve shutting down processes to make sure that even without employees or information systems there is no danger of physical harm to plant, equipment, or personnel.

4. *Delayed Impact*   The full impact of some disruptions is felt immediately. Other disruptions can take time to affect a company, depending on factors such as the magnitude of the disruption, the preparation undertaken, and the inherent resilience of the organization and its supply chain. NUMMI's just-in-time inventory system meant that, under normal circumstances, it would have been disrupted within hours of the West Coast port lockout. The parts inventory NUMMI accumulated in preparation kept the plant operational for another four days before it was shut down. In the aftermath of the unanticipated 9/11 attacks, car makers felt the impact of border delays and halted airfreight within days.

5. *Full Impact*   Once the full impact hits, performance often drops precipitously. When inventories of critical parts ran out after the West Coast port lockout began, NUMMI halted production. Apple tried to ship slower computers in response to the 1999 Taiwan earthquake that disrupted memory chip supplies, only to be rebuffed by customers. Retailers are often unprepared for an increase in demand during panic buying.

Examples include gas hoarding during fuel shortage periods, stockpiling food items before a snow storm, and buying lumber for boarding windows in anticipation of hurricanes.

In some cases, when the disruption hits a company facility directly, the full impact is immediate. For example, the Union Carbide facility in Bhopal was off-line immediately after the accident; GM's Oklahoma City automobile assembly plant came off-line immediately after it was hit by a tornado; and Wall Street firms stopped trading exactly when the 9/11 attack occurred.

6. *Recovery preparations* Preparations for recovery typically start in parallel with the first response or shortly after they commence. They involve qualifying other suppliers and redirecting suppliers' resources, as Nokia did in the aftermath of the 2000 Philips fire; finding alternative transportation modes as NUMMI did when it used airfreight to get parts during the 2002 West Coast port lockout; and determining what parts are available and selling products built from those parts, as did Dell after the 1999 Taiwan earthquake.

7. *Recovery* Restarting production, distributing restored supplies, repairing damaged infrastructure, or reconnecting damaged IT systems can take significant time. In the aftermath of the Kobe earthquake, many companies recovered slowly because of lack of utilities and employee absenteeism (as employees picked up the pieces of their own disrupted lives). Serious structural damage in the port of Kobe took two years to rebuild.

To get back to normal operations levels, many companies make up for lost production by running at higher-than-normal utilization using overtime and suppliers' and customers' resources. After the West Coast port lockout, NUMMI made up for its one-week plant closure and posted record sales by year's end, despite the work stoppage. Cantor Fitzgerald, the bond trading house, lost hundreds of employees and all its systems in the World Trade Center on 9/11. It was back to trading when the stock exchange opened for business on September 17, 2001, and it was back to its pre-9/11 level of bond trading within two months.

8. *Long-Term Impact* It typically takes time to recover from disruptions, but if customer relationships are damaged, the impact

can be long-lasting and difficult to recover from. For example, Kobe's network of small-time shoe makers, responsible for some 34 million pairs of shoes a year, lost 90 percent of their business as buyers shifted to Chinese factories in the wake of the quake, and most buyers never came back. Other examples discussed earlier include Ericsson's exit from cellphone manufacturing following the Philips fire and the bankruptcy of many rural English hotels and motels in the wake of the FMD. In some cases, the delayed impacts are indirect. For example, during the three months that followed 9/11, many people who would have normally flown took to the roads instead. One result was that 353 more people died in automobile crashes than the average for that time of year.[22]

During the West Coast port lockout, Dell, P&G, and Intel were disappointed by the attitudes of some suppliers, who saw the labor troubles as an "act of God," for which the supplier was "sorry," that "everyone is stuck in the same boat," and that "nothing can be done until it is over." Dell, P&G, and Intel felt that suppliers should have anticipated the strike and could have done more to reroute stuck traffic, expedite shipments, and ensure faster resumption of the flow of goods. Dell attributed suppliers' inaction to cultural differences, with Dell having a much higher sense of urgency. For some of these suppliers, the disruption did not end with the resumption of port activities. Both Dell and P&G fired unresponsive suppliers.

Totaling the Potential Damage

Many companies can recover quickly from disruptions, even large-scale ones, if they are prepared and know what to expect. When assessing the possible impacts of low-probability disruptions, two somewhat less obvious potential effects should be taken into account. First are the various potential cascading effects that may result from governments' (or other institutions') responses. Understanding such reverberations requires understanding the structure of the supply chain. The second effect is rooted in the competitive positioning of the company; if it is in a highly contested commodity market, it may have less time to react than if it has a unique product that its customers must have.

Causes Spread to Effects and Effects and Effects

The fire in Philips's Albuquerque plant affected its customer, Ericsson, far worse than it affected Philips itself. Moreover, the impact of the Philips fire spread beyond Philips's customers. Ericsson's disrupted production and loss of market share meant cutbacks in purchasing from all of its suppliers.

Anadigics, another chip-making supplier to Ericsson, suffered a 33 percent decline in revenues late in 2000, months after the actual fire.[23] Ericsson canceled large volumes of orders for Anadigics' chips in the final quarter because of the lost market share following the disruption. Thus, a fire at one chip maker led to the disruption of another chip maker by disrupting a mutual customer.

In the case of the West Coast port lockout, the effects spread from the ports to suppliers and customers on both sides of the Pacific. Both of these examples demonstrate the cascading of disruptions across the globe.

The FMD provides another example of unexpected cascading effects. Although the disease does not taint the meat, consumers in many regions avoided beef nonetheless. McDonald's saw a year-over-year $300 million decline in European (5 percent) and Asian (6 percent) sales in the first quarter of 2001.[24] British leather production plummeted by 50 percent as millions of potentially infected cattle were slaughtered. This disrupted the flow of raw material to leather suppliers who provided material to manufacturers such as Nike (shoes), Louis Vuitton (handbags), and Jaguar (car seats). These manufacturers were forced to look for new sources of leather supply. With the loss of many of its customers, U.K. leather producers have never recovered to pre-FMD levels.

Competition and Resilience

A crucial factor in the potential long-term damage from a disruption is the time it takes for a company to get back to normal versus the "grace period" that the market would give it. The time to recovery is a function of the company's resilience, while the grace period is a function of its market position.

The company's market position with regard to its competition determines how much latitude it has with its customers and how fast the supply chain must get back to pre-disruption levels before customers defect. In commodity market situations, in which the company's customers can switch suppliers with little difficulty, the company has little time to recover before it starts losing customers. Consequently, a firm selling to a commodity market—in which there are many other suppliers and firms compete on the basis of price and customer service—is vulnerable if it cannot respond quickly to a disruption.

This is the most dangerous scenario. It is, for instance, the situation that many of the world's older hub-and-spoke airlines are in today. Their market has been disrupted with the entry of discount carriers, offering a virtually identical product, causing the hub-and-spoke airlines to lose pricing power. Shackled by inflexible union work rules, they are unable to respond and seem destined to lose in the long term. To a somewhat lesser extent, U.S. automobile manufacturers are also in this unenviable position. They are facing stiff competition, yet they are unable for historical reasons (such as restrictive long-term labor agreements and entrenched bureaucracy) to respond quickly and adequately to competitive disruptions.

High resilience in a competitive market offers the potential for positive long-term effects—creating market share gains in the face of a disruption. Nokia did just that, gaining the market share that its less resilient competitor, Ericsson, lost. Thus, the long-term performance of Nokia a year after the Philips plant fire was actually above the pre-disruption level of sales.

For companies that have market power through unique product offerings, or an otherwise monopolistic position, the effects of disruption are still dependent on how fast the company recovers. To the extent that customers cannot or do not defer their purchases during a disruption, the company will lose sales if it does not respond quickly. Although not fatal, this can be costly, given the high profit margins enjoyed by companies in this situation. For example, pharmaceutical companies enjoy gross margins of 90 percent or more on patent-protected products. Consequently, they ensure that their retailers and warehouses are always stocked with enough inventory so they can withstand most disruptions, since the cost of a lost sale is so high. Moreover, if a monopolist does not respond to customers' needs during a disruption, customers might seek regulatory remedies or redesign their businesses in the long run to avoid the monopolist.

Winning from Disruptions

In many cases, one company's problem is another company's opportunity. When a competitor stumbles, quick response can lead to increased market share when new customers try the company's products or services and stay with them.

The Northridge, California, earthquake in January 1994 knocked out four freeways and destroyed highway overpasses and parking structures, in addition to damaging numerous buildings and other infrastructure components. One of the expressways that closed, the Santa Monica Freeway, connects Los Angeles to its international airport and carries 300,000 cars a day. The earthquake made Los Angeles's already-congested highways considerably worse.[25]

The disrupted traffic created an opportunity for Metrolink, the L.A. regional rail system, and for the Metropolitan Transit Authority (MTA) for Los Angeles County. Immediately after the quake, Metrolink ridership increased by a factor of twenty.[26]

Rather than simply enjoy the extra revenue, the two transit authorities cooperated to enhance the service, using the boost in ridership to introduce and market the service to potential long-term customers. Authorities added parking lots at commuter rail stations and enhanced the schedules. Metrolink (commuter rail) and MTA (intracity buses) collaborated to improve connectivity and coordination between their two systems and introduced a connecting shuttle service. The two authorities also made changes to accommodate bicyclists. Metrolink relaxed its rules, letting riders bring bicycles on the train so that riders could bike the short distances to and from the train stations. Similarly, MTA added bike racks to its buses.[27]

Many of the new riders stayed after the roads were repaired. Three years after the quake, transit ridership in the quake-affected regions remained more than four times the pre-quake levels. When Metrolink celebrated its 35 millionth rider, the winner was, appropriately, a woman who began riding the train because of the quake.[28]

Gaining new business when a competitor is disrupted involves seizing the moment and allowing new customers to experience the product or service. The 1997 strike at UPS was an opportunity for FedEx to demonstrate its service to several new customers. Unfortunately, the FedEx network was overwhelmed by the volume diverted to it, and FedEx had to implement several restrictions to its service in order to maintain the reliability of its operation. It was able, however, to pick up several new customers, such as Unique Photo Inc., in Florham Park, New Jersey, whose CEO was impressed enough with the service he got during the UPS strike to give testimonials in FedEx press releases.[29]

Similarly, Dell's agility during the 1999 Taiwan earthquake allowed it to manage the demand for its computer systems by adjusting the component prices. Such adjustments allowed it to sell what it had and not have to disappoint customers. Apple at the same time was locked into long-term agreements and prior orders that it could not fulfill. Apple lost market share while Dell gained share.

Dell used a similar strategy during the West Coast port lockout. All through that period it worked with LCD flat screen monitor manufacturers to reduce their price by increasing Dell's volume of purchase of these monitors. In comparison to the bulky CRT monitors, LCD monitors take much less room and can therefore be economically flown rather than shipped by ocean. The result was increased demand for systems with LCD monitors and reduction in demand for systems equipped with the old CRT monitor, a trend that continued after the lockout ended. Most important for Dell, overall system sales continued to grow even during the lockout.

Missing the Opportunity
Some suppliers miss such opportunities. With the recall of millions of Firestone tires, and the massive media coverage surrounding roll-

over accidents with Ford Explorers, sales of Firestone tires in the United States dropped more than 15 percent. Moreover, Ford severed its 100-year relationship with the supplier. Major tire makers such as Goodyear, Michelin, and BF Goodrich rushed to woo newly safety-conscious tire buyers. "The recent unfortunate events will remind consumers of the importance of brand and quality," said Michelin's chief executive Edouard Michelin.[30]

At the top of the list of potential beneficiaries was Goodyear, since Ford announced that Explorer owners could go to any of the Goodyear's 5,000 dealers for free replacement tires underwritten by Ford. In response, Goodyear boosted production at seven plants. But executives at the Akron, Ohio, tire company also believed that the quality of their tires could command a premium and boosted prices by 7 percent in January 2001 and again in June 2001 to profit from the demand surge. "We expect it to be profitable. It has to be," said Goodyear spokesman Chris Aked.[31]

At the same time, with hot sales of new automobiles and the replacement of Firestone tires, Goodyear failed to satisfy dealers' orders in a timely manner. Goodyear did not give dealer orders priority, even though the tire replacement market is significantly larger than the new car tire market (a car gets one new tire set at the factory yet several replacement sets during its lifetime). Consequently, dealers suffered a high rate of stock-outs[32] and started to rebel, looking for other brands to sell.

Even more important, once the Firestone recall fell out of the headlines, drivers replacing tires on their cars reverted to the behavior that now characterizes most markets—buying at a discount what is on sale. In other words, they reverted to treating tires as commodities that can be differentiated mainly based on price and availability. The public simply did not think that Goodyear tires were better than other tires, regardless of what executives in Akron believed. By the first part of 2002, Goodyear had lost the entire market share it had gained during the crisis, and more.[33] In the summer of 2002, Goodyear started to reduce prices on several models to restore their competitiveness, leading to some recovery in sales.

Disruption Consequences

This chapter highlighted several important characteristics of disruptions: the seemingly unrelated consequences and vulnerabilities stemming from global connectivity; the fear and related government actions and overreaction that may intensify the impacts of low-probability/high-impact disruptions; and the stages that the various disruptions typically go through.

Disruptions affect supply chain performance both immediately following the event and over the long term. A 2000 study of 861 public companies[34] found that with the announcement of a supply chain malfunction such as production or shipment delays, the company's stock price tumbled nearly 9 percent on average. Furthermore, that stock lost 20 percent of its value within six months of the announcement.

A survey of 20 leading companies conducted by MIT's Center for Transportation and Logistics in 2002 and 2003 analyzed companies' supply chain response to terrorism. Part of this survey examined how companies assessed their vulnerabilities in terms of measuring the possible impact of supply chain disruptions.[35] Although few companies had developed systematic methods of assessing vulnerability at the time, several companies described quantitative and financial estimates for the consequences of supply chain disruptions, albeit not tied to a specific type of disruption. General Motors estimated that each day of a supply network disruption costs $50 to $100 million; Masterfoods Inc. claimed that an ill-timed disruption could cause the firm to "lose the franchise" with customers, or miss a critical retail promotion point (e.g., "back to school"); and Boston Scientific determined that a significant disruption to the manufacturing of a few key products could precipitate a cash-flow crisis leading to insolvency.

To further explain how supply chains are affected by disruptions, chapter 5 provides a short primer on supply chains and their management, the relationships between trading partners, and the ways in which supply chains are vulnerable.

II

Supply Chain Management—A Primer

5

Basic Supply Chain Management

The twin supply chain management challenge facing retailers, distributors, manufacturers, and suppliers is to maximize customer service while minimizing costs. For most supply chain operations the service challenge can be expressed in terms of availability: having the right product at the right place when the customer wants it. The cost challenge is to make that happen at low cost.

Matching supply with ever-changing and unpredictable demand is what separates Wal-Mart from Sears, Dell from HP's PC business, and Zara from Marks & Spencer. Supply chain disruptions, at their core, impair a firm's ability to satisfy demand because of a reduction in the firm's manufacturing or delivery capacity. But stock-outs and lack of product resulting from wrong orders also represent a failure to satisfy demand, albeit because of a wrong forecast rather than a disruption.

Demand in certain industries is notoriously unpredictable. Consequently, much can be learned from understanding how leading operators in these industries design their supply chains to mitigate such problems. Chapter 6 is focused specifically on supply chain designs aimed at mitigating forecasting difficulties. This chapter, however, first explains the structure and dynamics of supply chains.

Manufacturing Operations

In 1927, Ford Motor Company began producing the Model A in its River Rouge plant. Spanning over 2,000 acres, the "Rouge" was the largest industrial complex in the world. In 1929, it employed more than 100,000 people and incorporated all phases of auto manufacturing. Through 1942, it generated its own power and made its own parts, even glass and rubber, in the process of producing 15 million automobiles. The company fed the Rouge from its own iron-ore mines in northern Michigan and Minnesota and from its coal mines in Kentucky and West Virginia. Raw materials were brought in on Ford-owned railroad lines and ships for processing at the Rouge mills.[1]

Henry Ford clearly did not want to depend on suppliers. But even though Ford ran a *vertically integrated* factory, where all stages of manufacturing were controlled by Ford, it still had the challenge of coordinating the internal parts of its sprawling system.

The main challenge facing Ford operations managers was deciding what to produce, how much to produce, and when to produce it. For example, if they planned to make 20,000 cars in a given week, then they needed to have the parts for all those cars. To complete the wheel assembly, for instance, Ford would need to have on hand 40,000 axles, 80,000 wheels, and 400,000 lug nuts (five per mounted wheel). They would need 80,000 tires (not including a spare), and the tire plant at the Rouge would need to have enough raw material on hand, which it would have to process weeks and months ahead of the car assembly, in Ford's South American plant. Even in 1927, each automobile had thousands of parts, each part made of other parts and raw materials. These parts took time to manufacture and thus managers needed to schedule production far in advance.

The first step in managing all the parts of a complex product such as the Ford Model A is to list them all. In manufacturing terminology, the list of all parts, and the quantities involved in manufacturing a product, is known as the *bill of materials* (BOM). Consider the manufacturing of a toy car.[2] The BOM and the processes involved are depicted in the process map in figure 5.1. In this example, two pins for the axles (Part #2) are cut (in Process 3 shown by the circled numbers in the figure) and four drums (Part #3) are drilled (in Process 4) to be welded (in Process 5) into an axle set (Part #6). Metal paint (Part #7) is applied to the axle set

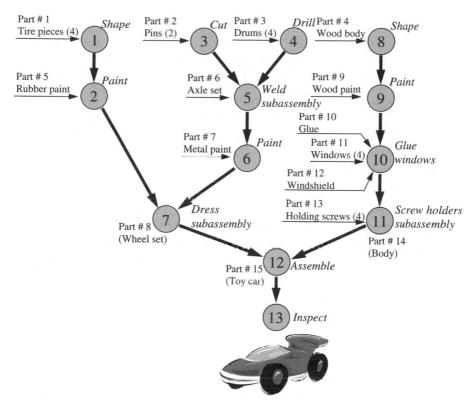

Figure 5.1
Bill of Material for Toy Car Manufacturing

which is then assembled with the four tires to produce a wheel set (Part #8). That part is then mated (in Process 12) to the car body (Part #14) to produce the toy car (Part #15).

Production planners use the BOM in the *material requirement planning* (MRP) process to identify the parts needed, the quantities required, the inventories of parts available, and the time when they should be ordered so that they will be available for the manufacturing process.

Modern supply chain processes involve significantly more complicated BOM and MRP processes. In most cases, the MRP uses special computer applications to control the tens of thousands of parts and processes involved. These applications identify situations in which several finished products rely on the same supplier, or on the same manufacturing process, with an eye toward efficiency—leveling the requirements and the work loads. The same MRP logic, however, can also be used to identify vulnerabilities of suppliers, plants, and processes. Thus, the BOM can be turned into a supply chain vulnerability map, as mentioned in chapter 2.

At the height of the high tech bubble, Lucent's main supplier of inductors to dozens of Lucent products cut off deliveries to all Lucent plants. The supplier had fixed capacity and a huge demand, and it had decided to divert its constrained output to a large consumer electronics firm. This resulted in an immediate scramble on Lucent's part using the BOM of all products to identify where the capacitors were used, identify the future demand for those products, use the BOM again to identify the resulting future demand for the inductors, and start looking for new sources of supply. Because of its immediate response, including the involvement of senior management with the supplier, Lucent was able to get the supply restarted, but the event served to highlight the importance of resilience to Lucent's top management. This case was one of the impetuses for the establishment of the Supply Chain Network organization (described in chapter 11), including a group of supply relationships managers. These actions made Lucent even more resilient, making such surprises less likely and diminishing their potential to affect Lucent.

Supply Chain Management

In the second half of the twentieth century, many manufacturers realized that total vertical integration had many disadvantages. A company could not be the best in everything. For example, it was difficult for Ford to be the best tire maker in the world while it focused on building the best cars in the world. Thus, companies started focusing on their core competencies, buying ready-made parts and services from suppliers whose core competency was, presumably, the part or service bought. The suppliers were able to concentrate on making specific parts, enjoying economies of scale by serving several customers, and focusing their expertise. That trend accelerated further in the 1980s and 1990s with the globalization and deregulation of commercial activities worldwide, leading to the widespread practice of *outsourcing*. In many cases production moved offshore, as certain regions of the world and certain countries, such as China, developed expertise and scale in many stages of manufacturing. It also led to the birth of modern supply chain management, which is focused on the flow of products through the global web of suppliers, manufacturers, distributors, transportation carriers, and retailers from raw material to finished goods in consumers' hands, and the recycling and disposal of these products.

Figure 5.2 depicts a simplified view of the main stages of garment manufacturing—from raw material to finished product. It starts with the use of cotton, wool, or oil-based raw material to produce fiber. The fiber is used as the main ingredient in the manufacturing of yarn. The yarn is textured, twisted, warped, drawn, woven, scoured, dyed, and finished into fabric. The fabric is rolled up, packed, and sent to apparel manufacturers. Then the fabric is cut, sewn, and finished to make apparel. The apparel is then shipped and sold in retail stores to consumers.

In some cases textile manufacturers control several of these steps in one location; in others they use specialized plants in disparate locations. Chapter 1 outlined the example of the manufacturing of Champion sports bras by Griffin Manufacturing of Fall River, Massachusetts, using material from the Far East that is processed in Massachusetts, Honduras, and Vermont before it is shipped to U.S. retailers.

Another example was described by Victor Fung, chairman of Li & Fung, Hong Kong's largest export trading company, in an interview with the *Harvard Business Review*:

Say we get an order from a European retailer to produce 10,000 garments. . . . For this customer we might decide to buy yarn from a Korean

Figure 5.2
Textile Industry Supply Chain

producer but have it woven and dyed in Taiwan. The Japanese have the best zippers and buttons, but they manufacture them mostly in China. Okay, so we go to YKK, a big Japanese zipper manufacturer, and we order the right zipper from their Chinese plants. Then we determine that, because of quotas and labor conditions, the best place to make the garment is Thailand. So we ship everything there. And because the customer needs quick delivery, we may divide the order across five factories in Thailand. . . . Five weeks after we have received the order, 10,000 garments arrive on the shelves in Europe, all looking like they came from one factory with colors, for example, perfectly matched.[3]

The term *supply chain* is a simplification of the supply *web* or *network* of suppliers, manufacturing plants, retailers, and the myriad supporting companies involved in design, procurement, manufacturing, storing, shipping, selling, and servicing goods. Figure 5.3 depicts a stylized supply network and the main flows associated with such a network.

These flows comprise the movement of parts and products downstream (from the suppliers to the retailers) and the flow of money upstream. These two flows define the supplier-customer relationship. Just as important is the flow of information; customers send orders and product requirements upstream and suppliers broadcast their inventory levels and their actions (such as shipping notices and invoices) downstream to their customers. Thus, information flows both ways.[4]

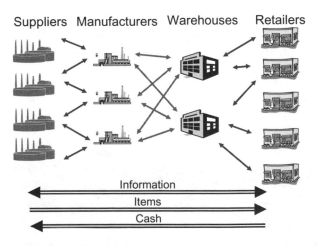

Figure 5.3
Simplified Supply Chain (Network) Diagram

When Ford managed its network of factories at the Rouge plant, there was little focus on inventory management across all stages in Ford's internal chain. Because Ford's revenue materialized only when cars were sold, the company emphasized availability of the finished product. It was a cardinal sin for plant managers not to have enough parts or raw material on hand, causing a production delay and lost revenue. Consequently, Ford's various subassembly and parts manufacturing units kept a large inventory of parts, subassemblies, and finished products. The same inventory management mentality prevailed though the 1970s until Toyota demonstrated the cost and quality advantages of lean manufacturing systems: relying on little inventory; just-in-time deliveries; strong relationships with suppliers; concurrent processes of product design, manufacturing and distribution; continuous quality improvements; and a culture of employee empowerment.

One of the fundamental tenets of modern supply chain management is the focus on controlling inventory levels. The role of inventory, and how companies manage it, is outlined in the next section.

Inventory

Firms have no intrinsic desire to have inventory of material, parts, or finished goods. Inventory requires management attention and costs money for each day it is held; so the question is, why hold inventory at all?

Some types of inventory cannot be avoided. Others serve a useful role that should be balanced against the inventory holding costs. Work-in-process (WIP) inventory cannot be avoided. WIP is the inventory of material while it is undergoing any process *that adds value to it*. Thus, the material on the production line, while undergoing the manufacturing process, is WIP inventory.

Typically, however, the time that materials and goods spend in any value-adding process is dwarfed by the time they spend between processes. For example, DuPont Inc. estimated that in 1993 it took about 168 days to get from raw material to a finished product in the supply chain for yarn. Unfortunately, value was actually added to the material only during eight hours of this time. The rest of the time the material was waiting for the next process to take place.

Inventory, however, does have an important function. Inventory's role is to *decouple* processes, disconnecting the various supply chain processes from each other. Decoupling means that processes can operate independently of each other; a tire factory can make tires when it is most efficient and the car factory can use the tires when it is most convenient. Without inventory, the two processes would need to operate synchronously; four tires (of the right size) would roll off the tire-making line just in time to be mounted onto cars in the assembly line.

Decoupling is required because the processes that constitute the supply chain have different characteristics and economies. Thus, to operate well, they need to run independently from the processes that precede or follow them. In the last example, the tire and automobile manufacturers may in fact synchronize their manufacturing processes. The difficulty for the tire manufacturer is that it must synchronize with many automobile manufacturers and also produce for the aftermarket. Thus, a complete synchronization with a single customer may increase its overall costs.

The problem is more obvious when selling to consumers, where it is impossible to coordinate the supply and the demand perfectly. In order to minimize inventory, just as a consumer would come to the store to buy a single package of detergent, a shipment of a single package would be delivered to the supermarket. But consumers do not notify the supermarket when they intend to go shopping and for what product. Furthermore, even if they did, it would be uneconomical to ship detergent in single packages from the factory to the supermarket. So, supermarkets keep inventory on the shelves *just in case* consumers may require it, thus decoupling the process of procurement and receipt of goods from the process of selling them to consumers. Similarly, a manufacturer may keep an inventory of raw material on hand just in case it gets an unexpected order and needs to use it in the manufacturing process. Given estimates of demand randomness and the costs of ordering and holding inventory, classical inventory theory gives procurement managers the tools to optimize the orders so as to minimize their total expected costs, including the cost of lost sales.

The Coordination Challenge

In the mid-1990s, the Swedish car manufacturer Volvo had excessive stocks of green-colored cars. To move them along, the sales and marketing department began offering attractive special deals, even selling at a loss, just to clear the inventory. So green cars started selling, but nobody had told the manufacturing department about the promotions. The latter noted the increase in sales, read it as a sign that consumers had started to like green, and ramped up production of green cars, exacerbating the problem and hurting profitability.[5]

In many cases, coordination is even more challenging when two companies are involved rather than two departments of the same company. Since it takes time from receipt of an order to delivery, companies need to forecast future demand at the time of placing the order. They need to communicate their material requirements to their suppliers, who, in turn, need to communicate and order from their suppliers further "upstream" in the supply chain. The forecasting challenge is discussed further in chapter 6.

Forecasting demand, however, is not the only challenge facing supply chain operations. Some of the challenges are structural.

The Bullwhip Effect

Most babies, oblivious to supply chain management issues, use diapers at a steady rate. Week to week, the number of diapers purchased by parents at Wal-Mart, K-Mart, Carrefour, or El Corte Inglés S.A. is, essentially, constant. In the early 1990s, however, Procter & Gamble, the manufacturer of Pampers, Luvs, and Hipoglos diapers, detected some puzzling sales patterns. Despite the stable birth rate in the United States, and the steady rate of babies' usage of diapers, P&G experienced significant fluctuations of orders from distributors to its factories. In fact, P&G's own orders to its material suppliers, like 3M, fluctuated even more.[6] It soon became clear that orders and inventory levels were subject to greater and greater variations as one moves further and further up the supply chain—from consumers to retailers to distributors to manufacturers to suppliers and their suppliers.

P&G called this phenomenon, depicted in figure 5.4, the *bullwhip effect*, denoting the increased amplitude of orders and the increased fluctuations of inventory levels the further one moves upstream in the supply chain. Hewlett-Packard (HP) uncovered a similar pattern when it examined the orders and sales rates of its printers at Office Depot. While sales at the office supplies store exhibited only mild variations over time, the orders that Office Depot placed on HP fluctuated much more. Furthermore, the orders from HP's printer division to its integrated circuit division had even greater fluctuations. Even Barilla, the Italian pasta manufacturer, has experienced widely fluctuating orders from its distributors in the 1980s, despite the constant level at which Italian households consume pasta. This led to random fluctuations in the distributors' inventory levels and 6 to 7 percent stock-outs.[7]

Several factors contribute to the bullwhip effect. The main factor is the lack of coordination between buyers and sellers along the supply chain. For example, a distributor may perceive a small increase in a retailer's order as an indication of future demand growth, rather than a temporary fluctuation. Anticipating that future orders may be even higher, the distributor orders too much from the manufacturer—not only enough to fulfill the order at

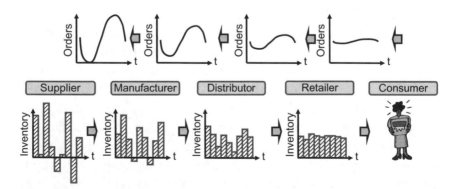

Figure 5.4
The Bullwhip Effect

hand but also to be ready for furture growth in the retailer's orders. The manufacturer now has a magnified order signal and, forecasting even higher future orders, may order an even larger amount from its suppliers. When the higher demand does not materialize at the retail level, the distributor ends up with too much inventory and then cuts back on orders, and even stops ordering completely, and the process repeats up the chain. Orders and inventory then fluctuate with ever-greater amplitude upstream in the supply chain as each echelon misinterprets the order signal.

Even worse, in many cases the sparks that trigger the fluctuations are set on purpose. For example, promotions and discounts cause customers to buy more during the promotions and buy less later. In fact, in the 1980s, Wal-Mart was known for taking advantage of local promotions that P&G was running. When P&G offered, say, a 10-cents-off Tide promotion in the New York region, Wal-Mart would buy all of the Tide it needed nationally in New York and then truck it to its stores in other regions.

The batching of orders and shipments can also start the fluctuations. Many companies order only once a month or once every two weeks, creating an order "spike" for their suppliers. In addition, suppliers' salespeople, motivated by quarterly bonuses, typically create incentives for their customers to order more than they need toward the end of each quarter, causing over-supply in the last month of the quarter followed by low order volume in the next month.

A somewhat different mechanism starts the bullwhip when products are in short supply, for example during the introduction of a new "hot" product such as the Sony Play Station or the Volkswagen Beetle. In these cases, manufacturers may put retailers "on allocation," meaning that each retailer gets only a fraction of what it orders. Cognizant of the practice, the retailers double and triple their orders; even though they know that they do not need and cannot sell the additional products (known in the trade as "phantom" orders). The manufacturer, facing even greater demand for the product than it anticipated may invest further to increase production. Unfortunately, it is bound to be disappointed when supply catches up with the real demand and the phantom orders disappear, leaving the manufacturer with extra product that needs to be sold at lower margins.

Overcoming the bullwhip effect requires careful coordination and continuous communication between companies and within departments and business units of the same company. Some of the programs used by industry to enhance communication and otherwise mitigate the bullwhip effect are described later in this chapter.

Coordination during Disruptions

The bullwhip effect underscores the importance of continuous communication along the supply chain in case of a disruption. Companies may order more from one supplier when another supplier is disrupted, or they may order more in anticipation of a labor strike or a port closure. If the suppliers do not get information about the temporary nature of these orders, they may assume that such orders indicate an increase in demand. They may, in turn, increase capacity or order even more from their own suppliers in anticipation, thus generating a strong bullwhip effect. The same phenomenon can take place when a company reduces its orders for certain materials or parts because of a temporary disruption. Such disruptions include plant closures for refurbishing (or new model introduction), industrial accidents, or work stoppages caused by strikes. If the temporary nature of such disruption is not communicated to suppliers, they may over-react and shift capacity to other uses or stop ordering parts from their own suppliers.

Reducing Inventory

Most large manufacturers did not awaken to the potential cost savings associated with inventory reductions until Toyota Motor Company demonstrated, in the 1980s, the magnitude of these savings and the range of other benefits associated with lean manufacturing. With its vaunted just-in-time system, Toyota coordinated activities throughout the supply chain, reducing both inventories and the bullwhip effect. Even more important, Toyota demonstrated that inventories mask quality problems and that lower inventories lead to higher product quality, thus exposing the hidden cost of carrying inventory.

The realization that inventory costs are much higher than initially thought pushed many other companies to integrate their supply chain more tightly, minimizing the inventory between the various stages. A tight supply chain relies on coordinated connections and synchronized processes between trading partners along the supply chain and it operates with less inventory.

Some approaches to channel coordination—getting all participants to work together to eliminate the costly fluctuations of orders and inventories—try to eliminate some of the middleman functions. For example, in Vendor-Managed-Inventory (VMI) programs, the retailers give manufacturers the point-of-sale data and the manufacturer, in turn, is responsible for replenishing the retailer's shelves. This eliminates the need for the retailer to forecast and order, reducing the chance of order amplification and eliminating a whole echelon of inventory. Barilla used a similar approach in its just-in-time delivery program. Rather than respond to distributors' orders, the company shipped to the distributors just the amount they shipped to the retailers, preventing the distributors from accumulating inventories and amplifying orders. The program successfully reduced distributors' inventories by 50 percent and, at the same time, practically eliminated stock-outs.[8]

Wal-Mart developed *cross-docking* processes in which goods come from the suppliers to Wal-Mart's distribution centers (DCs) and are moved immediately to the stores. This process reduced DC warehousing costs and, more important, eliminated an echelon in the distribution chain. Rather than ordering from the store to the DC and from the DC to the suppliers, the stores were, in fact, ordering directly from the suppliers.

Bose Inc., the Massachusetts manufacturer of high fidelity audio systems, achieved a similar end result by bringing key suppliers' representatives in house and giving them authority to function as an integral part of the Bose material and purchasing systems. The process replaced traditional buyers, planners, and salespeople with "in-plant" supplier personnel responsible for ordering material, parts, and services from their parent companies, according to

Bose's needs. The elimination of suppliers' sales people and buyers' procurement personnel resulted in lower inventory of parts and raw material, as well as more responsive suppliers.[9]

The Japanese concept of *kanban* cards—cards signaling that a particular part is needed—helps control inventory by eliminating the bullwhip effect through control of the ordering process; each stage in the manufacturing process can get the part that it needs only by releasing a kanban card upstream. The total number of kanban cards in the system is controlled, thus ensuring that forecasts are not inflated; each stage in the manufacturing process can order only as many parts as it uses and only when it needs them. This is the underpinning of the "lean" manufacturing systems. Material arrives just in time to be used in the next stage of production, rather than wait just in case it is needed.

There are many other ways in which supply chain participants have cooperated to tighten their supply chains, creating just-in-time flow of material and better information sharing in their quest to reduce inventory without reducing service levels. All these processes are based on similar ideas: Reduction in the number of decision-making echelons and tight coordination and synchronization, leading to lower inventory levels and improved service. The specific programs include Continuous Replenishment Programs (CRP) and Efficient Consumer Response (ECR) used in the grocery industry; Quick Response (QR) programs used in the apparel industry; and Collaborative Planning Forecasting and Replenishment (CPFR) used in the consumer-packaged goods industry.

Vulnerability of Tight Supply Chains

Many modern-day manufacturing plants operate with only a few hours' worth of safety stock, relying on constant communication with their parts suppliers, transportation carriers, and warehousing operators to avoid parts' stock-out. But by removing inventory from the supply chain, every participant becomes more dependent on others. Furthermore, the system as a whole becomes less resilient. This became painfully clear to manufacturers such as Toyota who, in 1995, had to close most of its manufacturing plant immediately following the Kobe earthquake because of a shortage of break shoes.

To avoid costly delays in a lean manufacturing environment in which little safety stock is kept, many manufacturers levy a significant penalty on transportation and logistics providers for late deliveries. For example, Ryder Integrated Logistics provides just-in-time transportation services to the Saturn plant in Spring Hill, Tennessee. It collects information from Saturn regarding each day's production schedule and delivers exactly the right parts from all the area's suppliers to the Saturn plant, just before the parts are needed on the production line. The contract between Saturn and Ryder Integrated Logistics specified a $5,000 penalty for each 15 minutes of a delayed delivery. This contract clause was designed as a deterrent; the actual costs Saturn would incur from a plant shutdown are actually higher.

Thus, lean manufacturing systems, with their low inventory levels, imply less redundancy and increased vulnerability. Although companies reduce their everyday costs, they may be increasing certain long-term vulnerabilities.

Some industries, such as fashion apparel and consumer electronics, face large demand fluctuations and uncertainties as part of their everyday business. Demand forecasting is especially challenging in such industries, yet the companies involved are also extremely cost conscious because they face unrelenting global competition. Thus, on the one hand, they cannot reduce their inventories because these inventories are necessary to buffer against demand uncertainty. On the other hand, they cannot build up inventories because the higher costs will render them uncompetitive. The next chapter examines how such firms deal with the need to reduce inventories and costs yet not increase vulnerabilities to demand disruptions. It offers some lessons in managing challenging supply chains, balancing demand and supply—lessons that can be used in preparing for other disruptions.

6

Demand-Responsive Supply Chains

The need to make or order products before demand is known with certainty is one of the basic challenges of supply chain operations. Too much product means that it has to be stored for a long time, incurring inventory carrying costs and likely being sold at a discount or a loss; too little inventory means lost sales and lost customers.

Typically, companies use forecasting techniques based on statistical models to predict demand and use the resulting forecast to produce or order the amount they anticipate their customers will demand. But even with the most sophisticated forecasting models, forecasts are inaccurate. And forecasting methods are even less useful for predicting low-probability events. Thus, it is instructive to study how companies facing significantly uncertain demand organize their operations. These companies minimize forecast errors by creating a more responsive supply chain so that they can react to demand fluctuations even when not anticipated.

Demand Disruptions

In mid-2000, IBM revamped its laptop computer product line, the venerable ThinkPad, releasing the T20 and A20 models. After losing $800 million in 1998 and $571 million in 1999, the IBM PC division used a conservative forecast of the sales of the new machines and kicked off a major ad campaign in conjunction with the release. However, to the delight of the IBM marketing department and to the horror of its operations department, the new

ThinkPads became an instant hit with consumers. Sales soared, leading immediately to product shortages. In mid-July, customers seeking 79 of the 108 ThinkPad configurations faced back orders of well over a month. The problem had no quick fix because component suppliers were geared for the original forecast and could not quickly ramp up their production of DVD and CD-RW components.

One of the most unfortunate problems with such "under-forecasting" is that IBM does not even know how many potential sales it lost to competitors, as would-be buyers were turned away by the publicity regarding the shortages. Erring on the side of overestimating demand, however, can also be detrimental, as items may have to be sold at discount, robbing the manufacturer or the retailer of its profit margin and even forcing it to sell at a loss. Such discounts are commonplace in both fashion apparel, which is subject to teenagers' whims, and consumer electronics products, which lose their appeal when a new model or gadget comes on the market. But even in mature products, like automobiles, discounting is common. For example, in 2004 American manufacturers were offering $3,000–$4,500 rebates on sales of sport-utility vehicles when demand ran below forecast, in part because of high gas prices.

In some cases, products flop completely, as was the case with the Ford Edsel. After unprecedented consumer research and an extensive ad campaign, Ford introduced the car on September 4, 1957. It quickly became clear, however, that consumers preferred the silhouette photos in the marketing brochures to the actual cars. Instead of the 200,000 Edsels that Ford was geared to sell, only 63,110 were sold—with discounts. Even after a restyling for the 1959 model year, only 45,000 Edsels were sold. Ford pulled the plug on the car one month after the 1960 model was introduced, again to disappointing sales.

New product failures are not confined to automobiles. In the consumer packaged-goods industry, almost 80 percent of all new products and new product variations fail within the first two years. In the industrial products sector, 30 percent of all new products fail.[1] And the results of such failures can be dramatic. In 2003 two pharmaceutical companies—Wyeth Inc. and MedImmune Inc.—jointly introduced a new flu vaccine that could be inhaled rather than injected. Unfortunately, it was not a consumer favorite even during the flu vaccine shortage of 2003.[2] Wyeth was able to sell fewer than 400,000 FluMist doses out of 4 million produced and had to take a $20 million charge in January 2004 to destroy[3] and write off the unsold stock. Wyeth has announced a plant closing and the elimination of several hundred jobs[4] while Med-Immune stayed in the market but produced only a few vaccines in 2004, contributing to the influenza vaccine shortage of 2004.[5]

The world of commerce is strewn with products that failed despite sophisticated customer research and lavish ad campaigns. The failure of New Coke, Crystal Pepsi, the Betamax VCR, the Apple Newton, and Microsoft's Bob demonstrate vividly the difficulties of forecasting.

Forecasting

Forecasting has always been a challenge to business. In the last part of the twentieth century, however, it has become at once more difficult and more important because of several trends that characterize almost all supply chains:

- *Globalization* As companies buy parts and sell products around the globe, their supply chains involve greater distances and larger numbers of partner companies on different continents and over many time zones. The result is longer lead times, a need to forecast further in advance of sales, and greater communication challenges.

- *Product variety and life cycle* As companies introduce more new products, forecasting becomes more challenging because such products have no "history." In addition, the sheer number of new products and the increasing variety of exisitng products mean that each is sold to an ever-smaller market segment, which is more sensitive to random variations (see further explanation below).

- *Demand homogeneity* As CNN and the Internet bring new trends and innovations to every corner of the globe, consumer tastes become similar. In other words, if Japanese teenagers turn thumbs down on a new gadget, it is not likely to catch fire in Kansas City or Barcelona. When markets "move together" like this, the amplitudes of their uncertain fluctuations are larger. Moreover, this trend makes it hard to dump obsolete inventory into secondary markets.

At the same time, forecasting is more important because most companies are facing fierce competition around the globe. Faster product cycles mean that inventory becomes obsolete more quickly, exacerbating inventory carrying costs. Companies that fail to deliver on time are in danger of losing their markets to competitors who are ready to take their place. Thus, forecasting mistakes may have long-term impact.

Many companies have responded to these trends by investing in refined forecasting tools based on statistical models. By and large, these software applications use data on past sales and, with sophisticated algorithms, try to forecast future sales.

Forecasts' Characteristics

Regardless of the sophistication of the underlying approach, the characteristics shared by all supply chain forecasts include the following:

- *Inaccuracy*   The most glaring attribute of all (point) forecasts[6] is that they are invariably wrong. This is simply a statistical reality. For example, forecasting the monthly sales of a certain yellow women's blouse in size 8 at a given price is bound to be wrong because there is a certain probability that it will equal almost any number. Since the forecast is a single number, the probability of the actual sales matching exactly the forecasted demand is practically nil.

- *Improvement with aggregation*   A second characteristic is that aggregate forecasts are more accurate than disaggregate forecasts. Forecasts can be aggregated, for example, over time, geography, or products. With aggregate forecasts, errors tend to cancel each other out, leading to more accurate forecasts.[7] While it is difficult to forecast the sales of a blue men's blazer size 42R on a given day in a given Boston store, it is easier to forecast the *monthly* sales of that blazer in that store, and even easier to forecast the monthly sales of that blazer throughout New England.

- *Time Horizon*   As anybody who follows weather forecasting knows, long-range forecasts are less accurate than short-range ones since fewer factors are known the longer the time frame is. Likewise, sales trajectories can diverge further and further from a projected forecast as time progresses. New fashions, economic changes, and competitors' actions make the distant future murkier than the near-term future. But many supply chain operations require long-term demand forecasts since orders involve long lead times.

- *Reliance on history*   Forecasting methods use historical data and experience. The competitive environment drives manufacturers and suppliers to introduce new products and new versions of old products continuously. In these cases, and when companies enter new markets, data are scarce, making it difficult to forecast.

- *Reliance on trading partners*   History, however, is not the only source of data; trading partners often have information that can help in forecasting and planning. For example, retailers can give their suppliers data on sales patterns throughout their stores so the suppliers can base their forecasts on actual consumer behavior rather than the retailers' order pattern.

- *Risk sharing*   While the sharing of data may lead to more accurate forecasting, companies can also share the *risk* of forecasting. Even though this will not improve the forecast itself, the practice can help supply chain partners mitigate the consequences of wrong forecasts and increase the profits of all trading partners.

Companies facing uncertain demand are doing more than investing in better forecasting tools. Acknowledging the inherent variability of demand and the limitations of statistical forecasting, they use these characteristics to design their supply chains to be flexible and to respond to ever-changing demand patterns, thus making them less dependent on demand forecasting. The flexibility to respond to demand fluctuations, created by these supply chain designs, also increases these companies' resilience to disruption—be it an unexpected demand surge or unexpected problem with their supply lines.

The next sections describe how companies build flexibility into their operations based on each of these six forecast characteristics.

Building Responsiveness with Range Forecasting

Instead of forecasting a single demand figure, progressive companies have turned to forecasting a range of potential outcomes. The range is used as a guide for supply contracting terms and contingency plans: what to do if demand is on the high end or low end of the range. More important, the use of range forecasting conditions the company to think in terms of uncertain outcomes or a range of possible realizations.

Companies can and do use range forecasting for more than just estimating future demand volume. For example, Agilent, Inc., develops a range forecast not only for future demand but also for supply volumes and prices for all of its products. Agilent is a $6 billion manufacturer of scientific instruments and analysis equipment, spun off from Hewlett-Packard in 1999. After developing all the possible outcomes for each new product, it assigns probabilities to each outcome that has more than a 10 percent likelihood of materializing and develops contingencies for these outcomes. Thus, Agilent's planning covers 80 percent of the potential outcomes.

Range forecasts are used in flexible contracting, procurement strategies, and financial planning. The objective is to increase the company's flexibility, as the range forecasts prepare the company for changing market conditions.

Flexible Contracting

Many companies use their range forecast as an integral part of flexible contracts with their suppliers. These contracts specify a range of performance expectations, giving the company built-in flexibility to ramp production up or down as demand materializes. In a typical supply contract, Hewlett-Packard specifies that its suppliers should be able to ramp up production by 50 percent with two weeks' notice and by 100 percent given one month's notice. Similarly, Jabil Circuit Inc., an electronic manufacturing services company, requires its suppliers to increase deliveries by 25 percent on a week's notice and 100 percent above normal on four week notice.[8] Such contracts communicate to the supplier the importance of flexibility.

When contracting for transportation services, it is common for U.S. companies to bid for capacity on certain origin-destination movements ("lanes") and then bid separately for "surge capacity." Surges occur when a company's business grows unexpectedly in certain regions of the country (as a result of weather, for example, or because of an unanticipated large order). Transportation carriers cannot be expected to have trucks or rail cars in reserve everywhere "just in case." They can, however, put in place certain operational procedures to identify available resources and move them around, helping them respond to surges. Such surge capacity is typically priced higher, in acknowledgement of the extra equipment repositioning required by the carriers to respond to the increased demand.

Rather than rely on specific contracts, Helix Technology Inc., a vacuum products company, relies on its long-term relationships with its suppliers, and a continuing assessment of the suppliers' capacities to ensure resilience and flexibility. In particular, Helix uses "quarterly capacity reports" via site visits to the supplier facilities to assess the supplier's capability to support it in case of a disruption or a significant change in demand patterns. This also contributes to "socializing" the suppliers so they can better understand the importance that Helix places on flexibility.[9]

Multi-sourcing

Typically, the forecasting range can be separated into an uncertain portion and a more predictable portion. Companies can be confident that they will sell at least at the low end of the forecast range while being less sure of, but prepared to sell at, the high end of the range.

For example, Hewlett-Packard manufactures DeskJet printers for North America in Singapore and Vancouver.[10] The plant in Vancouver is more flexible, faster, and closer to the market, but manufacturing costs in Singapore are lower. So HP assigns the more stable, high-volume production to Singapore while using the Vancouver plant for the uncertain portion of the demand range. The Vancouver plant is used for short production runs to satisfy temporary demand surges. It is also used during each printer's end-of-life, when demand is falling off and becoming very uncertain (as a result of a new model introduction, a competitor's offering or other changes in the marketplace). At that point, HP can even stop production in Vancouver altogether without being burdened with several weeks' worth of inventory in the pipeline from Singapore.

Financial Planning

Ford Motor Company, like other manufacturers in the automotive and heavy manufacturing sectors, cannot easily change its automotive production capacity. While range forecasting is used to let suppliers understand the variety of possible outcomes that Ford foresees, Ford uses the range forecasting internally for financial planning. Ford knows that at the low end of the demand range it will have to offer rebates to potential buyers, while at the high end it may have to use overtime to manufacture the extra vehicles that consumers demand. Analyzing the possible financial outcomes helps Ford hedge and plan its borrowing, cash and dividend policies.

In general, the value of range forecasting is that it conditions all the organizations involved in a particular supply chain to the likelihood that the demand, and therefore orders, staffing levels, capacity utilization, and other factors may defer from the expected forecast number.

Building Flexibility with Risk Pooling

One of the largest geographic markets for Cadillac, the upscale division of General Motors Corporation, is Florida. Customers' experience when buying a Cadillac in Florida used to be similar to the less-than-satisfactory experience of car buyers everywhere. The process involved negotiations in which the dealers tried to sell what they had on their lot and the customers tried to compensate for buying the set of options and color they did not really want by haggling over price. If customers insisted on buying exactly what they wanted they had to wait about two months[11] for the vehicle to be built to their specifications.

To enhance customer service, Cadillac decided in the late 1990s to move to a new sales regime. Instead of letting dealers order whichever cars they thought customers desired, Cadillac shipped only demonstration vehicles to the dealers, giving customers the opportunity to test-drive the cars. Cadillac itself used its Florida-wide database to forecast sales of different vehicle combinations and shipped them to a central Florida distribution center (DC). When a customer placed an order at any dealer, Cadillac shipped the car from the DC immediately, getting it to the dealer overnight.

Thus, instead of the dealers ordering from the factory, they were ordering from the DC. The DC had exactly the vehicle that the customer wanted about 75 percent of the time; a significant achievement given the large number of models, colors, and options available. When the right vehicle was not available at the DC, Cadillac was able to build the desired vehicle within three weeks, which is less than half the industry average, because it had to deal with a smaller number of special orders.[12]

Why Risk Pooling?

In the example above, Cadillac had its customers' desired configurations "in stock" most of the time because its forecast for all of Florida was inherently more accurate than any individual dealer's forecast. Assume a customer wanted a crimson pearl Cadillac DeVille with dark gray interior, the Bose music system, and a touch-screen GPS, but no XM radio; memory mirrors, but no night-vision display or rain-sensing wipers; lumbar support for the driver seat but no heated/cooled front seats; with a trunk mat, but without a universal garage door opener; and so on. The chances of a customer finding that particular car at a local dealership are very low. The chances that such a car may be available centrally in Florida, however, are high because Cadillac only had to forecast that somebody, somewhere in Florida, may want such a car.

Thus, Cadillac *pooled* the forecast risks across all its Florida dealers, forecasting Florida demand in the aggregate. As mentioned in the discussion of forecast characteristics, aggregate forecasts are more accurate than individual forecasts, because random forecast errors tend to cancel each other out. Harley Davidson, the American motorbike manufacturer, has instituted a similar system in Europe, leading to significantly improved customer service and reduced inventories.

Part Variability Reduction

Another common risk pooling strategy is to reduce the number of components used to make products. When multiple products share common components, the company can aggregate the forecasts for the products to create a more accurate forecast for the common components. For example, Intel's Systems Group found it possible to simplify their parts usage by using common components, reducing 20,000 different part types to 500. In one case, they were using a mix of 2,000 different types of resistors, capacitors, and diodes; after analyzing their designs, they found that they needed only 35 types.[13]

Using a component or a part in a large number of finished products pools the demand risk. The demand for each part is the aggregate demand for all the finished products that use it. If there are many products, each facing its own independent demand pattern, a change in the demand for one product is likely to be offset by an opposite change in the demand for another. Such aggregation makes forecasting more accurate, enabling companies to keep all the parts they use in stock without excessive levels of inventory.

Product Variability Reduction

A large number of product configurations increases forecasting difficulty. For example, the 2000 Mercedes E Class allowed customers in the U.K. to specify any combination of two body styles, nine power trains, 121 paint/trim combinations, and 41 include/exclude options, for a total of 3.9 trillion possible car varieties. Clearly, a company cannot forecast and stock trillions of car varieties. Some manufacturers combat these forecasting difficulties by restricting the number of options they offer. Thus, many automobile manufacturers put forward "packages" of options rather than offer a smorgasbord of add-on features. Honda, in contrast to Mercedes, allowed buyers of its popular Accord model in 2000 to choose among two body styles, four power trains, 30 paint/trim combinations, and two options, for a total of only 529 permutations. One can imagine the problem facing Mercedes dealers when trying to decide what to buy in order to stock their lot. The smaller number of packages, compared to an exponential explosion of fully customized configurations, allows for better risk pooling, lower variability, and thus better forecasts, resulting in higher customer satisfaction and lower inventory carrying costs.

The risk pooling in this strategy aggregates the desires of a large number of potential customers into a smaller number of product variants. The challenge with this strategy is to make sure that the vast majority of customers can be satisfied by a more limited range of options. Very few manufacturers today are in the position of Henry Ford, who suggested that customers can have its venerable Model T "in any color as long as it is black."[14]

Shortening the Forecast Horizon

Reducing the lead time from product conception to its introduction into the marketplace shrinks the time lag over which the firm needs to forecast customer needs. The main steps involved are described in figure 6.1. Each of these steps involves multiple processes. For example, product development encompasses first the development of the product idea, market research, and final specification. Then the engineering process involves multiple cycles of building a prototype, testing it, sending it over to the manufacturing department, studying their objections, and repeating the process with a new prototype. Once the design is agreed

Figure 6.1
Sequential Processes

upon, the ramp-up phase may involve tooling for the new product, manufacturing test batches, and finally production. In many cases, when nonstandard parts are involved, one waits for the suppliers to go through the same process. Production and logistics involve procuring and processing the parts and raw material, manufacturing the product, and distributing it.

In order to shorten the lead time involved, quick response manufacturing (QRM)[15] processes involve rapid prototyping to speed up product development, rapid tooling to speed the ramp-up process, and rapid manufacturing to speed the production process. These methods are based on concurrent engineering—performing many of the development tasks in parallel, as shown in figure 6.2, in order to reduce the overall lead time through more efficient coordination between the various departments involved. To this end, the engineering iterations are conducted both with suppliers and with manufacturing personnel, with input from the procurement and logistics departments.

Companies who practice concurrent processes can react quickly to market changes when planning a new product. In addition, they can better respond to disruptions when products have to be changed quickly, parts rerouted, or products redistributed.

Some companies, such as Lucent Technologies, established such concurrency by creating a single supply chain organization. Others used physical proximity. For example, Luen Thai Holding Ltd. has been cobbling together a textile "supply chain city" in the southern Chinese city of Dongguan. It is a vast campus that represents all stages of the textile supply chain, aimed at speeding the time to market for customers like Liz Claiborne Inc. Instead of working

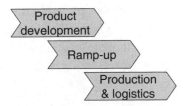

Figure 6.2
Concurrent Processes

with factories around the globe, Liz Claiborne designers are co-located with engineers from the fabric mills and apparel manufacturers. The aim is to shrink the iterative design process and reduce the time from concept to retail store from the current 10–50 weeks to just 60 days.

Creating History with Test Batches

Nine West, a subsidiary of Jones Apparel Group, has emerged as a leader in specialty women's shoe retail through a multistep supply chain design. The new process reduces downside risks and increases upside potential.

Fashion retailers such as Nine West face a common forecasting challenge. Each time a new style of shoe is introduced, Nine West faces unknown demand. Each shoe model is unique and thus it has no historical sales pattern to support demand forecasting. Typically, the result was widely missed forecasts, missed sales targets, and missed profits. When Nine West had a style that its customers really wanted, it ran out of stock. But at the same time, it had too much stock of slow-moving styles and had to discount them. It even developed a well-oiled process of getting rid of the unwanted inventory through outlet stores and discount retailers.

To improve its forecasts and be able to base its manufacturing decisions on sales data, Nine West developed a new process. After placing an order with a supplier, the first 1,000 pairs of shoes of a new style were flown to five representative U.S. stores where their sales were monitored closely for a few days. That information was then used as an indicator to forecast the sales of the entire line, increasing production if the sales were above expectations and decreasing it if the sales were lower than expected. If a new shoe "bombed" completely during the tests, Nine West would not only halt production; it would also send any already-produced shoes directly to outlet stores and discounters, saving the transportation to and from its own facilities.

Nine West is not the only manufacturer/retailer using this approach. A similar *accurate response* system used by the fashion skiwear manufacturer Sport Obermeyer cut the cost of over-production and under-production by half; enough to increase profits by 60 percent.[16] While such accurate response systems were designed to help companies respond to demand/supply imbalances caused by demand fluctuations, they allow companies to react quickly to imbalances rooted in supply problems as a result of a disruption, since they entail flexible contracts and close working relationships with suppliers.

Collaboration to Improve Forecasting

Collaborative efforts based on lean supply chain principles—such as vendor-managed-inventory (VMI) and the Kanban system—are aimed primarily at reducing the bullwhip effect. They all involve information sharing. Wal-Mart Stores recognized that providing information to its suppliers can help these suppliers become more efficient, reducing their cost and therefore their prices. To this end, Wal-Mart developed in the early 1990s a computer application known as Retail Link. The tool, which is currently Internet-based, provides secure access to detailed daily sales data, trend analysis and more, to Wal-Mart's many suppliers and partners. "Retail Link provides rapid access to near real-time information," said Linda Dillman, Wal-Mart's CIO. She added that the system's information capabilities range "from predefined management reporting to fully customizable inquiries."[17]

Actual sales data help suppliers understand the real demand for their product, regardless of the retailer's order pattern, negating one cause of the bullwhip effect. Such data can help suppliers better plan their production, promotions, and product introductions.

Tackling the difficulties in forecasting, however, requires more than data sharing; it requires a cooperative process of identifying discrepancies and fixing the trading partners' forecasts so that their actions can be aligned. Many such processes have been developed over the years. The Collaborative Planning, Forecasting, and Replenishment (CPFR) process is one of the most comprehensive such methods.

Collaborative Planning, Forecasting, and Replenishment
Superdrug Plc operates more than 700 stores throughout the United Kingdom, offering its customers an average of more than 6,000 product lines. Despite selling health and beauty aids—items for which the demand is relatively stable and therefore should be known—inventory levels at Superdrug were running in peaks and valleys and didn't always match sales levels. These supply-demand mismatches created out-of-stock situations in some cases and excess inventory in others. Not surprisingly, most of the problems occurred during sales promotions and new product introductions.

To solve the problem, Superdrug turned to CPFR, a process developed by an industry consortium of retailers and consumer packaged goods manufacturers.[18] Its partner in the collaboration process was Johnson & Johnson (J&J), the giant health-care products manufacturer and one of Superdrug's most important suppliers. Both trading partners had a keen interest in increasing forecast accuracy.

A pilot process involving several J&J products was launched in August 2000 and ran through the end of that year. Each week, the two trading partners would exchange their sales forecasts and orders forecasts. Next, a special-purpose CPFR software engine[19] would process the data and return any discrepancies between the data sets. A joint group then decided which forecast was correct and who should adjust. The data were adjusted and the process repeated the following week.

CPFR resulted in a 13 percent reduction of Superdrug's inventory levels, while improving in-store availability by 1.6 percent. Superdrug cited many other, less quantifiable but possibly even more important benefits of its collaboration process, including better relationships with J&J, a factor that can create flexibility to respond to future disruptions.

The potential of close supplier relationships to enhance resilience was demonstrated by Toyota's suppliers in the aftermath of the fire in the sole plant of Aisin, Toyota's P-valve supplier, discussed in chapter 13.

Risk Sharing

While sharing the risk of an erroneous forecast with supply chain partners cannot improve the forecast itself, it can mitigate the consequences of forecast mistakes and lead to higher expected profits for all trading partners. Risk sharing can be imbedded in supply contracts in many forms, including buybacks, revenue sharing, and real option-based contracts.

One of the most common forms of risk sharing arrangements is the *buyback agreement*. In the book industry, for example, publishers buy back unsold books from retailers.[20] By doing so, publishers share the risk of having too much inventory rather than let the retailers shoulder the entire risk. This arrangement encourages the retailers not to be unnecessarily conservative in ordering books and it can increase the profits of both the supplier and the retailer.

Similarly, the practice of "price support" provides reimbursements from the manufacturer to the retailer when the price of a product falls as a result of the introduction of new models. This practice, prevalent in the consumer electronics industries, is similar to a buyback agreement in its effect on both trading partners.

For the retailer, such arrangements are advantageous because having higher inventory allows it to sell more if demand is high. At the same time, the retailer gets financial support from the manufacturer if the product is not selling and must be discounted below cost. For the manufacturer, these arrangements work because the manufacturer sells more up front with a better chance of higher sales. Even if it must bear some of the risk of low sales, its expected profits are higher.

Blockbuster Increases Sales with Revenue Sharing[21]

Until 1998, video-rental stores bought movie tapes from the major studios for about $66 a tape and rented them to customers at $3 a tape. This meant that it took 22 rentals just to cover the tape's direct cost and a lot more in order to return a profit. Unfortunately for the retailers and the studios, consumers' interest in movie rentals peaks at the time of the release and wanes shortly thereafter as newer movies are released. Because tapes required so many rentals to reach profitability, retailers purchased tapes in accordance with long-term, not peak, rental patterns. Thus, retailers were nearly always out of the most popular movies during peak demand, leaving consumers frustrated and both stores and studios losing potential income.

In the summer of 1998, Blockbuster Video solved this problem by restructuring its supply contracts. Instead of paying $66 a tape, it negotiated with Paramount Studios to buy each tape for only $9 but give the studio 50 percent of the rental revenues. Even though Blockbuster gave away 50 percent of the $3 rental fee, the remaining $1.50 let them cover the direct costs in just six rentals. At this price, Blockbuster could justify buying many more copies of tapes, because the risk of not being able to recover the tape purchasing costs during the peak demand period was greatly reduced. The larger purchases led to many more rentals and satisfied customers. In fact, the average inventory of tapes of major movie releases in Blockbuster stores increased from 24 to 124 tapes per title, as compared with an average inventory of 12 tapes at independent stores.

The results were spectacular. Blockbuster's market share increased by five percentage points in the first year following the establishment of the new supply contracts (an amount that roughly equaled the share of the number two retailer, Hollywood Studios). Blockbuster's market share continued to increase from 24 percent in 1999 to 40 percent in 2002. The new arrangement was very profitable for the studios as well, because minting more tapes costs very little; the largest cost is in creating the content in the first place.

Two outcomes of this revenue-sharing scheme stand as testament to its success. First, the practice became widespread throughout the industry for all the large chains and studios. The second outcome was that Blockbuster and the studios were sued for unfair trade practices by independent retailers—a sure sign that the scheme provided Blockbuster with a competitive advantage.[22]

Reducing the Dependence on Statistical Forecasting

Companies facing uncertain demand cannot rely only on statistical forecasting, even when using increasingly sophisticated algorithms. As the examples in this chapter demonstrate, they must use inherently flexible supply chain designs, allowing them to anticipate and respond to inevitable demand changes instead of planning for a fixed forecasted amount.

The major benefit of range forecasts and flexible contracts is that they condition all the supply chain partners to think and act in terms of multiple possible scenarios. Such nimbleness is likely to earn its rewards also when responding to a disruption.

Reducing the number of parts and product variants allows companies to use aggregate forecasting, which is more accurate. Aggregation creates inherent flexibility—inventory can be deployed to serve multiple products, multiple markets, or multiple retail outlets. It allows a company to move parts and products from surplus areas to areas where they are needed. The same procedures and mindsets can be used when responding to disruptions.

Reducing time-to-market means that a firm can better respond to changing market conditions because it forecasts over a shorter horizon. It also means that it can recover faster from a disruption because its business processes are concurrent and the various functions are accustomed to cooperating with each other.

Using test batches to gauge market demand reduces uncertainty and allows firms to make manufacturing and distribution decisions based on actual data. The benefits of such practice are that firms can re-route their goods to where they are actually needed. For disruption-planning purposes, however, one of the main benefits of this approach is that it conditions the firms and its suppliers to react quickly and to test continuously for uncertain outcomes.

The benefits of collaborative relationships and risk sharing contracts vis-à-vis disruptions are similar. Collaboration strengthens the relationships between the trading partners, making it easier to respond to disruptions. Risk-sharing contracts ensure that trading partners understand each other's processes and share data, leading to faster response in case of disruptions.

These examples demonstrate how firms can create supply chains that are responsive and can react nimbly to supply/demand imbalances in an environment of high demand uncertainty. Such supply chains are also more resilient and can withstand supply disruptions better. Most companies invest in these and related schemes designed to make them more flexible and less prone to forecasting errors. The increased resilience offered by such supply chain designs may provide an extra impetus for moving in these directions.

Another system for creating flexibility—based on postponement and late customization—combines many of the principles outlined in this chapter to create flexible organizations that can withstand significant disruptions. This topic is discussed in chapter 12.

III

Reducing Vulnerability

7

Reducing the Likelihood of Intentional Disruptions

Disruptions can be random, accidental, or intentional. Chapters 2 and 3 dealt with some of the methods for assessing and reducing the likelihood of random and accidental disruptions. Reducing the likelihood of intentional disruptions means increasing security. Efforts to reduce the likelihood of high-impact intentional disruptions involve several principles that, at their core, are as applicable to reducing the likelihood of a damaging theft, or a computer virus, as they are to reducing the likelihood of a successful terrorist attack. The specifics and the intensity may differ, but many of the security principles are universal.

They're Out to Get You

Left unattended for only a few moments, an American Airlines courier van parked at a loading dock outside Heathrow Airport in London was stolen just before lunch on Sunday, January 12, 2003. The van wasn't holding a typical shipment of overnight parcels. It held a valuable consignment of Intel processors that had just arrived from Miami.

The thieves knew exactly which van to take and exactly which cargo in the van to remove; they took $7.5 million in high-end Pentium IV chips while ignoring the $2.5 million in low-end Pentium III chips also in the van. At several hundreds of dollars per chip,[1] Intel's fastest processors are worth their weight in gold. A 26-pound box of chips can be worth half a million dollars; a pallet can hold $10 million to $60 million, and a truckload holds hundreds of millions of dollars worth of chips at retail prices.[2]

But to add insult to the injury, many of the stolen chips were not simply sold to anonymous PC makers. Instead, they were first over-clocked and *then* sold. With chips, speed is money. Like other semiconductor makers, Intel marks each computer chip with its officially rated speed and sells it according to the marked speed. Counterfeiting the rating, by re-marking a few numbers on the back of an Intel processor, can add $100 to $200 to the sale price of the processor. This profit potential has attracted a steady stream of counterfeiters since computers became commonplace with the introduction of the Intel 286 processor in 1982. A string of arrests from Singapore to Europe to Australia to the United States has highlighted the magnitude of the problem.[3] The added challenge for Intel is that running the chip at higher-than-rated speeds may cause frequent crashes and shorter chip life spans. Re-marked chips not only cannibalize sales of the higher-margin, high-performance chips, but they also create higher warranty costs because customers turn to Intel when these chips fail, and these failures can damage the brand's reputation.

Securing the Chips

Intel's supply chain stretches around the globe, including almost 300 corporate locations. Motivated by rising theft in the mid-1990s, Intel launched an initiative to reduce and eliminate the problem. It mapped its supply chain to identify all the places where chips could be stolen. To prioritize its security investments, Intel developed a "threat scoring model," classifying facilities into three risk categories with the highest category getting the most attention.

With facilities secured, Intel turned its attention to its shipments because those shipments move outside of Intel's control. It developed a process to assess the security of its suppliers' premises and their security procedures; it began measuring freight carriers' security and putting those metrics into its negotiated supply contracts; it insisted on background checks on drivers, because drivers are routinely out of reach of Intel's controls; and it introduced "security through obscurity" by shipping its chips in plain unmarked boxes so that potential thieves don't know that there is Intel inside.

To defeat counterfeiters, Intel implemented a long list of defensive measures. It replaced removable painted numbers with more permanent laser-etched numbers; developed retail packages with holograms and other hard-to-copy markings; and created software to detect any mismatch between the chip's internal rating and operating speed. "Re-marking in the next year [2000] is going to be significantly more difficult than a year ago," said Craig Johnson, a member of an Intel task force working to combat re-marking.[4]

As an added security measure, Intel changes the routing of its shipments at irregular intervals to make it more difficult to spot its distribution patterns. It has also instituted regular security drills to test the preparedness of its employees. Former Intel CEO Andy Grove named his book *Only the Paranoid Survive*.[5] Grove may have been motivated not only by the need to keep on top of changing technology but also by such attacks on his company. In keeping with that philosophy, he instilled a culture of skepticism and wariness that promotes preparedness.

Security Principles

The overarching principle underlying all security measures is that they must work in concert with the company's main mission—conducting business and making money. Because companies are run by executives who are charged with this mission, the challenge for security professionals is to "make the business case" for investments in reducing the likelihood of disruptions. The business case is easier to make when the investments are an integral part of the business, supporting and enhancing the main mission. In addition, the processes put in place are more likely to be followed and thus be more effective.

In the short term, a company's risk profile is determined by the location of its facilities and the nature of its business. For most companies, these location decisions were made well before modern threats were a reality. As companies make such decisions today, many realize that they involve not only long-term cost and service levels but also new risk factors.

Based on its risk profile, a company should identify the possible disruptions and prepare a set of processes to reduce the probability of each one. These processes should be based on the following principles:

- Use layered and balanced methods.
- Separate the threats from the baseline activity.
- Collaborate and build partnerships.
- Build a culture of awareness and sensitivity to security.
- Drill, drill, and drill.

These principles lead to a set of defensive actions that overlap with and complement each other. After first outlining an example of a comprehensive security framework at work, the next section examines each of these principles in turn.

"Never Again" in Boston[6]

Boston's Logan International Airport was the departure airport of the two Boeing 767s that struck the World Trade Center on September 11, 2001. Burdened with the responsibility for the weak security processes that allowed these two terrorist teams through, Logan's managers were determined to turn the airport into a model of security.

To begin with, Massport, the agency that runs Logan, identified the ways in which the airport can be attacked, including attackers entering over a perimeter fence, posing as passengers, or impersonating airport workers. An attack could also include a bomb inside passengers' luggage or an assault on the airport terminals themselves.

The next step was to prepare a layered defense against each one of these modes of attack. The first one was a possible entry through the airport's perimeter. Since the airport abuts private homes on one side and the busy waters of Boston Harbor on the other, the standard security approach of setting a "clear zone" beyond the airport perimeter was not feasible. Instead, the airport decided to enlist the people who conduct normal business outside its perimeter as the first layer of the defense team. Massport asked the people who know the environment best—neighboring home-owners and fishermen—to report any suspicious behavior to the airport authorities; they even gave cellphones to clam diggers. As a second layer of defense and detection it installed smart surveillance equipment, consisting of motion detectors and remote monitors, so a perimeter breach can be identified immediately.

But the security needed to be balanced. That means that protecting against a perimeter breach would only mean that perpetrators will try to find another way to enter the airport. To forestall entry to the airport as part of the stream of passengers, the detection procedures start when the passenger books the flight. The passenger's name (including spelling variations) and billing information are checked against airline databases and FBI information to identify profiles of risky travelers requiring more in-depth checks.

As in other airports, police patrols do not allow any vehicle to park unattended at the terminals' curbsides. The state police at Logan also routinely alter the traffic flow patterns throughout the airport to make it more difficult to plan an attack. In addition, Logan police officers patrolling the curbsides and terminals were trained in behavior pattern recognition, designed to identify people who may pose a risk. Officers were also trained in the proper approach and questioning of suspicious passengers. A scaled-down version of this training was also given to the 15,000 employees at Logan and to 1,000 Transportation Security Administration (TSA) personnel working at Logan.[7]

The screening of passengers is augmented by TSA managers working the front of the security queue, looking for suspicious patterns. Additionally, special TSA teams conduct random checks of screened passengers at their gates. These teams not only introduce an element of uncertainty into any potential attack, but they also provide extra manpower deep at the heart of the terminals if a problem arises.

To make sure that their security measures do not interfere with the airport's main mission, Massport scans all bags after they are checked in, rather than at the front of the airline desks. The reason is that such scanning can be more efficient and takes less time.

Massport also invested in special operator training so luggage is not delayed unnecessarily and does not miss the plane. The goal is to support the main mission of the airport, which is moving people and their luggage efficiently from the curbside to the planes. With the same goal in mind, the airport also instituted a comprehensive quick response system, so it will not have to shut down the terminals if security is breached as a result of non-threatening carelessness or a mistake. For example, an arriving passenger may remember belatedly that something was left on a plane and rush back through an exit. In most airports, this would trigger a "total airport shut down" that would require re-screening of all the people in the airport. Such was the case in Atlanta Airport on November 16, 2001, when a football fan rushed past guards and down an "up" escalator to reach a flight to catch the University of Georgia game in Mississippi.[8] On April 8, 2002, Cincinnati airport was shut down because of a screener's mistake. Similarly, security officials ordered the evacuation of United Airlines Terminal 8 and two adjacent terminals in L.A. Airport and re-screened all passengers after a passenger got off a plane and went back into a secure area on September 4, 2004. Similar incidents took place in several other airports.

Such procedures interrupt the entire airport for several hours, causing delays throughout the U.S. air transportation system. Instead, when such a security breach takes place at Logan, the airport managers come together immediately at the scene, review surveillance, and determine whether a shutdown is required, or if a more limited response will suffice.

More than forty agencies, airlines, and service providers with operations in the airport participate in the daily business at Logan. High-level representatives of all these organizations meet daily for a security briefing. The briefing covers current threats, new procedures, new personnel, and intelligence from outside sources.

In the winter of 2003, to prepare for the worst, the airport conducted a major disaster exercise, involving all the area hospitals, local emergency responders, and city and state officials.

Logan's layered defenses are modeled after the scheme used in Ben Gurion Airport in Tel Aviv, modified to reflect the lower risk and the lower tolerance of the American public to privacy intrusions. To check arriving passengers, Israeli security starts with a checkpoint well before passengers and their companions enter the airport grounds, continuing with roaming security personnel watching the curbside. When entering the terminal all passengers are interviewed at special security stations before they are even allowed to approach the airline counters. Passengers pass through another checkpoint before getting to the police's passport control station and then through the usual litany of metal detectors, X-rays, and hand screening checks. El Al, the Israeli airline, adds another layer of security with on-board trained air marshals on every flight, in case a hijacker should ever make it on board.

Supply Chain Security

Following the principles laid out above, one can start thinking methodically about how to apply them in efforts to increase security and reduce the likelihood of high-impact intentional disruptions.

The immediate components of the supply chain for any company include its own sites—plants, warehouses, and offices. As mentioned above, strategic decisions such as where facilities are located determine much of the company's disruption risk profile. Chapter 3 focused on assessing the likelihood of earthquakes and weather phenomena; such methods can be used to choose sites less likely to be disrupted by such events. Choosing a site that is less likely to be a terrorist object involves geopolitical considerations in the choice of country and region. Within any country, and within the United States, such considerations should include avoiding proximity to likely targets such as national symbols and important infrastructure components. Aon Re, the U.S. reinsurance arm of Aon Corp. demonstrates a potential client's vulnerability to a terrorist attack by simply placing the company's existing locations on top of a database of about 5,000 possible terrorist targets across the United States. "Most clients are shocked when they see the analysis," says Michael Bungert, Aon Re's chief executive.[10]

Choosing a location where unions are not dominant may increase the likelihood of harmonious labor-management relationships and reduce the likelihood of labor disruptions, particularly in industries characterized by a history of acrimonious labor-management interactions. Consequently, in 1993, the German automaker Daimler-Benz put its first U.S. factory in Alabama because of the low penetration of labor unions in that state. Alabama is a so-called "Right to Work" state, where unions cannot force workers to pay union dues. By 2004 the state hosted factories for DaimlerChrysler, Honda, and Hyundai, employing nearly 84,000 workers. Good labor-management relationships are important not only for avoiding strikes. In the context discussed here, labor can be the most important asset of a company; it can play a critical role in awareness and prevention. On the other hand, it also represents a crucial vulnerability—representing "the enemy from within." Thus, security considerations add weight to employee selection and monitoring procedures already used by most companies.

Since a company lives within its supply chain, security and resilience considerations are important in the process of choosing trading partners, suppliers, transportation carriers, and other providers. Adding "external" considerations to suppliers' choice, it should be noted, is not new. For example, after the technology bubble burst in the early 2000s, many companies required a review of the financial viability of software vendors before purchasing their products, in addition to the usual functionality, quality, pricing, and service considerations.

TAPA, a high-technology industry initiative described in chapter 8, includes a supplier certification program in its Freight Security Requirement document. The program is aimed mainly at certification of logistics suppliers, including trucking and warehousing companies. Insurance companies, such as the Chubb Corporation, help their customers choose "safe" suppliers by tallying the losses on various lanes of commerce and by each logistics provider. Similar processes, whether through industry consortia, insurance companies, or informal networks, can help certify and select all manner of suppliers.

Layered and Balanced Defense

Automobile companies design safety systems to ensure that a driver's survivability in a head-on collision does not rely on a single defensive measure. Instead, the front of the car is designed to crumple and absorb energy, airbags are designed to inflate and cushion, and the seat belt is designed to stretch just enough to slow the forward momentum of the driver. (In addition, to avoid specific dangers, the engine block is designed to slide under the passenger compartment and the steering wheel shaft is designed to collapse.)

This is the principle of layered defense. It is based on a series of measures, each of which may work, say, only 75 percent of the time. The chance that four such independent layers will fail, however, is less than half of 1 percent.

Most security processes embed the principles of layering. Perimeter fencing, burglar alarms, closed-circuit television monitoring, and access control have become commonplace since 9/11 in many corporate locations. In addition, getting into most large corporate locations requires a pre-arranged appointment and an employee escort while on the premises. Similarly, safety measures for operating a chemical processing tank are based on several layers of safety devices and procedures such as pressure and temperature meters with shutoff valves, cooling mechanisms, overflow tanks, and water sprinklers.

Defensive measures, however, need to be balanced as well as layered. Investing in a highly secure front door to deter house burglars is not effective if the back door or the windows are vulnerable. Thus, a defensive scheme needs to address all disruption possibilities at a level commensurate with the vulnerability of the firm to these disruptions, including all potential random, accidental, and intentional threats.

Few companies need to have the same level of defense as an airport, a nuclear plant, or a food distribution center. But the principle of investing in layered and balanced defensive measures holds for all.

Separating the Threat from the Baseline

The vast majority of events faced by companies are benign. To find out the few that pose a threat, companies need to develop ways to differentiate between risky and normal patterns. For example, to secure their cyber space, corporate information technology managers use special applications that monitor Internet traffic. These programs single out viruses, hackers, and spy-ware, which move in irrational ways compared to normal traffic (e.g., rather than moving in the most efficient way, their circuitous flow is designed to hide their origin). When an attack is successful, its pattern is added to the library of aberrant patterns and disseminated, so that firewalls and virus-killer applications can identify the pattern and trap it. Similarly, spam detection software uses a "scoring" function to rate each incoming e-mail message and decide whether it should be classified as spam or as a legitimate message, based on such information as the subject line, sender profile, known spam originating servers, and match-up with stored spammer databases.[11]

Most other security measures (and, more generally, disruption-avoidance measures) are based, in one form or another, on recognizing abnormalities or "outliers" in an otherwise regular pattern. For example, it was the hesitant behavior of Ahmed Ressam when he tried to enter the United States at Port Angeles, Washington, on December 14, 1999, that attracted the attention of Diana Dean, a 19-year veteran U.S. customs inspector. "There was something in his eyes," she said. When asked for further identification, Ressam tried to flee, only to be caught with more than 150 pounds of explosives[12] stashed in the wheel-bed of the trunk of his rented Chrysler 300M and written plans for bombing Los Angeles International Airport.

Clearly, it would be unrealistic to expect every guard in an office building reception desk to be endowed with the intuition of a veteran customs service inspector. Yet normal patterns of behavior do exist for business operations and their surroundings—basically, people need to have a purpose to be in any given location or perform any given activity—and several companies have trained their entire work force to recognize people and activities that do not fit into the normal patterns.

An important use of pattern recognition in the context of supply chain management is in understanding the normal flow of shipments in and out of a company's facilities. With today's technology, most companies have some idea where their shipments are at any point in time. GPS-equipped vessels and trucks transmit their locations, and because the company's databases contain information about which shipment is on which vessel or truck, the shipments can be followed through their predetermined shipping plan. Once a pattern of "normal" deviations from the plan is established and associated, for example, with severe weather or port congestion, outliers can be identified and investigated. In fact, existing supply chain visibility software applications are designed to perform this task automatically. The applications integrate the data from carriers and other logistics service providers into a system that can alert companies if their shipments are going to be late—an important function in the just-in-time world.

Another example of threat segmentation based on pattern recognition is the "profiling" of potential threats at airports. For example, El Al Airlines[13] would generally pay little attention to a Hebrew-speaking Israeli passport holder who is a frequent flier traveling with his family. It would vigorously interrogate, however, a young foreigner traveling alone on a one-way ticket.[14] The questions touch on trip purpose, history of activity and places of stay just before coming to the airport, names of associates who are traveling together and their relationships to the traveler, employment history, and more. The questioners listen to the answers but monitor the passenger's behavior at the same time, looking for telltale signs of lying and nervousness.[15]

More generally, pattern recognition is the bedrock of all process control functions. Deviations from normal behavior in a manufacturing process or a shipping pattern can be detected by using well-developed statistical models of process control (see chapter 9).

A very important vulnerability results from complexity. As systems become more complex, they become more difficult to design, build, and ensure for proper operation without hidden exposures. In addition, outliers are more difficult to discern from the normal pattern of events when the underlying "baseline" events or transactions are complex. One of the most spectacular examples of complexity leading to a dangerous disruption was the September 23, 1998, collapse of Long Term Capital Management (LTCM). The hedge fund invested in derivatives so complicated that even some of the people at LTCM who created them, including economics Nobel Laureates Myron Scholes and Robert Merton, apparently thought they had a "sure system" and did not adequately defend against certain market risks.[16]

Collaboration

By themselves, most company security professionals cannot deal with intentional threats around the globe. Because the supply chains on which their companies rely span dozens of countries under a variety of regimes, companies need to collaborate with their local suppliers, customers, logistics providers, and other trading partners in order to be effective. Learning from other companies' experience, and from the experience accumulated in various regulatory and law enforcement agencies, is also crucial for reducing the likelihood of accidents.

Working together with trading partners along the supply chain creates a safe and secure chain of custody for shipments. Working with other companies within the same industry, including competitors, leads to benchmarking and learning from others' experience. And government agencies bring not only resources to fight terrorism, corruption, sabotage, and other crimes, but also a wealth of knowledge regarding proven processes.

Beyond all that, some firms collaborate with and "deputize" their own work force by creating a "security culture."

Security Culture

After 9/11, Quaker Foods, a division of PepsiCo, awoke to the new importance of security. Realizing that locks and fences were no longer adequate, Quaker created an antiterrorism task force. "We didn't know how to protect our plants from professional criminals who weren't afraid to lose their lives," said Steve Brunner, a former Quaker Oats executive who was a member of the facilities and distribution center antiterrorism task force. "The threat was different from anything we'd dealt with before."[17]

Quaker wanted to do more than provide security against loss at each of its 11 facilities. It also wanted to prevent tampering with the Quaker food products that millions of Americans eat every morning. At first, Quaker implemented standard security measures such as reducing access points, requiring electronic badges, and moving parking lots further from buildings. Even so, the company felt that the new measures were not enough.

"We determined that the only way to make our total security plan successful was to harness the eyes, ears, mind, spirit and support of every employee," said Dan Wombold, senior manager of HR and community relations for the Iowa plant. Workaday employees make useful extensions of a corporate security net. "They know who belongs and who doesn't," said Al Hartl, president of Retail Wholesale Department Store Union (RWDSU) Local 110, whose members make up roughly 875 of the 1,300 workers at Quaker's Cedar Rapids, Iowa, plant.[18]

The key was plant-wide employee training that covered safety, identification of threats, and instructions on what to do about suspicious objects or people. Employees were told whom to contact about potential situations. Managers were trained to take seriously any security issues raised by frontline staff. Of particular concern was the etiquette of dealing with strangers. Because managers, engineers, or vendor representatives might have a legitimate right to enter different parts of the company, Quaker needed vigilance without confrontation. Thus, Quaker developed a training program for its employees on how to approach strangers.

A similar concern, rooted in law rather than etiquette, caused Logan Airport to clear its procedures for approaching strangers with the Massachusetts Attorney General's Office and the American Civil Liberties Union. Logan managers wanted to make sure that they would not be seen as discriminating or encroaching on privacy rights when approaching suspicious travelers.

"The human side of security is the most important element," Quaker's Wombold said. "Instead of relying solely on security guards, we will have 1,300 Americans who are committed, observant, alert and will know how to handle any dangerous situation."

Quaker is not the only company to realize that security is everybody's business. Bob Byrne, IBM's director of security for product group support stated: "One very important distinction is that security in IBM is the responsibility of the process owners. It's not IBM security who has a responsibility to execute on all of these security requirements."[19]

Building a culture of security and involving employees in the task is something that labor and management can work on together, because their interests clearly coincide; this cooperation can lead to cooperation on other issues. Such improvement in labor-management relationships came about from the efforts undertaken by CSX and its unions to improve safety.

A particularly high accident rate led to a large number of injuries in the rail yards of CSX Railroad in the mid-1980s. The yards are particularly dangerous because they are large facilities in which giant locomotives and lumbering rail cars get assembled and disassembled over a vast maze of tracks. To combat the trends in injuries, the railroad initiated joint management-labor teams to investigate the problem, suggest solutions, implement them, and follow through. The teams came up with a slew of processes, from a "buddy system" where each worker was responsible for the welfare of another, to a campaign of safety and security that involved sending brochures and leaflets about safe workplace practices to employees' homes, thus enlisting spouses in the campaign. The result was not only a marked reduction in accidents and injuries, but a much better labor climate in the tough union environment of U.S. railroads. In part, that improvement in the labor climate was attributed to employees' spouses being impressed with the level of care the company exhibited toward its employees.

Better collaboration and trust between management and labor is particularly important for flexibility and resilience because it facilitates fast response. Trust enables either party to contact the right person for help, without needing to build confidence, establish a chain of command or verify authenticity. Creating trusting relationships between labor and management, however, is not always easy. Joint work to develop security and resilience is one mechanism for creating trusting relationships, which can extend to and benefit other areas of business.

Train and Drill

One of the dangers of disruption avoidance measures is that they become routine. With the daily challenges of running a business, it is easy to relax and fall into a habitual pattern of security and safety procedures. The twin dangers of this trend are that employees become complacent, and that stable patterns are easy for malicious perpetrators to study and overcome.

The theft of the Intel Pentium IV chips at Heathrow in 2003 was clearly well planned and based on accurate information regarding the shipment routing and content. As mentioned before, some companies change their shipping patterns, using different carriers and different routes, in order to make it more difficult for would-be thieves, saboteurs, and terrorists to perpetrate an attack. Such changes not only keep the "other side" guessing, but they also serve to keep security personnel, and the rest of the company, more alert.

In commercial settings, however, firms need to balance the trade-off between the frequency of changing processes to avoid predictability and maintaining standard processes to achieve efficiency. Because it takes time for employees to learn, debug, and optimize a new process, frequent changes hinder efficiency.

Even when processes are not changed, it is important to reinforce continuously the existence of risks. Exercises, tests, and other events designed to reinforce security processes and a culture of vulnerability awareness should be used routinely. Quaker, for example, follows up its security training with randomized vigilance checks, such as putting a strange object or person in the factory and testing how long it takes for employees to notice. Winners of such checks are celebrated, further encouraging a cultural norm of security. More elaborate versions of testing how long it takes for employees to find an unattended package are the "Red Team" exercises mentioned earlier, in which a team of outside experts tries to penetrate the company's defenses.

Not all attacks use brute force or technical feats of hacking. Attackers can leverage the system itself for malicious purposes by exploiting natural social tendencies. For example, when a leading UK retailer wanted to test its security system in 1998, it hired an outside expert to try to break into key facilities. A few weeks later, the expert delivered a series of photographs showing himself with his hands on the retailer's main computer controls. With a flick of a switch, he could have brought down the entire company's computer system.

To gain entry into these sensitive areas, the expert didn't use a James Bond–like array of gadgets. Rather, he simply approached locked doors that he wanted to enter wearing workman's overalls with his arms full of fluorescent lighting boxes and a confident smile on his face. The polite, helpful employees of the retailer opened the locked doors for him one by one, all the way to the heart of the data center.[20]

Integrating Security into the Business

Businesses face many risks; the increased danger of terrorism is only the latest one. But antiterrorism security measures have been mandated by the government or added to the list of qualification for doing business in some sectors. When security measures are added to ongoing business processes after the fact, or in response to a specific incident, they are largely ineffective and are viewed by operating managers as a hindrance. To be effective, security has to be "built in" as an integral part of business processes. Although such a goal may seem an added burden and detrimental to good business practices, two examples of integrating new requirements into business processes with great success may show the way.

These examples, which were also viewed as hindrances at one time, are safety and quality.

The Safety Movement

The toll in lost life and limbs at manufacturing, construction, transportation, mining, and other industries during the first part of the twentieth century was horrific. Workplace accidents were commonplace and calls for safety measures by workers and their unions were met with howls of protest by executives who decried the added costs of such measures. During the twentieth century, however, unions won safer working conditions and many of their achievements were anchored into laws monitored by the U.S. Occupational Safety and Health Administration (OSHA) and the European Agency for Health and Safety at Work. More important, few business leaders today see safety as an added burden on company operations; their employees, the communities they work in, and the public at large have simply come to expect safe working conditions.[21]

To achieve safety, companies have followed a set of procedures aimed at identifying unsafe conditions: reporting, investigating, and learning from accidents; collaborating with authorities; and, most important, creating a "safety culture." Such a culture entails the development of an atmosphere in which safety is everybody's business—not the responsibility of the safety officer, the union, or the insurance company. Workers who report unsafe conditions and unsafe behavior should not be considered whistle-blowers but should rather be acknowledged and rewarded.

There are plenty of examples of companies that instituted a strong safety culture, like the "buddy program" adopted by the CSX Railroad for yard workers. Koch Petroleum Group in Pine Bend, Minnesota, for instance, introduced a behavior-based safety (BBS) system that included a set of tools and procedures designed to promote workers' responsibility for their own safety, as well as for their peers' safety. Additionally, the organization's formal management systems and leaders' management practices facilitate safety by recognizing and reinforcing appropriate behaviors.[22] Ryder Systems Inc., the Miami-based logistics company, is striving to instill safety in everything it does. It starts every company meeting with a safety message, regardless of the participants or the topic of the meeting. ABF, the Arkansas trucking company, awards prizes and publicly recognizes safe driving by inducting safe drivers into its "million miles club" of accident-free driving. Organizations operating in high-risk environments, such as nuclear plants and air traffic control systems, have long worked to introduce safety culture into their operations.[23]

The Quality Movement
In the 1950s, Ford executives were famous for not disclosing where they worked to casual acquaintances in order to avoid the inevitable litany of complaints about the quality of Ford's cars. For a long time, U.S. and European automobile companies were convinced that building quality into their product was simply too expensive. They believed that cars were sold based on looks and performance and that the trade-off between cost and quality indicated that quality was just not worth the investment.

In the 1980s, Toyota Motor Corporation turned this perception on its head using the principles advocated by Edward Deming.[24] Toyota demonstrated that it was feasible to build quality cars at low cost. One of the guiding principles of the Toyota manufacturing system was that doing things right the first time saved the costs of reworking flawed products, reduced the need for testing at every stage of manufacturing, cut the need to compensate unhappy customers, and decreased warranty and after-sales service. Furthermore, the public appreciated the reliability of Toyota cars, leading to meteoric sales growth for Toyota automobiles. This notion was popularized by Bill Crosby's book *Quality Is Free*,[25] which became the mantra of businesses all over the world.

The quality movement roadmap to security was not lost on several authors after 9/11.[26] Focus on security measures can enhance the efficiency of the supply chain in the post-9/11 world just as the focus on quality enhanced efficiency. The quality movement has focused on building quality into the product rather than trying to inspect for defects later; it stressed process integrity so that if there is a problem on the production line, the line stops and the problem is corrected before multiple defective products would roll off the assembly line. Most important, it stressed that to build quality in products or services, the entire organization should be enlisted and be part of the effort. The security lessons are obvious: fighting problems at the source (for example, securing freight origins and departure ports); continuous monitoring for anomalies (for example, in shipping patterns and people's behavior); and the development of security culture throughout the organization.

The success of the quality and safety movements was not limited to the introduction of new processes and new institutions. More important, these movements also succeeded in changing corporate attitudes and company cultures on a large scale. These changes suggest that such cultural changes are possible and point the way to how security can be enhanced.

Continuous Effort

Quality efforts, safety programs, and security processes cannot succeed if they are viewed as a one-time "project." Instead, they require continuous updating and reinforcement. In particular, security against malicious attacks has to account for the fact the "other side" can learn how to overcome routine measures. Part of such an effort involves making changes to the environment, updating plans, and frequent training, so that security and response plans are well rehearsed. Another part of the security effort involves auditing of the company's own operations for security, in the same way that quality and safety audits are performed. More and more global companies extend this practice to their suppliers. They carry out supplier training sessions—frequently for multiple suppliers in the same region. To make sure that security standards are developed and maintained, Seagate, IBM, HP Hasboro, Gillette, Target, and many others conduct pre-engagement security audits as well as ongoing (including unannounced) on-site security audits. The continuous effort against malicious perpetrators also involves updating the security measures themselves in response to new counterfeiting, theft, and sabotage incidents, as demonstrated by the following example.

On May 20, 2002, the FDA found 1,004 bottles of Johnson & Johnson's blockbuster anemia drug Procrit without the required paperwork certifying the authenticity of the drug. Tests showed that counterfeiters had relabeled inexpensive low-dose vials to look like pricey high-dose vials, with twenty times the active ingredient, in order to remark the price from $22 a vial to $475 a vial.

With the health of millions of cancer, kidney disease, and AIDS patients potentially at risk, J&J decided it would not release any of the $1.2 billion of the product in its warehouses until the company had addressed the problem.[27]

First, J&J alerted distributors, hospitals, and doctors—sending 200,000 letters and repeating the process eight times—to tell customers how to recognize the counterfeits. The letters also provided updates and explained J&J's new anti-counterfeiting measures. J&J also tightened its distribution chain, warning distributors that they would lose their accounts with the company if they bought the medicine from other sources. The company asked its customers to watch for mailings or faxes that were from unknown companies and forwarded these suspicious offers to the FDA for investigation.

As an anti-counterfeiting measure, Johnson & Johnson adopted technology used by the U.S. Treasury, using the color-shifting ink found on $20 bills, which looks green or silver depending on the angle of the light. About six weeks after the FDA call, J&J was shipping vials in repackaged boxes with the new ink and improved seals. Within 13 weeks, J&J had repackaged the entire six months worth of inventory.

Less than nine months after J&J introduced the color-shifting ink and improved box seals, the first crude fakes appeared. But J&J continues to upgrade its anti-counterfeiting features: Color-coded wrappers and vials and new seals ensure that no one can confuse the dosage or reuse the vials. "We hope to keep one step ahead of them, to make sure even if they do figure out what we have on this label, in six months we will have something different so they won't be able to duplicate that," said Elizabeth Hansen, a J&J package development engineer.[28]

Justifying the Investment

In November 2001, MIT Institute Professor and Nobel laureate Robert Solow assessed the impact of increased corporate investment in security by surmising that "Last year there were 100 elves working in the North Pole preparing toys for the Christmas season, while this year, 95 of them will be making toys and five will be guarding the perimeter fence."[29] Such a comment embodies the view that increased security outlays are going to be a burden on corporations, leading to lower productivity, increased costs, and lower profits.

Justifying security measures faces the same problem that any other project involving cost avoidance does: "Nobody ever got promoted by avoiding costs." Since costs avoided do not show up on any financial statement, or in any incentive system, and costs incurred *are* visible (including security outlays), there is little natural incentive to invest in cost avoidance.

The result is that continuous security efforts can be hampered by their own success. When Sun Microsystems suffered a spate of freight thefts in Europe, it used a multi-pronged effort to stem the losses.[30] Sun hired escorts for trailers carrying high-value Sun gear and monitored logistics personnel to reduce inside-job leaks of information about high-value shipments. With these measures, Sun cut its losses to zero.

Later, when managers asked why the company was spending so much money for escorts when they were no longer having hijackings, security managers faced the classic catch-22 of security: how to put a value on avoiding a problem that you don't have because you spent money to avoid it. Sun's security managers benchmarked other companies, quantified the likely loss rates if they stopped using escorts, and successfully justified their security measures.

According to Steven Lund, Intel's director of corporate security, Intel uses statistical models to estimate the amount, frequency, and expected losses for each facility. Intel also commissioned a study by RAND Corporation to understand further the patterns of losses and costs in the high-tech industry.[31] The study found that indirect costs resulting from theft (including lost sales, costs to customers, and investigation costs) totaled two to five times the replacement costs of the stolen goods. In analyzing the relationship between security expenditures and losses at a group of 18 firms, RAND also found that, at the level of security expenditure at the time, each 1 percent in added spending on security provided more than a 7 percent reduction in losses.

Cross-industry benchmarking efforts and careful analysis of all the costs involved in a breach of security can help companies make the business case for security investments. They also help direct such investments and size them in accordance with the disruption they are trying to thwart.

8

Collaboration for Security

Collaboration among companies plays two important roles in reducing the likelihood of disruptions. First, it allows them to learn from others so they can each use the best experience available to operate securely. Second, because many disruptions arise from outside the "four walls" of a company or propagate to and from others in the supply chain, collaboration allows for coordinated prevention efforts among trading partners. Collaboration is, of course, also crucial for resilience, providing early warning when something goes awry somewhere in the process and enabling coordinated mitigation efforts if the supply chain is disrupted.

The focus of this chapter is on collaboration for security—aiming to reduce the likelihood of a disruption. In addition to cross-industry cooperation, this chapter describes the role of public-private partnerships in preventing disruptions from crime and terrorism. Such partnerships are imperative given the role of government authorities in intelligence gathering, alerts, and deterrence.

Industry Collaboration for Security

Risk sharing between trading partners can mitigate the bullwhip effect, avoid costly misalignments, and increase the expected profits of all participants. To enhance security, however, companies should band together not only with suppliers and customers, but even with competitors. Such collaboration might include sharing information on threats, creating a coordinated interface with law enforcement agencies, sharing security best practices, and developing industry-wide security standards.

Tapping Expertise with TAPA

Intel's efforts in freight security did not go unnoticed by other high technology companies. It started with several of Intel's customers, the original equipment manufacturers (OEMs), who asked to learn from Intel's experience. The result was that in 1997, Intel joined with other high technology companies to form TAPA, the Technology Asset Protection Association.[1] The nonprofit TAPA provides a venue for sharing knowledge about cargo security and developing standards for freight security in the high-tech industry. Overall, TAPA had in 2004 some 450 members representing all echelons of the high-tech supply chain, including chip makers like Intel, AMD, and Xilinx; device makers like Apple, Cisco, and Dell; and contract manufacturers like Celestica and Solectron.

In the late 1990s, the benefits of business collaboration were well established. Companies were working together with their trading partners to combat the bullwhip effect and working together with competitors to coordinate lobbying efforts, invest in basic research, and participate in standard-setting bodies. Working together to coordinate security was a logical extension.

Collaboration and information sharing, however, are not the natural tendencies of security professionals. Most senior security officers in large multinational companies are veterans of law enforcement agencies and the military. Befitting its global presence, Intel hires not only ex-FBI, CIA, and U.S. Customs personnel, but also veterans of other respected security services such as Israel's Mossad, the British MI5, and the Hong Kong police. Steve Lund, Intel's director of corporate security, had 15 years of law enforcement experience, including six years as an FBI special agent, prior to joining Intel. Such operatives are not always inclined to share processes and methods with each other, and they are even less inclined to collaborate with people outside the security community. Consequently, it took some time for TAPA to coalesce and for its members to realize the value of sharing security methods as well as data and metrics on disruptions, attacks, and losses. The most potent argument for cooperation was probably that such sharing allowed the security professionals to make the business case for security investments inside their own companies.

TAPA first created standards for freight security. For example, TAPA created a set of contractual terms and conditions that members may use to ensure that freight carriers protect shippers' high-tech, high-value goods. In 2001, TAPA created standards for auditing freight carriers and even created an independent audit program. The methodology includes risk scoring and a set of risk-dependent compliance criteria; to attain certification for serving the highest-risk facilities (those carrying large volumes of expensive products), transportation carriers must meet 70 freight security requirements.[2] TAPA explicitly avoids blacklisting carriers; it only highlights which carriers are compliant and provides a basis for understanding the security strengths and weaknesses of each carrier.

Unfortunately, TAPA's prescriptive approach to carrier security created some tensions with the carrier community. For example, many large carriers think that they know better how to secure their own operations and should not be subject to their customers' ideas of security, particularly because shippers do not shoulder the cost of increased security. In addition, carriers complained that several shippers used the TAPA security guidelines in order to obtain price concessions from carriers who were not in complete compliance. Such frictions may be part of the normal commercial environment between carriers and shippers, and many of these frictions may subside as carriers are able to integrate security processes in their regular operations, finding business benefits in such measures.

In 1999, a regional TAPA organization was formed for Europe, the Middle East, and Africa (the EMEA region). TAPA EMEA created a confidential incident information web space, called eTAPS, for reporting losses. This enables TAPA members and European law enforcement officials to spot emerging patterns in supply chain crimes without giving away confidential data.[3] Building on this success, in 2000, TAPA Asia and the TAPA Worldwide Council were formed.

Coordination with local authorities has yielded results. For example, in May 2004, a cooperative effort between TAPA EMEA and London's Metropolitan Police led to a substantial number of arrests involving organized crime gangs who were targeting high technology components being transported through Heathrow Airport[4] (affectionately known as "Thiefrow Airport" among security professionals).

Additional lessons in the value of collaboration among direct competitors can be learned from service industries, even though they do not handle physical products.

Pooling the Data

When Kevin Lewis sat down at the high-stakes blackjack table inside an Atlantic City casino in 2003, he planned to win big. In the 1990s, the former member of an infamous group of MIT students[5] had helped his team win millions of dollars at blackjack by keeping track of the aces and face cards played. (Card counting can substantially change the odds of blackjack in favor of the player; that is why casinos refuse to allow card counters in.)

But winning was not in the cards that day. Moments after Mr. Lewis sat down, the pit boss got word of Lewis's card counting past. "It was obvious that somewhere and somehow I had been made," said the 30-year-old Lewis, who bolted before the pit boss could summon help.[6] Kevin's departure was a result of close cooperation among many of the world's casinos.

Unwelcome gamblers come in all shapes and sizes. They include card counters, false shufflers, bottom-dealers, and card switchers. They also include users of gadgets designed to change the winning probabilities of slot machines, force them into free game mode, or even empty them altogether. The MIT students' team used pairs of blackjack players. One would play for low stakes but count cards without drawing any attention to himself. Halfway through the dealer's card shoe, the player could tell how many aces and face cards were left in the shoe. If the shoe was "rich" with aces and face cards, making for higher winning probability, a signal would be given to the other member of the team, who would start betting heavily. With the odds thus tilted, the team made millions of dollars.

While not illegal, card counting can cause casinos heavy losses and "bring down the house." Casinos are entitled to deny privilege to anybody, even if the only reason is that the person wins too often. To avoid such losses, casinos share information about known card counters to ensure that any card counter expelled from one casino in Atlantic City or Las Vegas cannot simply go to the next casino on the strip.[7] With the advent of high-speed pattern recognition software, card counters' faces can be captured by surveillance cameras and recognized automatically as they enter the casino, if they match the face of a known card counter in the database.[8] Naturally, the most important part of the system is the information stored in the database. Cooperation between several of the world's leading casinos means that a card counter would be recognized as soon as he or she entered any of the 140 casinos around the world that participated in the system in 2004.

Another example of data pooling is the joint activities of sixteen Scottish whisky distillers who decided to collaborate on preparedness for disasters and on security problems plaguing them all. In 2002, they hired a single security firm and reported all their theft data to it. The data revealed that all sixteen had consistent losses on one particular delivery route. But since the losses were all "below the radar"—that is, too small to engender insurance claims—the pattern did not surface without the collaboration.[9]

Watching for Weak Links in the Supply Chain
Other industries have formalized collaboration to avoid supply chain disruptions. The Critical Materials Council (CMC) monitors the semiconductor materials supply chain, watching for short- and long-term potential materials shortages.[10] Sematech, a global consortium of semiconductor makers, created the CMC after a 1993 fire at a Sumitomo chemicals factory threatened 50 percent of the world's supply of the black plastic used to encase silicon chips. The council also helped the industry rally its resources after

a 2000 explosion at a Nisshin Chemical factory created a potential shortage of hydroxylamine, a specialty chemical needed for
cleaning silicon wafers. The CMC assessed the impact on the
integrated circuit manufacturing community and worked with
hydroxylamine suppliers and other industry associations to ensure
an adequate supply. The efforts resulted in other suppliers, including BASF and EKC, agreeing to increased production in order to
make up for shortages.

The CMC models the myriad facets of the semiconductor and
electronic component supply chains, with special emphasis on the
raw materials, specialized chemicals, and equipment used to make
semiconductors. The group created its own software package to
analyze trends in the chip industry, including supplier capacity,
supplier markets, product demand trends, business dynamics, and
assumptions regarding the productivity of technology.

As part of monitoring twelve critical materials used by semiconductor makers, the council has, over the years, examined the
impact of political instabilities in Zaire[11] on the supply of cobalt;
the potential need to develop new helium supplies in Russia; and
the impact of changing manufacturing technologies of xenon gas
supplies. Although the CMC works at the behest of the chip industry, the council looks at the impacts of other industries on critical
supplies. For example, the 2000 shortage of tantalum was due to
extremely high demand for small electronics (e.g., cellphones and
PDAs) and was exacerbated by a simultaneous growth in demand
for the metal by the aerospace and power plant industries.

The CMC does more than watch for potential shortages resulting from suppliers' problems. It also looks at shifting patterns of
R&D investment and capital expenditures to understand future
material supply. For instance, as semiconductor manufacturing
becomes more capital intensive and suppliers merge with each
other, the CMC assesses the vulnerability of the industry that may
result from a disruption at one of the decreasing number of suppliers, and it works to develop alternative sources of supply.

The consortium provides a venue for information-sharing
between materials suppliers and materials customers (chip
makers). Confidential workshops help members of the semicon-

ductor industry share technological roadmaps, capacity investment decisions, and forecasts, helping all participants plan and avoid disruptions.

The Power of Many

An employee-based "community watch" program enlists all the employees of a business to watch for and report security-related anomalies. Similarly, bringing together multiple companies in an industry to share data leverages the experience and resources of every member company.

Industry associations play a similar role to that of TAPA's in many industries. The Toy Industry Association developed comprehensive safety standard for toys; the American Chemistry Council developed Responsible Care, including a set of guidelines for handling chemical products from inception in the research laboratory through manufacturing and distribution to ultimate disposal; the Automotive Industry Action Group has launched training in 2004 for crisis management and business recovery for its 850 members; UPS, FedEx, the USPS, and DHL, together with smaller parcel carriers, formed the Postal and Shipping Coordination Council, aiming to foster communications and quick response in the event of a large-scale disruption; and Limited Brands and Nike address common security issues through the Retail Industry Leaders' Association (RILA).

In a fashion similar to the corporate-employee alignment created by internal safety and security programs, external collaboration also aligns corporate interests with those of the government, trading partners, and the community: The collaborative security dialogue often leads to other areas of collaboration.

Alan Fletcher, group manager for global operations and investigations at Target Stores, says that security concerns not only brought deeper collaboration between Target and its suppliers, they also served as the basis for initial collaboration between Target Stores and Wal-Mart, who are bitter rivals in the marketplace. He says, "One of the committees I have been working on is developing a 'Best Practices' guide for all shippers bringing merchandise into the U.S. The committee is made up of, for want of a better term, competitors who work together to design the guide for the rest of the industry." Fletcher expects the standards not only to improve security but also to simplify work with all suppliers, forwarders, and customs officials.[12]

Public-Private Partnerships (PPPs)

One of the fundamental differences between past conflicts and the war on terror is that with the latter, "the private sector is on the frontline of the homeland security effort: Its members are holders of information that may prove crucial to thwarting terror attacks; stewards of critical infrastructure that must be protected and dangerous materials that could be used to do harm; and important actors in responding to attacks."[13] Nowhere is the challenge more evident than in securing maritime commerce.

Every year, almost 12 million maritime containers pass through U.S. borders, on board more than 200,000 ships. Anonymous, ubiquitous, and carrying upward of 25 tons each, these containers move seamlessly, without being opened, from factories to trucks, to ships and trains, and ultimately to their final destinations throughout the United States. Although owners of the containers do have some information on where the containers are and where they are going, such operations-oriented information is not enough. To assess how secure these containers are, the needed information includes the containers' histories: Where they have been, who handled them, and what has been in them. During the eight-year lifespan of a shipping container, it might have traveled to more than 100 different ports all over the globe from Addis Ababa, Jeddah, or Lagos to Montreal, Los Angeles, or New York, and it may have been handled by hundreds of operators. In the past, such information was not a concern; when a carrier needed to load a container, it simply picked the next empty box off the stack.

After 9/11, the vulnerability of the United States to container-based attacks became evident, as the Customs Service admitted that its inspectors examined fewer than 2 percent of the containers entering the United States. Containers could be used to transport bombs or to carry chemical weapons or radioactive materials. Or the shipment carried inside could be contaminated with biological agents.[14]

The devastating results of an explosion on board a ship at port were made evident in Halifax on December 6, 1917, when the Belgian relief ship *Imo* collided with the small French ship *Mont Blanc*, carrying a full cargo of explosives. The *Mont Blanc* exploded in the largest manmade blast before the nuclear age. The barrel of one of her cannons landed three and a half miles away and part of her anchor shank—which weighed more than half a ton—flew two miles in the opposite direction. More than 1,900 people were killed immediately and 9,000 more were injured, many permanently. Nearly 325 acres, including almost all of Halifax's north end, were destroyed.[15] The effects of a port explosion were also made evident on April 16, 1947, when a ship loaded with ammonium nitrate exploded in the port of Texas City. The explosion caused on-shore fires at chemical and other industrial plants, a devastating tidal wave, and two more ship explosions. The Texas City disaster caused 600 deaths and 3,500 injuries, representing a casualty rate of over 20 percent for the 16,000 residents of the city. One-third of the city's houses were condemned as a result of the damage from the explosion and the fiery aftermath.

Containers have also been used by terrorist groups, especially Al Qaeda, to transport people as stowaways. On March 14, 2004, two suicide bombers entered the Israeli port of Ashdod in a container, and ten port workers lost their lives before the attackers were killed. And on October 18, 2001, a 43-year-old Egyptian stowaway named Amid Farid was caught at Italy's Gioia Touro port aboard the German vessel *Ipex Emperor*. He was comfortably installed in a container converted into a luxurious suite complete with a soft bed, a small kitchen, cellular telephones, and enough food, water, and batteries to last him three weeks.

Although container security occupies the minds of government officials, the majority of the international transportation infrastructure is in the hands of the private companies that own the shipments, containers, ships, railroads, trucks, and terminals around the world. Government agencies, therefore, need private cooperation in order to reduce the probability of terrorist attacks. And private companies need the benefits of the intelligence and enforcement resources owned by governments. Both public and private sectors need each other to secure trade lanes and infrastructure.

Secure Freight-Handling Processes

In addition to the large number of containers entering the United States every year, there are 12 million trucks, almost a million planes, and over two million cars entering the country annually. Searching each and every one of these conveyances is not practical. Relying on the principle of identifying outliers from existing patterns, the U.S. Bureau of Customs & Border Protection (CBP) has launched its C-TPAT (Customs-Trade Partnership against Terrorism) Program. C-TPAT invites companies to apply and become "known entities" to the CBP. Companies must pass a four-step certification process, after which they are entitled to reduced import inspections at the various ports of entry. This amounts to a significant advantage to C-TPAT certified companies, with estimated pass-through times of two to three days compared to 12 to 14 days for non-certified companies' imports. The principle behind the system is that when shipments from a certified importer are transported by a trusted carrier, the probability that those shipments are suspect is much lower than for shipments from non-certified companies, and hence these shipments do not need to be checked as often.

C-TPAT is focused not only on each company's security but on the security of its suppliers. It states that companies that apply for C-TPAT certification have to "develop and implement a program to enhance security throughout the supply chain in accordance with C-TPAT guidelines, and communicate C-TPAT guidelines to other companies in the supply chain and work toward building the guidelines into relationships with these companies."[16]

To make sure that its processes do not hinder commercial activities, the U.S. government incorporated certain industry initiatives into its programs. For example, after 9/11, the government approved many of the TAPA certification processes as C-TPAT-compliant and built on the processes developed by the TAPA companies.[17] As with TAPA, the key is collaboration. "From the agency side, what compelled the agency early on to take this route of C-TPAT is again a recognition of a need to get the private sector—just about anyone and everyone who moves something through the border—involved in the protection of the border alongside us," said Robert Perez, of the Bureau of Customs and Border Protection and a director of C-TPAT.[18] He then added, "The certified partners in this arrangement are afforded more efficient and predictable flow of goods—that's a huge benefit for . . . everyone involved . . . and protection of their brand names and their product. I don't think anyone wants their name associated with the next terrorist action in the United States."

Other Public-Private Collaborative Efforts

Although 9/11 sent a wake-up call for authorities about the deadly seriousness of container security, the war on narcotics trafficking has already driven long-running efforts to improve the security of ocean shipping. Companies in the Toy Industry Association (TIA) have a history of partnering with the government to prevent the use of toy shipments for smuggling drugs. Mattel was among the first companies to join the Business Anti-Smuggling Campaign (BASC).[19] BASC works with 1,000 manufacturers in selected foreign countries to prevent the smuggling of drugs inside commercial goods. Such initiatives have shifted their focus and added efforts to prevent the import of dangerous materials as part of C-TPAT.[20]

To complement C-TPAT, the U.S. CBP has launched the Container Security Initiative (CSI), aimed at detecting and intercepting risky cargo before containers can reach U.S. ports where they can be detonated or activated. To this end, CSI mandates advance notice of the manifests of all shipments bound for U.S. ports 24 hours prior to loading. Each incoming container is then scored by various algorithms, which assess the shipper, consignee, payment methods, and the previous routing history of the container to come up with the potential threat posed by the shipment and the container itself. The program lets customs officials direct interdiction efforts to the highest-risk containers.

Such processes can be highly effective. For example, in 2001 German authorities complained to UPS, the giant parcel and logistics company, that drug seizures among German-bound UPS international shipments were an order of magnitude higher than drug seizures on other carriers. The German authorities were factually correct; what they did not account for was that UPS used its own scoring algorithms based on shipping documentation to identify international shipments that were likely to contain drugs. The information was then transmitted to the German Federal Customs Administration, which used the results to direct their searches, resulting in a very high rate of drug seizures.

In addition to mandating advanced shipping notices, CSI calls for changes at foreign ports—increasing the security of the facilities that store, handle, and load U.S.-bound goods. Based on mutual agreements with international ports, US CBP inspectors have been placed at participating foreign ports to help identify and interdict suspicious cargo and containers prior to loading and departure.[21] This is analogous to quality control practices that are aimed at detecting defects early, before they become a significant problem.

As of February 2004, 5,500 companies were C-TPAT-certified, representing all aspects of the global supply chain—major U.S. importers, carriers, brokers, forwarders, foreign manufacturers, and terminal operators. Over 3,000 U.S. importers have joined CSI, representing approximately 40 percent of all goods imported into the United States by value. All of these C-TPAT partner companies have entered into agreements to work with CBP to implement specific security measures and best practices, in order to protect their supply chains, from the factory loading docks of their foreign vendors to their arrival in the United States.[22]

In many cases, cooperation between the government and the private sector is not part of any particular program. For example, CSX Railroad has its own security force that coordinates its effort routinely with local, state, and federal security personnel. This is the case with many of the companies interviewed by MIT for this study—their security personnel seems well connected with government security and law enforcement agencies—in part because these security personnel include many former employees of such government agencies.

An example of multiparty public-private joint operation takes place every week in the port of Boston. It starts with a short radio notice for all ships in Boston harbor that dangerous cargo is on the way. The dangerous cargo is about 35 million gallons of highly flammable liquefied natural gas (LNG) contained in a hulking tanker more than 900 feet long. As the tanker moves through the harbor and the narrow channel, it is turned by tug boats under the Tobin Bridge and towed into the Mystic River to its berth in Everett. This movement is coordinated by more than 40 federal, state, and local law and safety agencies, as well as private sector companies. A boarding party on deck works with a helicopter in the air, a police cruiser on the shore, and armed coast guard patrol boats and cutters front and aft to orchestrate the move, which requires shutting down operations at Logan Airport as the ship passes under the glide path. Similarly, the Tobin Bridge is closed to traffic as the ship is turned underneath.

But the operation itself is just the tip of the iceberg. The ships are built to the highest standards of structural soundness and manned by experienced crews. The Norwegian facility in which the crews train has developed special instruction sessions on the approaches to Boston Harbor and ways to deal with various disaster scenarios there. The loading takes place in Point Fortin in Trinidad, a facility that has been certified by the coast guard. Coast guard officers routinely ride with the ship from Trinidad to Boston—the high seas equivalent of air marshals.

Other programs developed in cooperation with private sector carriers and shippers in the United States include the following:

- *Free and Secure Trade* (FAST) allows C-TPAT-qualified importers and carriers who use pre-screened drivers to move low-risk cargos freely at selected border crossings between the United States and Canada and the United States and Mexico.[23]

- *Operation Safe Commerce* (OSC) funds business initiatives for developing security technologies. Much of the initial work has focused on the potential of incorporating radio frequency identification (RFID) tags in shipments and low-cost GPS receivers and wireless networking systems in containers to track shipments.

- *Smart and Secure Trade Lanes Initiative* (SST) is an industry-driven supply chain security program. A combination of secure business processes and advanced technologies (anti-intrusion sensor devices and satellite tracking systems combined with a backbone of RFID technologies and networked software),[24] it aims to provide end-to-end shipment visibility and security.[25]

- *The Maritime Transportation Security Act of 2002* (MTSA) requires vessels and port facilities to conduct vulnerability assessments and develop security plans that may include passenger, vehicle, and baggage-screening procedures; security patrols; establishing restricted areas; personnel identification procedures; access-control measures; and/or installation of surveillance equipment.

Programs around the World

Like the United States, many countries and international organizations around the world have recognized the security threat posed by the movement of containers. Established in 1948, the International Maritime Organization (IMO) is a U.N. agency responsible for improving the safety and security of international shipping and preventing maritime pollution. It is the author of Safety of Life at Sea (SOLAS), the most important of all treaties dealing with maritime safety.[26] Following 9/11, the IMO adopted amendments to SOLAS in the form of an International Ship and Port Facility Security (ISPS) Code, designed to parallel U.S. requirements, making these in essence world-wide standards. The ISPS Code requires ships on international voyages and the port facilities that serve them to conduct security assessment, develop a security plan, designate security officers, perform training and drills, and take appropriate preventive measures against security breaches. Vessels must carry the International Ship Security Certificate (ISSC) and may be denied entry into a port if they do not have a valid ISSC. Many of these requirements and conventions went into effect on June 1, 2004.

The World Customs Organization (WCO) is an independent, intergovernmental body with 164 member countries. In December 2004, the WCO accepted the first draft Framework of Standards to Secure and Facilitate Global Trade, based on the following principles:

- harmonizing advance electronic manifest information among all member countries to allow a common and consistent risk assessment

- using non-intrusive detection equipment to affect examinations

- focusing on the accrual of benefits to nations, customs and business

In a fashion similar to the US C-TPAT and CSI initiatives, the WCO convention allows for companies that fulfill their criteria to be classified as "authorized traders" and receive tangible benefits, such as faster movement of low-risk cargo through Customs.

The European Commission introduced in July 2003 a series of measures to address security issues and manage the European Union's external borders based on a harmonized risk assessment system. The commission proposed a number of measures to tighten security around goods crossing international borders, which are similar in nature to the C-TPAT and CSI and the SOLAS/ISPS and WCO initiatives and standards. It requires information on goods prior to import or export from the European Union; it provides reliable traders with trade facilitation measures under the "Authorized Economic Operator" program; and it introduced a mechanism for setting uniform community risk-selection criteria for controls, supported by computerized systems.

The Asian Counter Terrorism Task Force, begun in October 2002 by the Asia-Pacific Economic Cooperation (APEC) organization, is a similar initiative to secure and enhance the flow of goods and people and to protect cargo, ships, international aviation and people in transit throughout the Asian trade corridors. The program follows similar U.S., E.U., and international guidelines. It calls for identifying and examining high-risk containers, requiring provision of advance electronic information on container content to customs, port, and shipping officials as early as possible in the supply chain, while taking into consideration the facilitation of legitimate trade. The APEC August 2004 Private Sector Security Guidelines provide voluntary standards for supply chain security.

Unfortunately, the December 26, 2004, tsunami served as a sad example of the consequences of the failure to establish international collaboration and cooperation processes. The tidal wave, resulting from a huge undersea quake in the Indian Ocean, took hours to reach certain parts of Asia and many more hours to reach Africa. Even though they had time, the affected countries had no monitoring or detection systems in place (see chapter 9), resulting in massive loss of life, property, and infrastructure. But other countries knew of the impending disaster.

The Japanese main earthquake observatory detected the quake and alerted its emergency-management system. That system ascertained within minutes that Japan faced no tsunami risk. Japanese officials didn't do much else with the information.

An Australian seismology officer in Canberra detected the quake and predicted a tsunami only 30 minutes after the quake. He sent warnings to Australia's national emergency system and the foreign ministry, but no messages were given to foreign governments "for fear of overstepping diplomatic protocol."[27] Had a formal process been established between first responders, or a communication networks established among the appropriate emergency management agencies of the countries involved, the death toll might have been significantly lower.

Increasing Security

Collaboration is a crucial requirement in the effort to secure shipment custody across supply chains that span many companies all around the globe. Suppliers, carriers, customers, port operators, and the government all have a stake in avoiding disruptions. Cooperation ensures a layered defense by instituting multiple checks of shipments while they are variously in the custody of the shipper, the logistics company, the port operator, or the consignee, using diverse government agencies in the process to enforce safe practices and secure trade lanes.

Industry associations create opportunities for benchmarking and adopting security processes that work well in each industry. They also facilitate security problem-solving at the system level, unlike the efforts of a single company that may only shift vulnerability rather than increase all partners' security.

Even before the Department of Homeland Security (DHS) was created in the United States, an advisory council of leaders from business, academia, and state and local governments was created by an executive order in March 21, 2002. Its members have been meeting monthly to advise the White House on how to strengthen domestic security and how to engage the private sector with all levels of government on this issue. The council was headed by Joseph Grano Jr., chairman and CEO of PaineWebber and a Special Forces veteran.[28]

The Next Step in Public-Private Partnerships—Increasing National Resilience

The U.S. government's efforts in fighting terrorism are focused on two fronts: (i) disruption of terrorist activities overseas (through the overthrow of the Taliban in Afghanistan, the war in Iraq, and many clandestine operations around the world), and (ii) increasing security at home, including supply chain security. Another element of preparedness, however, is not yet getting the same attention from the government. This element is resilience—developing the capability to recover quickly after an attack.

In July 2004, the U.S. Department of Agriculture received an anonymous e-mail that containers of Argentine lemons loaded on the New Jersey–bound CSAV[29] container ship *Rio Puelo* were contaminated with a "harmful biological substance." Dozens of federal, state, and local agencies sprung into action and the coast guard boarded the ship on July 29 at the Ambrose Anchorage, 11 miles out of New York harbor. It took over a week for everybody involved to agree that there was no contamination and the ship could proceed to its destination at Port Elizabeth. By then all the lemons had rotted.

The government actions in this incident raised alarms in the maritime shipping community. It demonstrated to vessel and port operators that the government has not yet balanced the commercial needs of the nation with its security needs and may be "overreacting" to threats, leaving to imagination the extent of "overreaction" following an actual port incident. The incident highlighted the fact that while the government does security, it does not do resilience. In other words, most of the government's effort is directed toward thwarting a terrorist attack. "The problem is that the U.S. government has not worked out protocols for how to restart the trade and transportation system after an event. That's the reality."[30] said Steve Flynn, senior fellow at the Council of Foreign Relations and author of the excellent 2004 book *America the Vulnerable*.[31] If the government were to close the nation's ports after finding a lethal cargo, for example, or even following a port explosion, the economic damage could be incalculable without clear reopening procedures. Developing such procedures will require another cooperative public-private effort. It may even involve a part of the government dedicated to "getting back to business" in addition to the Department of Homeland Security.

9

Detecting Disruptions

Baxter International faced a major crisis when its kidney dialysis filters became implicated in the deaths of patients. For some time, however, Baxter could not find anything wrong with the filters and therefore was not sure if the company had a significant problem on its hands.

Detecting a disruption means distinguishing a true problem from the sometimes considerable variations of normal day-to-day business. This is one of the most important tenets of reducing the likelihood of disruptions—the ability to identify outliers in the normal pattern of events.

The speed of detection may be crucial in avoiding disasters. The "nightmare scenario" among security professionals is not a nuclear holocaust or a dirty bomb. Instead, it is an attack in which the target does not realize it is under attack (or does not realize the severity or magnitude of the attack) until it is too late. And the result can be devastating.

The influenza pandemic of 1918 killed 40 million people world-wide;[1] 28 percent of the U.S. population was infected and 675,000 died[2]—and this was before the age of globalization and jet travel. Not realizing the magnitude and severity of the disease, Baltimore's health commissioner, when asked on October 4, 1918, about closing schools and banning public gatherings, told the Baltimore *Sun*, "Drastic measures . . . only excite people, throw them into a nervous state and lower their resistance to disease." Only after thousands of deaths, Baltimore, like most other U.S. cities, slowly came around to sterner measures, closing schools and outlawing public gatherings.[3]

Detecting Dialysis Deaths

Elderly kidney-dialysis patients sometimes die. So, in mid-August 2001, when four elderly patients became seriously ill and died shortly after dialysis treatment at a Madrid hospital, the deaths did not make the news. In accordance with standard rules, however, the hospital sent a notice to the maker of the $15 dialysis filters used in the treatment process. That maker was U.S.-based Baxter International, which had recently acquired Althin Medical AB, the Swedish maker of the dialysis products.

This seemingly random event was followed a week later by another incident, made more ominous because of its timing. Six more dialysis patients died in Valencia, Spain. Regional health officials investigated and discovered that all six Valencians had received their treatments from systems using the same single lot number of Baxter dialysis filters. Although the media published the news of the connection, other events, notably 9/11, soon overshadowed the story.

Even though Baxter did not make headlines, the company was neither oblivious nor apathetic to those first deaths in Spain. As a precaution, Baxter recalled the two lots associated with the deaths, halted distribution of that line of filters, conducted an internal investigation, and commissioned independent tests from TUV Product Service, a widely used international certification and inspection service. On October 9, after weeks of testing, TUV and Baxter announced that neither could find anything wrong with the filters, local water supplies, or equipment. "We do not see any connection between the dialysis and the deaths," said Frank Pitzer of TUV.[4]

Even as Baxter and TUV were announcing that the filters were safe, more people were dying. On October 13, Alan Heller, the recently named head of Baxter's renal division, was at a conference in San Francisco. There, he picked up a voice mail that told of terrible events being reported on TV in Croatia.[5] In an average week, three to six dialysis patients die in Croatia from the inevitable complications of kidney failure. However, between the 8th and 13th of October, 23 Croatian kidney patients in eight different centers had died. Twenty-one had used a Baxter-made dialysis filter. The event made world headlines and prompted an emergency meeting of the Croatian cabinet.

Baxter immediately dispatched a team of medical specialists to Croatia to spearhead the investigation.[6] "It is nearly impossible at this early point in time to identify with any certainty the causes of these patient deaths since there are many variables involved in these incidents," said Dr. Jose Divino, the leader of Baxter's investigative team.[7] Baxter spokeswoman Patty O'Haer told the Reuters news agency that "data from hospitals show that there was more than one common element to all the patients, including what we call disposables—needles, dialysis and the solution used in the process."[8] Nor were the deaths identical; some patients died during dialysis and others after; some had heart attacks, while others suffered strokes or developed breathing problems.

Despite the unclear evidence, "I knew that there was too much there to be a coincidence," Heller said.[9] Baxter immediately recalled the filters and launched a full-scale investigation into the cause of the problem. More than two dozen staffers were assigned to scrutinize the filters for evidence of defects or tampering.

At first, Baxter could find nothing wrong. Then an engineer at Baxter's Swedish filter-making plant noticed an anomalous bubble in one filter. The bubble seemed to be from the perfluorocarbon liquid used on some filters during the manufacturing process. Although the liquid was inert and nontoxic, it vaporized at a low temperature. Baxter investigators theorized that this could create small gas bubbles in the patient's blood that then precipitated the deaths. After tests on rabbits replicated the symptoms, the company announced, on November 2, that it believed that this liquid was the cause of the disaster.

To this day, Baxter does not know exactly why any of the perfluorocarbon liquid was left inside the filters. The processes Baxter used at the acquired Swedish plant had been used for nearly a year and were used by other manufacturers. Perhaps the ultimate irony is that the offending liquid was used specifically for quality-control processes.

In all, more than 50 deaths were connected with the perfluorocarbon bubble. Although the majority of victims were from Spain and Croatia, other patients in Italy, Germany, Taiwan, Colombia, and the United States also succumbed to the effects of the faulty filters. Baxter discontinued manufacturing the problematic product line. Some 360 workers in Sweden and Florida lost their jobs. Baxter's $100 million acquisition of Althin in 2000 resulted in $189 million in damage to the company's bottom line in 2001 to cover the costs created by the defective filters.

Detecting Disruption in Global Organizations

Baxter, like many global businesses, faces numerous challenges in detecting problems associated with its products. The first basic challenge is to realize that there is a disruption. Some rate of product failure can be expected simply as a result of random causes, and it may be difficult to ascertain that there is a systemic problem. The second challenge is to identify the cause. Products may fail for numerous reasons, many of them involving exogenous factors or improper use. In addition, most products are built from parts provided by many suppliers; finding the root cause of a failure requires detection across multiple company lines, each of which has a stake in making sure that its parts are not at fault. In many cases, finding the root cause is the only way to ascertain that there is a problem. These challenges both delay the detection of the problem and create further confusion during the disruption. For most business disruptions, detection delays cost money. In Baxter's case, the delay in detecting the problem with the filters cost lives.

How Do Organizations Detect Disruptions?

The challenge Baxter faced in its detection efforts was the difficulty in spotting a pattern that would indicate an aberration in daily variations of common random events. Although dialysis prolongs the life of kidney-failure victims, it does not cure the disease. Approximately 10 to 20 percent of dialysis patients succumb each year to the severity of their medical condition. An estimated 218 dialysis patients are expected to die every day during 2005 in the United States alone.[10] Of course, this does not mean that exactly

218 people will die every day.[11] The daily number will fluctuate just because of the laws of probability and a spike in the number of deaths may simply be one of those fluctuations. In a region where the average number of daily deaths is low, the variability will be high. For example, in a region where the average is, say, two deaths per week, one can expect seven weeks a year with no deaths at all and approximately 17 weeks a year with three or more deaths.[12] Spotting a problem in this context takes more than simply looking at higher-than-average death rates.

The process that many organizations use to distinguish between common highs and lows of any process (such as the temperature of an industrial boiler, the number of chips yielded per wafer, or terrorist "chatter") and "outlier" events warranting special scrutiny is called statistical process control (SPC). With SPC, a company calculates upper and lower control limits—recording, for example, the normal range of variation of the number of daily and weekly deaths while the process is considered under control. Watching the process to identify unfavorable trends can help the company detect situations when the process is, or threatens to get, out of control. Thus, the numbers help a company, like Baxter, know when some rate of deaths is "too many to be a coincidence."

Even when a problem is suspected, companies face a further challenge. Any given problem might have many potential root causes. Possible causes for the dialysis-related deaths included a statistical fluke (handled by SPC), contaminated water at the dialysis clinic, faulty Baxter dialysis equipment, contaminated needles, contaminated tubing, contaminated IV fluid, product tampering, physician error, or defective Baxter filters. Because the majority of these causes were outside of Baxter's control, it was easy for the company to miss the true cause until it became more evident, in Croatia, that the filters probably played some role in the problem.

When Does an Organization "Know" Something?
With headquarters located in Deerfield, Illinois, with manufacturing and research facilities located in dozens of countries (including the acquired products division in Sweden), and with customers located throughout Spain and 99 other countries,

Baxter faced the not-uncommon challenge of communication in a global enterprise. For example, the president of the Althin division learned of the problems in Croatia from a voice mail message that described the media firestorm developing in Croatia, rather than learning it through internal communications channels or from customers directly.

Detecting problems can take time because of the many ambiguities involved: is there a problem? where is it? and so on. Thus, the search for a cause is part of the detection process. The first set of independent tests commissioned by Baxter took four weeks to examine the cytotoxicity, intracutaneous reactivity, systemic toxicity, and hemolysis of the filters in accordance with ISO 10993 standards.[13] These tests found nothing. The second investigation took more than two weeks to pinpoint the probable cause to be the perfluorocarbon liquid used at the Althin factory in Sweden.[14]

Many victims' families and their lawyers argued that the latter deaths, in Croatia and elsewhere, could have been prevented. But this view fails to acknowledge the complexity and difficulty of identifying the cause of sporadic phenomena in an intricate product and service supply chain. In Baxter's case, only 10 percent of the filters were even susceptible to the fault and only a few dozen filters out of many millions produced actually had the fatal fault. It took weeks to discover the faulty filters, with the death-toll steadily increasing. An epidemic such as SARS or a potential biological terrorist attack could take days or weeks before it is identified.

Because early detection helps halt the spread and minimize the consequences of such an event, the city of Boston instituted an early warning system during the anthrax attacks of 2001: Fourteen Harvard Vanguard treatment centers reported data every day on 250,000 patients, with a database management system looking daily for suspicious patterns of flu-like symptoms. In 2002, the U.S. Center for Disease Control (CDC) announced plans for a similar system against bio-terror attack—looking for signs of anthrax, smallpox, or other disease outbreak in the aches, pains, and sniffles of 20 million patients.[15] The system is based on Statistical Process Control (SPC) principles, looking for worrisome patterns such as geographical clusters of routine symptoms like respiratory infections and small rashes accompanied by fever, symptoms that may signal a bio-terror attack in progress.

One of the methods for early detection includes monitoring the daily purchasing of over-the-counter medications at pharmacies around the United States. The rationale is that people tend to self-medicate when they feel sick, before they visit a doctor's office. Thus, a spike in aspirin and cold medication sales might be an early indication of a flu outbreak or bio-terrorism attack in progress.[16] In addition, the CDC and DHS have invested heavily in systems to monitor the water and food supplies, as well as air quality, in order to identify pathogens quickly.[17]

Although it was the fear of bio-terrorism that prompted the CDC and the DHS to create the national monitoring systems mentioned above, the systems' greatest value may prove to have nothing to do with terrorists. The need for such monitoring systems was demonstrated in 1993 when Milwaukee's water supply was fouled by the cryptosporidium microbe that entered the water system from cattle lot runoff. More than 400,000 people became ill and 100 died, in part because it took days for disease trackers to realize an epidemic was under way. The CDC, however, was able to identify quickly and point to the cause of a rash of suspicious lung-related complaints in Queens, New York, in late 2001. The breathing problems of the area's residents were caused by fumes from the burning American Airlines jetliner, flight 587, which crashed there on November 12.

Companies face yet another level of challenge: bridging the gulf between having the data about a disruption and "internalizing" these data. Internalizing the data means absorbing them and communicating them internally so that relevant parties know of the situation with enough clarity to be able to contemplate possible actions. Several examples illustrate how difficult it is to bridge this gap and how long it may take to transmit the message, thus readying the organization for a response.

During the Kobe earthquake, Texas Instruments (TI) in the United States knew of the event even before the Japanese Prime Minister did. The quake broke a trans-Pacific data link and set off alarms that instantly alerted managers in the company's corporate data center in Dallas, Texas, and TI's attempts to contact the Kobe facilities uncovered the cause within minutes.

In contrast, it took Japanese government officials four hours to decide that the event warranted disrupting the schedule of higher-ups and to route the news through the chain of command up to the prime minister. After the quake, some faulted the central government for its slow response to the events in Kobe; clearly, low-level Japanese officials (and the local government in Kobe) knew about the quake immediately. The delay in informing the prime minister demonstrates the difficulties in getting a large organization to the point that it internalizes the event and starts thinking about a response.

Similarly, in the case of 9/11, there is no single identifiable moment one can point to and say "this is when the U.S. government knew about the terrorist attacks." Instead, all that can be said is that different parts of the government knew different facts at different times and only after accumulating enough facts did enough of the government know enough information about the events to take action. In fact, when told of the attack on the morning of 9/11, U.S. president George W. Bush did not immediately internalize the meaning of the news and famously kept reading stories to children for seven more minutes.

Even before the attack itself, and regardless of all the events that were its precursors (see chapter 3), the U.S. 9/11 commission has found out that U.S. Federal Aviation Administration officials received 52 warnings prior to September 11, 2001, from their own security experts about potential al-Qaida attacks, including some that mentioned airline hijackings or suicide attacks. The report comments that aviation officials were "lulled into a false sense of security" and "intelligence that indicated a real and growing threat leading up to 9/11 did not stimulate significant increases in security procedures."[18] In other words, the FAA officials did not internalize the warnings.

The way most organizations are structured, information percolates up the chain of authority and commands percolate down to the people who implement them. This process takes time and is imperfect, but it works for non-emergency situations. In an emergency, people have to be empowered to bypass the normal structure of information. Unless the organization has created the requisite culture of distributed decision-making power (see chapter 15), there are numerous barriers to deviations from the normal process (such as actions without explicit authority), especially in the early hours when information is unclear.

Baxter did not expect to have problems with its filters. Regulations and painstaking procedures cover all phases of the design, development, and testing of medical devices. Manufacturing processes are, likewise, heavily regulated and monitored both by the company and by health authorities. Perfluorocarbon liquids are, in general, so inert and nontoxic that some of them have even been proposed as artificial blood substitutes. Yet the particular perfluorocarbon used by the Althin division of Baxter had never been explicitly tested for internal use by the supplier, 3M. Althin and Baxter never expected that liquid to get into patients; in theory, manufacturing processes ensured the removal of the test fluid.

Detecting and internalizing the unexpected is hardest because it often means questioning long-held assumptions about what is possible and moving information outside the normal channels. One of the keys to detection and fast response is the process of escalating knowledge, including the decisions regarding what to inform superiors about and when to do so. Some corporate cultures do this better than others.

Escalations and Warnings

As managers monitor ongoing processes, they continuously face the question of "common" vs. "special" aberrations. Although statistical process control charts can give an indication of an aberration, it typically takes a manager to decide the nature of the irregularity. Is it just a minor disturbance in the process monitored—be it the central processing unit workload, the boiler's temperature, or the number of SUV rollovers—or does the abnormal reading indicate a real problem? Managers can either (i) do nothing and wait for additional data, (ii) investigate the situation, (iii) notify their superiors ("escalate" the notification), or (iv) take immediate action.

When deciding among the various courses of action, managers have to balance the chances and outcomes between two types of errors: If the problem is serious and they do not escalate or react, the delayed reaction may cause severe damage; if they alert their managers and trigger actions that prove unnecessary—because there was no real disruption—they will cost the company money (in dispatching technicians, activating emergency responses, or stopping ongoing industrial processes) and appear to have faulty judgment.

Companies such as Baxter face an especially hard-edged trade-off on detection sensitivity. If Baxter recalled its products every time a suspicious death occurred it would have to cease selling its products, but missing a defect in a medical device can cause preventable deaths. There are no hard-and-fast rules for deciding when to alert and escalate. The more empowered and informed field personnel are, the more likely they are to make the right call.

Some companies are turning to automated processes to help them detect disruptions quickly. Consider SVS Inc., which processes gift-card transactions for 170 large retailers, including Radio Shack, Barnes & Noble, and Zales Jewelers, as well as restaurant chains and gas stations. As the largest gift-card and stored-value transaction processor, SVS handles 450 million transactions every year; downtime is costly and critical to the livelihood of the business. "In our business, SVS absolutely requires their online systems to be available 24 × 7," says Pat Guenthner, vice president of the Louisville, Kentucky, Data Center.[19] Because of that, the company invested in a monitoring system that lets technicians scrutinize remotely any increase in CPU utilization as a result of looping or other problem processes. Using SPC, the system also monitors transaction failure rates to identify developing disruptions. A rule-based system lets SVS define when to alert technicians, when to alert managers, or when to send an e-mail that might be seen in the morning instead of an emergency page in the middle of the night.

The Nokia and Ericsson case illustrates the value of fast detection and internalization of a disruption. Philips alerted both Nokia and Ericsson about the fire at its New Mexico plant at the same time. It was a relatively low-level alert with accompanying reassurances about fast recovery. Whereas Ericsson waited, Nokia acted immediately, alerting an internal troubleshooter of the potential problem and placing Philips on a "watch list." Nokia's heightened awareness allowed it to identify the severity of the disruption faster, leading it to take timely actions and lock up the resources for recovery.

Detection and Alarms

In many cases, disruptions are inevitable and warnings should be given immediately. In other cases, the proverbial writing is on the wall and the challenge is to internalize the impending disruption and take actions to mitigate the consequences.

When tornado sirens sounded at the GM plant in Oklahoma on May 8, 2003, the workers took shelter and none of the plant's 3,000 workers was injured, despite extensive damage to a number of GM's buildings. When Hibernia Bank learned that Hurricane Lili was bearing down on the Louisiana coast in October 2002, it implemented its "Hurricane Plan" emergency procedures. It pre-positioned these recovery teams, arranged for lodging for teams and emergency data center staff, and alerted their backup hot-site IT service provider.[20] In these cases, there was no question that the danger was imminent.

The impending war between the United States and Iraq was no secret in the spring of 2003. Dow Corning internalized this news and realized that this event would disrupt future shipping in the Atlantic—not directly through acts of violence, but indirectly because the U.S. government would monopolize much of the trans-Atlantic transportation capacity as it ferried tens of thousands of troops and their weaponry, ammunition, and supplies. In anticipation, Dow Corning accelerated its own shipments and built up inventories that helped it weather the subsequent reduction of available shipping capacity.[21]

On the other hand, in September 2000, the government of Britain did not immediately grasp the impact of the ongoing fuel strikes. Truckers, angered by a new fuel tax, blockaded refineries and fuel depots, thereby creating shortages at filling stations. On the surface, this event—which unfolded nightly on British television screens—seemed to be simply an inconvenience for the driving public. What the government failed to realize fully was that fuel shortages affected food deliveries, too. The result was that the country came within four days of food rationing before the government woke up to intervene in the dispute. Prime Minister Blair warned the strikers that police and troops would be used to clear the blocked fuel depots.[22]

At their early stages, many disruptions may seem innocuous. Suppliers, business partners, customers, and even governments may release reassuring information. Realizing the magnitude of a large disruption at an early stage requires analytical capability to understand "what does it mean?" and a deep understanding of the system in which the business operates. It is this understanding of the system that enables managers to recognize the sometimes distant and unlikely relationships between the firm and various external threats and disruptions.

To improve early detection, vulnerable companies have instituted special monitoring devices and, in some cases, added new capabilities. For example, following the closure of its Louisville hub resulting from an unexpected snowstorm (see chapter 13), UPS built its own meteorology department. The department issues detailed forecasts regarding key airports where UPS operates—routinely besting the U.S. meteorological service in its forecast accuracy.

New technologies may help companies deal with fast-developing disruptions. In 2004, seismologists in Los Angeles were testing a warning system that could detect an earthquake at its epicenter and send an electronic alert to authorities, companies, and the public. Because the electronic warning signal travels at the speed of light, it reaches parts of the affected areas seconds before the shock waves. Authorities and companies can use these precious seconds to secure or shut down critical processes immediately before the shaking starts, the power goes out, and the pipes rupture.

A tsunami detection system has been in place in the Pacific Ocean since 1948. It is based on signals from eight deep-ocean sensors mounted on buoys and about a hundred coastal monitors, all tuned to detect wave patterns characteristics of a tsunami. In the United States the National Weather Service operates a program called TsunamiReady, promoting emergency awareness, and coastal communities at risk have installed warning systems and disseminate information about evacuation procedures. The system is credited with saving hundreds of lives when Crescent City in Hawaii was evacuated before the tsunami generated by the 1964 Alaska earthquake reached the island. The government of Japan is spending $20 million per year on a completely automated system of tsunami warning based on additional sensors and automatic connection to media outlets for warning. Unfortunately, nations around the Indian Ocean have not installed such a system. The December 26, 2004, tsunami hit Indonesia, Thailand, India, Sri Lanka, Bangladesh, the Maldives, Myanmar, and even Somalia on the east coast of Africa, killing over 175,000 people and causing billions of dollars in damage. While Indonesia was hit within minutes of the quake, the tsunami took two hours to reach Sri Lanka, three hours to reach India, and six hours to reach Somalia. Yet no warning ever sounded.[23]

Monitoring systems can also provide past data to help catch near misses and developing patterns of disruption. For example, Amazon.com monitors seven variables in real time as it processes the ebb and flow of orders and packages to customers. Amazon gathers tracking data from transportation carriers such as UPS and FedEx, who deliver Amazon.com's shipments to customers. Amazon.com knows, for example, that packages that get fewer than three scans are more likely to get lost or cause the customer to call Amazon.com about the shipment. The data not only helps Amazon.com detect problems; it also helps the company fine-tune which carrier it selects for which packages, thus improving its service.

Increased Detection Sensitivity as a Benefit for Business

A system of early detection put in place to avoid low-probability disruptions can, of course, routinely alert managers to smaller problems and day-to-day negative trends. Monitoring near misses can point to systemic process problems that are likely to manifest themselves as future disruptions.

Many of the initiatives of the Department of Homeland Security in the United States are focused on providing electronic monitoring of shipment integrity and shipment status. "Smart" container seals can show telltale signs of tampering, and radio frequency-based shipment identification (RFID) tags can help determine the content and location of shipments.[24] Naturally, smart seals, along with closed-circuit cameras and theft-detection electronic tags in terminals and loading docks, can also help deter theft and vandalism.

The location technologies that let shippers and consignees know where shipments are (creating "visibility," in the parlance of supply chain professionals), can reveal ominous tampering with shipments. Most of the time, however, shipment visibility applications are part of automatic event management systems used to alert consignees of late (or early) shipments and incorrect shipment content. Such shipment visibility systems can also be used to reroute shipments to areas where demand is unexpectedly high and away from areas where demand is lower than expected, or reroute shipments to cover late arrivals. Thus, shipment visibility systems designed for the primary purpose of detecting tampering can also be used to create flexibility in responding to day-to-day demand variations.

The Challenge

Is it anthrax or Sweet'n Low? Cyanide or almond paste? In the past, firefighters dealing with unknown substances leaking from turned tankers or rail cars had to wait hours to find out. But now, with the possibility of a bio-terror attack, emergency crews might have only minutes to determine if they're dealing with a terrorist attack, a college prank, or a media-induced panic.[25] Dozens of companies, federal laboratories, and research institutions around the world are racing to develop detection methods for warnings against nuclear, biological, or chemical attacks. The aim is to develop "smoke detector"–type systems—accurate systems that are "always on," sounding an alarm when they detect radiation, biological, or chemical hazards in shipments, buildings, water, or food supply.[26]

Such early detection can give firms and the government time to implement containment and recovery operations and to prepare customers and the population at large for the disruption. In many cases, however, companies invest in early detection systems because of the tangible day-to-day management and control functionality that such systems provide. With early detection managers can still recover and expedite a late shipment, order another, or alert their customers to the problem. Thus, the same functionality that helps create a smooth, cost-efficient flow of goods and services also helps firms monitor their systems for disruptions.

Prepared or not, however, when disaster strikes, the first line of defense is typically redundancy: Having extra inventory, surplus capacity, or alternative supply sources can give a firm time to organize its response and recovery. This is the subject of the next chapter.

10

Resilience through Redundancy

Between September 18 and October 9, 2001, a series of letters were deposited at a mailbox in New Jersey. Poison-pen letters in a very literal sense, the envelopes contained a fine powder of deadly anthrax spores along with a short handwritten anti-American missive. Addressed to a variety of U.S. government offices and American media companies, the lethal letters created a scare, killed five people, and infected 19 others.

As these letters made their way to their fateful destinations, they left behind a deadly residue. Sent to addresses in New York, Washington, D.C., and Florida, the letters entered the United States Postal Service's (USPS) massive network. The fine anthrax dust leaked from the envelopes to contaminate the Brentwood Processing and Distribution Center in Washington D.C., the Trenton Processing and Distribution Center in New Jersey, and a host of minor mail handling facilities in New Jersey, New York, Washington, and Florida.

The Brentwood facility is an imposing 633,000 square-foot brick building.[1] Inside, 2,500 workers work 24 hours a day, seven days a week to handle much of the torrential flow of letters coming to and from the nation's capital. Some three and a half million items pass through Brentwood every day.

On October 21, 2001, two workers at the Brentwood facility were hospitalized with suspected (later confirmed) cases of anthrax. The USPS immediately shut down the facility for a thorough inspection. To their horror, they found anthrax spores on the mail-sorting equipment. The two sickened postal workers died the following day. It took two years to decontaminate and refit the cavernous facility.[2]

In the meantime, the government's mail had to get through; the USPS had to find an alternative to Brentwood's lost capacity. "Neither sleet nor rain nor anthrax will keep these carriers from their appointed rounds," promised Sue Brennan, a spokeswoman for the U.S. Postal Service.[3] The USPS quickly rerouted Brentwood-bound flows to two other distribution centers in Capitol Heights and Gaithersburg in Maryland.[4] By most accounts, mail delivery the day after the closure was normal.

The USPS survived the closure of the 633,000 square-foot Brentwood facility, the 300,000 square-foot Trenton facility, and other smaller facilities because of the massive overcapacity built into its system. Such redundant capacity was not the result of planning for disaster. Instead, it was the consequence of the reduction in the volume of mail resulting from the increasing use of the Internet to pay bills, write letters, and send greeting cards. Since USPS workers are subject to civil-service employment laws, the USPS cannot adjust its operations quickly for the falling business volume, resulting in massive overcapacity.

Profit-oriented companies can hardly keep massive amounts of capacity idle and just waiting to be used, but some forms of redundancy are used by all businesses.

Inventory for Redundancy

The basic form of redundancy used by all businesses is safety stock. Although the extra inventory of parts and raw material on the one hand and finished product on the other can protect a company against small changes in the demand and supply patterns, it is expensive. Keeping extra supplies of parts and products not only ties up capital but also requires managing this inventory, including warehousing it, maintaining it, and preventing damage or pilferage. In addition, many products can become obsolete while they are stored in inventory, as new, better, and less expensive products are introduced into the market.

Extra inventory is also often the culprit in hidden manufacturing problems. With extra inventory, it is all too easy for production managers to tap the parts' inventory in order to replace a defective part, or to fulfill a customer order from the inventory of finished goods, rather than to investigate the source of the problem. But with little or no extra inventory, each problem causes an unfilled customer order or a stoppage of the production line, requiring immediate management attention leading to a corrective action. As Toyota Motor Corporation has proved, reducing inventory (and using just-in-time discipline) leads to improved quality.

Thus the dilemma: Although inventory can be used to protect against disruptions, it is expensive; more important, it can lead to relaxed manufacturing, procurement, and logistics disciplines at the expense of quality products and delivery.

SOSO Inventory

As a major provider of medical supplies, Johnson & Johnson serves many hospitals and pharmacies. Because the demand for its products ebbs and flows with the flu, hay fever, and cold seasons, as well as outbreaks of various diseases, J&J keeps safety stock in several warehouses for use when demand for any of its products exceeds the forecast. One of J&J's customers is the Pentagon. Normally, the Pentagon buys medical supplies in predictable patterns that J&J can supply from its manufacturing plants and warehouses. In case of a war or a major disaster, however, the Pentagon knows that it will need huge amounts of medical supplies very quickly.

For that reason, J&J is under contract with the U.S. government to stockpile certain quantities of medical supplies. (Indeed, the U.S. government has increased funding for the strategic stockpiling of vaccinations and medications from $41 million in 2001 to $400 million in 2005.[5])

To meet this contractual obligation, J&J has two major challenges: how to keep the extra inventory fresh and up-to-date, and how to ensure that the extra inventory will not infect its processes with sloppiness, leading to expensive quality problems. J&J solves the problem with a "sell one stock one" (SOSO)[6] inventory discipline.

Under the SOSO strategy, J&J does not let the Pentagon's inventory molder in a dedicated warehouse; instead, the inventory is commingled with the rest of J&J stock. To keep its commitment, J&J defines a "red line" for each product; when the inventory for a particular product falls to the red line, J&J computers signal the ordering hospital or pharmacy that J&J is out of stock. Because going below the red line requires Pentagon approval,[7] this inventory cannot be used to compensate for day-to-day variations. Consequently, J&J's everyday processes have to operate as if such inventory does not exist, thereby reducing the danger of sloppiness.

Using a SOSO strategy can mitigate some of the costs of keeping extra inventory. Commingling ensures that the stock is fresh, and requiring high level approval (CEO, board, or the Pentagon in the case of J&J) for tapping into the SOSO inventory ensures that the inventory will not undermine the company's quality processes.

In many regards, the Pentagon is using J&J's SOSO stock in the same way that the Department of Energy uses the Strategic Oil Reserve. These reserves were not established to mitigate price fluctuations; rather, they serve as backup inventory of a critical material in case of a national crisis.

Naturally, when companies are aware of potential disruptions, they can accumulate inventory to cushion the effect. This can be in anticipation of either a one-time phenomenon or a continuing situation. For example, prior to the West Coast port lockout in October 2002, Wal-Mart stockpiled some three to five weeks' worth of inventory to prevent the disruption from affecting holiday sales, and NUMMI accumulated several days' worth of parts supply. And when companies enter into an agreement with a supplier whose deliveries are less than predictable (because of distance, location, or process peculiarities), those companies can change their policies to increase inventory by using a higher "reorder point" in their inventory management. Unilever, for example, increased its North American safety stocks of Q-Tips by

10 percent as part of contracting all the production to a Puerto Rico plant (see chapter 13).

Redundant Capacity

Instead of using inventory for redundancy, some enterprises use redundant *capacity* for mission-critical business units. Boston Scientific manufactures an array of high-tech medical devices such as drug-coated stents that prop open the arteries of heart patients and help keep them blockage-free. For these specialized products, the company uses an array of sophisticated manufacturing systems to laser-cut nickel-titanium tubes into the delicate yet strong meshes that then receive the company's patented coatings. The nature of the product, and FDA regulations, specify meticulously clean and controlled production conditions. Each lot of stents must be traceable, requiring some 40 pages of paper-work to certify when, where, and how the devices in the lot were manufactured.

Were Boston Scientific to suffer from a disruption of its manufacturing facilities (e.g., a fire, industrial accident, or contamination), the company knows that the time to fix and recertify a disrupted facility could leave the company without a major portion of its revenues and profits and allow its aggressive competitors to take Boston Scientific's market share.

After assessing its vulnerabilities, Boston Scientific built redundant production lines for some of its most important products. These alternative manufacturing facilities are kept FDA-certified and ready to go in the event of a disruption. The company also has personnel who maintain the skill levels needed to operate those redundant lines. Although such redundancy is not inexpensive, the company realized that failing to maintain redundancy risks the entire company and decided to protect itself against that risk. Other companies aim for less than 100 percent capacity utilization rates on their existing production lines, reasoning that the unused capacity acts as a cushion to absorb unanticipated large orders.[8]

Yet other companies, such as Helix, a maker of high-performance vacuum pumps, rely on their suppliers to provide extra capacity. Helix used Demand Flow Technology,[9] in part, to segment its manufacturing processes into short, easily taught steps that in an emergency can be transferred to others (see further discussion in chapter 11). Having analyzed the capacities and capabilities of suppliers, Helix knows that it could quickly teach certain suppliers to make its products.

Shadow Flights

Every veteran business traveler knows the frustration of a delayed or canceled flight. But some airplane operators face especially large consequences for disrupted flights. If the corporate motto is "When it absolutely, positively has to get there overnight," then a canceled flight is not an option. Even a delay of a few hours may mean that someone's package will miss a crucial deadline, disrupting a customer's business and possibly leading to customer losses well beyond the price of shipping an overnight package.

To avoid such problems, FedEx invests in an unusual type of redundant capacity. Every night, two completely empty planes take off—one from an East Coast airport and one from a West Coast airport—and fly to Memphis.[10] In the wee hours of the morning, these planes make a similarly lonely return journey. In the event of a problem anywhere in the United States, these planes can swoop down, land, and pick up packages from a grounded aircraft. About forty more planes are flown deliberately half-empty for the same purpose. Finally, 14 planes (10 in the United States and 4 overseas) serve as spares on the ground that could be pulled into emergency service. Although these planes could not mitigate a major disaster, this fractional redundant capacity does alleviate many potential disruptions.

Inspecting Your Own Faults, Quickly

Located on the quake-prone West Coast, Intel's Oregon chip-making plant is vulnerable to an earthquake. The cost of downtime for this one plant is measured in hundreds of thousands of dollars per hour, putting a premium on fast recovery. The structure itself is built to the highest standards and can withstand most earthquakes, but the plant cannot open for business following an earthquake before inspectors check for hidden damage and dangerous structural faults. Worse, in the aftermath of an earthquake these inspectors would be terribly overworked. With thousands of buildings to inspect, and priority given to facilities like hospitals and schools, Intel knows it would face a three-day wait before being allowed back in its own buildings.

To save itself millions of dollars from the added downtime, Intel trained its own dedicated building inspectors for post-earthquake duty. Rather than rely on and wait for government-provided inspectors, the company can immediately inspect and certify its own buildings to reduce the delay. As a side benefit to the community, Intel plans to let these inspectors help the government examine and certify other buildings after Intel's are inspected. For Intel, the cost trade-off of the redundant training versus the severe costs of downtime creates an obvious business case for employing the inspectors.

Redundant IT Systems

Before September 11, 2001, the area in and around the World Trade Center served as an information nexus for many financial services firms. Companies like Merrill Lynch, Smith Barney, Morgan Stanley, and Deutsche Bank all had major trading installations supported by a massive information technology infrastructure in and around the WTC. After the terrorist attacks on the towers, and the towers' subsequent collapse, some 20 million square feet of offices were destroyed or rendered unusable and the entire local information technology infrastructure lay in ruins.

When the south tower of the World Trade Center collapsed on Deutsche Bank's New York facility, the German banking giant lost a major connection to the U.S. markets. Despite the loss, COO Hermann-Josef Lamberti said, "we were able, on the very same day, to clear more than $300 billion with the Fed." Redundant IT systems in Ireland took over when the New York systems were destroyed.

Other firms, such as Merrill Lynch, also quickly shifted operations to backup centers and redundant trading floors near New York City. According to Paul Honey, Merrill Lynch's director of global contingency planning,[11] "within just a few minutes of the evacuation, Merrill Lynch was able to switch its critical management functions to their command center in New Jersey." Moreover, everyone in the company knew of the redundant facility and was trained to call in or transfer their work to that location.

In businesses that transact billions of dollars a day electronically, building full redundancy is not a difficult decision. But the same is true for most modern corporations: The loss of their information systems means loss of the business. As compared with other redundancies, keeping redundant databases with shadow transactions and redundant application systems is relatively inexpensive given the potential damage from loss of data or the information technology infrastructure.

Redundancy as a Resilience Strategy

Redundancy of any kind helps companies continue serving their customers while rebuilding after a disruption. Indeed, most companies are accustomed to protecting themselves against small fluctuations, mostly in the demand for their products, by keeping spare inventory.

But over the last two decades, many companies have worked diligently to cut costs by reducing exactly this type of inventory, resulting in tightly connected supply chains and higher quality of products and services. Thus, when creating a special safety stock for protection against high-impact/low-probability events, companies should take care not to reverse the gains of such "lean" supply chain operations. In fact, some companies may decide to keep a lean supply chain with little inventory and a single supplier, even for a critical parts. Their rationale is that, on balance, the full cost of coordinating several suppliers and keeping safety stock may be judged to be too high. That was Toyota's consideration following the Aisin fire described in chapter 13.

Yet safety stocks are a part of most resilience and business continuity plans. Even a relatively small amount of inventory can provide a disrupted company with time to prepare its response. A high level of redundancy, however, may be too expensive. Only when the stakes are especially high and the costs of extra capacity are relatively low, as in the case of information technology, should companies keep complete redundant capacity.

Service companies, in particular, typically keep extra capacity because the costs of service failures are high—service is what these companies sell. Furthermore, service companies cannot keep an inventory of their product (e.g., if a package was not delivered on time, that service cannot be recovered and offered to the customer later). Consequently, a disruption will lead to an immediate service failure unless there is extra capacity or some other redundancy or flexibility in the system ready to kick in when the service is about to fail.

Resilience through Flexibility

Regardless of how it is used, redundancy entails additional costs to any enterprise. It reduces efficiency and therefore is not congruent with management's goals and objectives. With quality processes, continuous improvements, and "six sigma"[12] programs all aimed at reducing waste and redundancy, it is difficult to argue for more redundancy. At best, redundancy can be looked upon as a "necessary evil," an insurance against risk. But with managers motivated by competitive pressures and by short-term Wall Street expectations, the result is likely to be insufficient reserves.

Operational flexibility, on the other hand, can also increase resilience, allowing a company to respond quickly to disruptions. Such capability is more difficult to develop than simply keeping extra inventory, having more suppliers, or keeping extra capacity, since it typically involves fundamental changes to the entire company as well as its supply chain relationships. It involves close partnerships with suppliers, who can be called upon to help; flexible contracts, allowing for changes in quantities and delivery schedule; flexible manufacturing facilities that can be used to produce multiple products; a multi-skilled work force with empowered employees who can move quickly from one task to another; and strong customer relationships ensuring continuity in troubled times. The rest of this book discusses these and other aspects of such corporate flexibility.

IV
Building in Flexibility

11

Flexibility through Interchangeability

Ultimate flexibility means having viable alternatives in any situation. Standardization of parts, processes, and production systems, so that these elements are interchangeable, creates options for using them where there is a shortfall. In the event of a disruption, firms can substitute alternative parts (or part suppliers), swap out damaged components, use alternative processes, or reroute the flow of business activities.

Copy Exact!

Intel has plants in places ranging from Ireland to Israel to China to the United States. With such a widely dispersed organization, disruptions that could affect Intel include rolling blackouts in California, earthquakes in Oregon, typhoons in the Philippines, terrorism in Israel, or freight hijackers in Malaysia.

When SARS struck in Asia in 2003, chip industry analysts worried about the virus's effect on computer chip making. Intel, Hewlett-Packard, and other multinationals reported potential SARS cases among Hong Kong–based sales and marketing staffers; almost all trade shows in Asia were canceled.[1] Possible disruption of Asia's entire electronics manufacturing base loomed large. For example, a Motorola plant in Singapore shut down when one of the plant's 532 workers became infected. Some feared that other plants, such as Intel's Shanghai facility, might also close as the infection swept across Asian cities and curtailed normal public activities. Intel, however, was confident that if it had to, it could withstand the closure of the plant with minimal consequences.

In a strategy called Copy Exact! Intel builds each of its semi-conductor fabrication plants to the same exact specifications, creating interchangeable processes and interchangeable fabs throughout the world. Copy Exact! began in the mid-1980s as a means of coping with the inscrutable complexity of semiconductor manufacturing. The smallest variation in temperature, pressure, chemistry, or handling can mean the difference between a wafer full of hundreds of expensive chips, worth hundreds of dollars each, and a useless silicon disk. Once Intel has a new semiconductor manufacturing process debugged at one facility, it copies that process—down to the lengths of the hoses on the vacuum pumps—to other Intel facilities.[2] This strategy also provides flexibility; Intel can transfer capacity and work-in-process back and forth between facilities to eliminate manufacturing bottlenecks and overcome disruptions in any given facility.[3]

When SARS erupted in Asia, Intel spokesman Chuck Mulloy said, "If there's a problem, we can move the capacity around—we have designed the system so we don't have chokepoints."[4] Copy Exact! transforms Intel's global portfolio of facilities into a large virtual fab. Wafers can be partially completed in one fab and flown to another for finishing, without affecting yield.

The Copy Exact! mentality extends beyond semiconductor fabrication to the assembly and test factories and to the contractors who support building PC motherboards. According to Intel's Steve Lund, "If something happens to a facility, we roll over to another subcontractor who can pick up the same assembly test and make sure that we get the same product at the same amounts for our shipping plans."[5] Copy Exact! even extends to Intel's IT infrastructure. Identical software and hardware architecture support a range of activities, such as ordering and production planning at 18 manufacturing, testing, and assembly sites across three continents.

Commonality Breeds Flexibility

Other companies also replicate factories and standardize manufacturing processes. General Motors (GM), for example, operates near-identical plants in Argentina, Poland, China, Thailand, and

Brazil for enhanced flexibility. The plants were built to a common template that uses the same design, processes, and technology.[6] At GM, the standardized processes include material systems, body shop, stamping, fabrication, painting, and general assembly. GM even standardized the human resources strategies as well as the financial and quality control systems. GM's interchangeability, however, is more subtle than Intel's replication of plant and equipment. "It is not necessary to make a cookie-cutter for all our operations," said James Wiemels, vice president, manufacturing, GM Europe.[7] GM's new manufacturing process starts with designing common primary locating points and assembling vehicles in basically the same sequence, even if a plant's process is slightly different.

Given the difficulties of predicting demand for a particular vehicle years in advance of building a manufacturing plant, the resulting flexibility helps GM cope with uncertainty in demand. For example, GM's Thailand plant came on line in 1997, in the aftermath of the collapse of several Asian currencies. The plant was initially intended to produce cars for the local market, but the slumping Thai economy caused GM to switch the plant to export production, making engines and cars that were sold in Japan, Europe, and Chile.[8]

In addition, to be able to adjust plants to changing requirements, none of GM's five flexible plants has fixed conveyer lines that carry car bodies in a pre-designed assembly pattern. Instead, each plant can be reconfigured over a weekend.

Shifting production from one disrupted facility to an alternative one requires more than standardization of the technical capabilities of the factories (including equipment, personnel, and processes); it also requires the ability to shift the flow of inbound material into the alternative facility and the ability to service the customers from that facility. Such capabilities require flexible supply contracts and flexible distribution capabilities.

To provide strategic flexibility across product lines, beyond the ability to move production among plants, GM, like most other large automobile manufacturers, uses a joint platform strategy. Several car models share similar chassis, engines, transmissions, and many other components that are opaque to the customer. The factory, then, can use a single set of fixtures and jigs to handle multiple models of cars. It also allows the company to produce components (such as engines and transmissions) before committing to the production of specific models, thereby delaying this commitment until demand can be forecast with greater accuracy. A similar strategy is used by most automakers. For example, the Volkswagen "B Platform" is the basis for a wide range of models, from the budget-priced Skoda Octavia to the midpriced VW Golf, Beetle, and GTI to the luxurious Audi A3 and TT. All share about 70 percent of their content.[9]

Standardization of Parts

Standardizing manufacturing processes is not the only way to create flexibility through interchangeability. When Lucent's Switching System group in Spain faced a looming deadline for a major project in Saudi Arabia, the company's Tres Cantos factory could not handle the project's needs for circuit packs and cabinets. Worse, differences across Lucent's product line meant that Lucent could not use its factories in Oklahoma City, Poland, and Taiwan to help out. In response, Lucent redesigned the products to use standardized parts and adjusted its processes so that several factories could contribute to the project. Standardizing the designs and processes let Lucent use multiple capacities, complete the project on schedule, and avoid disrupting an important customer.[10]

The Saudi project made Lucent realize the high, ongoing cost of the company's proliferation of independent designs, components, and suppliers. To make this point internally, Lucent Supply Chain Networks (SCN) president Jose Mejia brought into one room all of the different types of product enclosures that Lucent used for their network systems and invited Lucent's senior supply chain executives to come take a look. The visual effect of seeing 47 different enclosures with similar functionality got the point across. As Mejia commented, "these products looked like they were made by different companies."[11]

In fact, Lucent's SCN organization was created by Mejia in 2001, in part, to solve this problem.[12] The organization was given broad responsibility for all supply chain costs, from research-and-development, to engineering, to manufacturing, to sales, and to distribution and installation.[13] SCN drove standardization throughout Lucent's operations with impressive results. The number of enclosures was reduced from 47 to seven; the number of shelves from several hundreds to three, the number of fan controller configurations from 92 to four platforms, and the number of specified filters from 466 to 15. The increased flexibility that resulted from this action helped return the company to profitability in the third quarter of 2003.

Lucent applied the same concepts of standardization to its supplier relationships. It went from spending 40 percent of its procurement expenditure with its 1,000 top suppliers to concentrating 80 percent of its supply expenditures with 60 top suppliers. Having narrowed the number of suppliers, Lucent then reached out to develop deeper relationships with them, putting emphasis on risk-sharing relationships to help seek new business for both Lucent and its suppliers. This included collaboration on proposal development, in which all parties shared the costs of investing in proposals and prototyping for potential customers (without bidding with other partners at the same time), thus winning or losing together.

In addition, the suppliers shared with Lucent the liability for failing to meet any contractual obligations to the customers. Inevitably, Lucent and its suppliers became intimately familiar with each other. The resulting trust and mutual awareness provided Lucent with even more flexibility, and together with its suppliers, Lucent could sense and respond more quickly to rapidly changing market conditions or to special requests. In particular, Lucent's average supply lead times to its customers were almost halved between 2002 and 2003.

When Toyota examined its use of P-valves following the Aisin fire (see chapter 13), it realized that it had too many different types of the small auto brake component. One hundred varieties of the simple part had complicated and delayed the recovery efforts after the fire. Toyota launched a redesign effort across its product line and reduced the number of different P-valve types to a dozen. This action was taken with two goals in mind:

- Increase corporate resilience by simplifying requirements from other manufacturers, in case the need ever rose again to bring new suppliers on line quickly.

- Simplify the forecasting requirements by using the same P-valve across several product lines, allowing demand to be aggregated over all the models that shared a given P-valve.

In some cases, existing standards are so commonplace that their contribution to flexibility is taken for granted. For example, when Ford recalled 6.5 million tires used on Ford Explorer SUVs, the standardization of automobile tire-mounting throughout the industry allowed Ford to quickly procure tires from other tire makers. Had tire sizes been nonstandard, the time required to provide a safe alternative for customers would probably have been months.

In general, the use of standard parts and commodity components presents a trade-off between the exact fit to a specific purpose (as presented by specially engineered parts) and the faster time-to-market and higher availability of standard parts. Using standard designs broadens the natural base of suppliers, letting the company procure from other suppliers in case one supplier is disrupted. It requires, however, higher levels of internal coordination while engineering new products.

Pliable People

The familiar brown uniforms of the UPS driver only hint at a deeper kind of uniformity at the global package carrier. UPS standardizes more that just the appearance of its 357,000 employees; it standardizes work processes to the minutest detail, down to telling package delivery truck drivers to snag the keys of the truck with the third finger of the right hand as they open the truck door with the left hand. Such uniformity creates flexibility for the giant package delivery company, which in 2003 handled shipments representing 7 percent of the U.S. GDP. That year it delivered an average of 13.6 million packages a day to eight million customers in 200 countries with its 88,000 brown vehicles and 575 brown planes.

Brown vs. Snow & Ice

UPS Worldport in Louisville is the central sorting facility for UPS air packages. Late each night, hundreds of planes come in and unload their packages. The packages are then sorted and loaded onto outbound planes, lifting off in the early hours of the morning to make deliveries all across the United States, when firms open for business. In 2002, the facility had the capacity to sort through more than 300,000 packages an hour, supported by computers twice as powerful as those running the New York Stock Exchange and with software capable of more than a million database transactions per minute.[14]

Sunday, January 16, 1994, began as a normal winter's day for UPS's bustling Louisville hub. Weather forecasts predicted a light dusting of snow as a cold front wound its way across Kentucky in the evening hours. But the forecast was wrong. Instead of one or two inches, the storm blasted Louisville with 16 inches of sleet and snow. With the blizzard came record cold temperatures—as low as 22 degrees Fahrenheit below zero (-30°C)—which froze the heavy snow to the roads. These arctic conditions paralyzed all transportation in and around Louisville.

What aggravated the conditions was that the city of Louisville was unprepared. Local snow plows had rubber-edged blades, which were designed to reduce wear and tear on the roads but such blades made them incapable of removing the thick ice laid down by the storm. Many of the plows broke down as they attempted to clear the heavy snow. The ultra-low temperatures made road salt ineffective. The city had no choice but to close all roads and institute a travel ban. Even ambulances became mired in the snow, forcing the city to use fire trucks instead. And even the fire trucks had trouble.[15]

The storm began at 8 P.M., just as some 100 UPS planes were preparing to take off all around the country loaded with packages bound for Louisville for sorting and delivery. As the weather took a turn for the worse, UPS realized that this would not be a normal night. The first order of business was to divert the airborne planes to alternative airports as Louisville's airport shut down. Next, the company had to attend to the hundreds of thousands of packages already sitting in its Louisville hub, each representing a customer eager for delivery.

Clearing the snow-clogged runways at the Louisville airport took less than a day, but the roads were a different matter. Local and state government declared a state of emergency and forbade nonessential travel for five days as the heavy snow bogged down vehicles and disabled two-thirds of the snow plows in the region. "We actually were up and ready for the next-day-air sort on Tuesday night, but of course, we had thousands of employees who couldn't get to work," spokeswoman Patti Hobbs said.[16]

But the company did not give up. "Our employees couldn't drive to work . . . but they could fly," Hobbs said.[17] With the airport open, UPS flew in employees from other UPS locations to help process the stranded packages and load the planes, getting out the packages stuck in the Louisville hub. The company negotiated with local authorities for a limited waiver of the travel ban so that the jet-commuting employees could be driven to nearby hotels for the night.

UPS could use workers from other facilities because of its uniform practices. UPS's sorting machines were interchangeable, the processes were interchangeable, and the people who were familiar with one location could operate any of them.

Standard processes also help UPS respond to demand fluctuations. For example, when the package volume booms every December, supervisors and managers help work the hubs—unloading, sorting, and loading packages. During a Teamsters strike against UPS in 1997, these seasoned managers kept the business going. The standardized processes mean that anyone who knows any UPS operation can contribute, and that means that UPS is flexible, whether it faces an unexpected blizzard or a busy Christmas season.

For UPS, widespread standardization not only provides flexibility but also underpins performance improvement processes.

Because every UPS outpost uses the same processes, the same machinery, and the same training, the company can cross-compare performance at different divisions, different regions, and different delivery routes. UPS then works to improve low performers (whether they are individual employees, a facility, or a region) and lauds and copies the high performers.

Going with the Flow

Helix Technology, a maker of vacuum instruments and equipment, uses Demand Flow Technology, an operational strategy descendent of lean manufacturing. The strategy is designed to increase manufacturing flexibility in a lean manufacturing environment. As part of the implementation of this strategy, Helix divided its manufacturing processes into small, well-documented pieces (sub-processes). Workers in "cells" are trained to perform the set of standard tasks constituting each sub-process. The result is a much-simplified set of work assignments requiring less training for each worker to achieve proficiency.[18]

In concert with other process changes, this strategy helped Helix improve asset utilization and accelerate material flows throughout its manufacturing processes. It had, however, a powerful disruption-related benefit as well. By atomizing the tasks, workers could perform a greater variety of sub-processes, each consisting of a set of simple subtasks. This created a flexible worker environment. The inherent cross-training means that many workers can substitute for one another. It also means that new or substitute workers can be quickly trained in the event of disruption. If one of its facilities is interrupted, Helix can even transfer tasks to suppliers, because the work has been so scripted that it can be easily transferred. More than 3,200 companies, including GE, Boeing, and Flextronics, use Demand Flow Technology to improve performance and flexibility.

Pilot Swapping

Other companies also use various types of standardization to create interchangeability, which in turns creates flexibility. Southwest Airlines flies nearly 400 airplanes—all of them Boeing 737s. The company operates a tight schedule with each plane spending only 20 to 30 minutes on the ground between flights and being expected to make seven flights each day, giving the company little time for recovery from disruptions. The use of a single aircraft type means that Southwest can swap airplanes and swap crews.

Southwest's penchant for standardization extends to the last detail; the company standardizes the cockpits, even as cockpit technology has evolved over the years. In more recent models of 737s, Boeing designed a "glass cockpit" with computer screens replacing old-fashioned analog dials. But in order to maintain interchangeability, Southwest asked Boeing to program the new displays to look like the old "steam gauge" dials and indicators that are so familiar to Southwest pilots.[19] Interchangeable cockpits mean interchangeable pilots and reduced training costs. If a plane has a maintenance issue or a pilot gets delayed, Southwest need not disrupt its time-sensitive flight schedule; any Southwest pilot can fly any Southwest plane on any Southwest route.

Other low-cost airlines use the same strategy. Ryanair, the European discount airline, uses only Boeing 737s, while JetBlue, the U.S.-based discounter, uses Airbus A320s on all of its long-haul flights and Embraer 190s for all short-haul flights. When EasyJet (which is Ryanair's main competitor in Europe) decided to buy Airbus A319 aircraft to add to its 48 Boeing 737s on October 13, 2002, its stock fell by 5 percent. According to the BBC, the market had "worries that the cost of mixing Airbus planes into Easyjet's Boeing fleet would prove expensive for the airline."[20]

Interchangeability

The benefits of interchangeability come from risk pooling. Assume that a computer manufacturer makes four types of PCs, each with a different case. Because demand for each of the computers is uncertain, the manufacturer needs to keep a certain level of safety stock of these parts to ensure that its production line does not run out of the parts too often. (That is usually expressed in terms of "fill rate," which is the percentage of occurrences when the needed part is available in inventory.) If the manufacturer, instead, decided to use the same case for all four computers, it would be able to cut its safety stock in half but still keep the same fill rate.[21] Alternatively, the manufacturer could keep the same level of safety stock, resulting in higher fill rates. The increased fill rate is rooted in the flexibility offered by the interchangeability of the cases. If the demand for one computer type increases, the demand for another may go down, and vice versa.

Standardization creates interchangeability, which creates flexibility to respond to disruptions. Standard factories (Intel, GM), standard equipment (Southwest, Ryan Air), standard components (Lucent, Dell), and standard processes (Helix, UPS) allow companies to respond to disruptions effectively. Companies can move personnel around, move work across their plants (and even their suppliers' plants), or change suppliers of parts and services.

In many cases, interchangeability implies "sameness" of parts or products so that they can be moved from surplus to deficit locations. But growing customer expectations, increased rate of product introductions, and strong competition mean that companies have to introduce more varieties of many of their products, thereby increasing the need for extra stock and diminishing the flexibility offered by interchangeability. The next chapter looks at a strategy of combining large production batches with the ability to offer many product variants, thus retaining flexibility while satisfying customer preferences.

12

Postponement for Flexibility

As consumer expectations grow, manufacturers try to satisfy every conceivable market segment. For example, in 2004 Colgate-Palmolive sold 35 varieties of toothpaste (combinations of long protection, toothpaste/mouthwash blends, herbal whitening, baking soda and peroxide, plaque and gingivitis prevention, kids' products, fresh breath, tartar control, and cavity protection). Procter & Gamble offers dozens of varieties of its Crest toothpaste: In 2004 it offered more than nine flavors and three consistencies (gel, paste, and striped combinations) in several formulations.

The multiplicity of products means that each one is selling at a relatively small quantity with the disaggregate demand for each being very volatile. Rather than pooling the demand risk, the multitude of products aggravates it, requiring manufacturers and retailers to keep large safety stocks in order to provide the high fill rates that customers demand. At the same time, global competitive pressures mean that companies have to reduce costs by manufacturing at low labor-cost locations, leading to long forecast horizons. They have to forecast demand accurately to avoid lost sales when there is not enough product, and avoid obsolescence and discounting when there is too much product.

Postponement or *mass customization* strategy allows manufacturers to satisfy many customer segments, yet it takes advantage of economies of scale in manufacturing and offshore outsourcing in order to reduce costs.[1] It is based on redesigning products and manufacturing processes so that a core component, common to a group of product varieties, is manufactured first. The focus in manufacturing the base component is on costs. Thus, it can be manufactured offshore and, if warranted, in long production runs to spread the fixed costs of producing a batch over a large number of items. The finished product is then manufactured or customized from the base product later, according to customer orders, rather than based on a forecast.

Such strategies are being used by many supply chains to provide high service levels for many product varieties at a lower cost than that involved in providing the same number of varieties directly from the factory. But they also provide an inherent flexibility that creates resilience in case of disruptions, since the base product can be tailored to changing demand for products and locations.

Gray Is the New Black (Hole)

In 1997, Marks & Spencer's annual profits exceeded £1billion for the first time in its history. Continuing the growth trajectory, brisk spring sales at Marks & Spencer made for a great start for 1998. The U.K.-based high street retailer was fulfilling its 1997 promise to shareholders "to become the world's leading volume retailer with a global brand and global recognition."[2] The profitable company was expanding globally and at home, causing journalists and academics to present Marks & Spencer as a role model for British industry.[3]

Facing increasing competition from more fashion-oriented yet lower-cost retailers such as Zara, The Gap, and H&M, Marks & Spencer took three strategic steps:

- It pressed its suppliers to procure material and finished garments in the Far East and Africa, thereby lowering its costs of goods.

- It increased the range of items it carried.

- It began shifting from its more conservative, timeless styles to more fashion-oriented styles and colors.

In early 1998, when M&S was deciding on its orders for the autumn/winter season of 1998, grays and blacks dominated the catwalks in Paris and Milan and seemed to be the hot colors of the year. Accordingly, the company ramped up production of the new apparel in those colors, using the slogan "Gray Is the New Black" in anticipation of the forthcoming holiday season.

But with its three strategic steps, M&S had exposed itself to three forecasting challenges:

First, it now operated a long supply chain, stretching from the Asian factories where its products were made to its U.K. distribution centers, and from there to its European stores; the result was longer lead times over which it had to forecast.

Second, it started carrying more items and therefore a smaller amount of each; the result was more volatile demand for each of the items.

Finally, with these challenges in place, it entered the much more mercurial market for fashion goods, rather than the steady market for functional clothing for which it was known.

As 1998 progressed, the first signs of the impending storm appeared: Retail sales fell somewhat during the summer, yet M&S executives remained hopeful.

Then the holiday season failed to deliver on the spring season's promise of a banner year. "We all thought that sales would recover in September and October, and in fact they have gone further south," said Sir Richard Greenbury, executive chairmen of Marks & Spencer at the time.[4] Declining sales created a three-month supply of unsold apparel. The company suffered £150 million in losses: £90 million because of pre-Christmas sales failures and a further £60 million lost from clearing the excess stock.

Marks & Spencer not only had three months of extra inventory, it also had the *wrong* inventory because of the company's gamble on gray. Andrew Stone, managing director of Marks & Spencer's British retailing division, acknowledged, "The customers don't want 12 million square feet of gray and black. They want a changing range through the season."[5] Worse, Marks & Spencer had canceled new orders when it saw the softening sales. Although the tactic seemed sensible at the time, the company's 1999 annual report described the impact, noting, "This damaged the balance of ranges because, as popular goods sold out, we lacked the usual injection of fresh merchandise and still had to clear unsold goods."[6] Stores full of unpopular, stale merchandise further hurt sales and caused pundits to charge that the former British icon was out of touch.[7]

Marks & Spencer's stock on the London exchange slid from a high of 650p in the last quarter of 1997 to less than 175p in the last quarter of 2000.

It took a long time for Marks & Spencer to realize the forecasting difficulties embedded in its new combination of Asian sourcing, increased number of styles, and, with these in place, its entry into the fashion market. The fashion apparel industry is notorious for supply/demand mismatches resulting from the fickle tastes of the young consumers who make up the bulk of the customer base. A study by the Industry Forum found that nearly one-third of orders in the fashion garments industry have forecast errors of more than 25 percent and that color choices suffer from even worse forecast errors.[8]

The Supply Chain Dilemma

At the time of year when retailers have to place orders for merchandise, they don't know the next season's demand. Consequently, they have to estimate what their customers may want and order the merchandise to meet this estimate. Furthermore, forecasting total demand is not sufficient; retailers must forecast the combinations of styles, colors, and sizes that will be sought in each store. If they order too many green blouses and not enough red ones, they may disappoint the customers looking for the red ones and be forced to sell the green ones at a discount or even at a loss. All too often, retailers will have either too much or too little inventory.

The problem is not limited to retailers. Suppliers of computer parts, agricultural ingredients, automotive components, and almost every other product are subject to the same market forces. Customers require the products faster than supply chains can respond.

To avoid disappointing customers, companies can order large amounts of everything, increasing the chances of meeting demand but at the cost of being burdened with excess inventory. With their razor-thin margins, most retailers cannot afford such a strategy.

A related approach is variable pricing. Automobile dealers charge extra for "hot" models while car companies give rebates on unpopular ones; airlines sell seats to business travelers at a premium while discounting seats for leisure travelers; and retailers charge full price for trendy items while discounting unwanted merchandise. In each of these cases, companies use price reductions "after the fact" (i.e., after the product has been built, shipped, and offered in the marketplace) to sell items that customers would not buy at a full price. Pricing is an important weapon in the struggle to balance supply and demand, but it does not create flexibility and resilience.

Chapter 6 explained the challenges of forecasting and outlined several supply chain principles that make companies less prone to forecasting errors. A combination of two of the principles mentioned there underlies the postponement strategy described in this chapter:

- Aggregate forecasts are more accurate than disaggregate forecasts (this is the principle of risk pooling).

- Forecasts over short time horizons are more accurate than forecasts over long ones.

Dye Another Day

Shifting demand patterns, in particular color preferences, are not a new phenomenon in fashion retailing. In the mid-1980s, Benetton, the Italian clothing manufacturer and retailer, faced that very problem. While it had relatively accurate demand forecasts for the total sales of each of its styles and sizes, Benetton continuously missed the forecast of which colors would catch the fancy of its fashion-conscious customers. It ran out of popular colors, lost sales, and disappointed customers, while having to slash prices on out-of-favor colors. To remedy the situation, Benetton changed its manufacturing and distribution process.

Most clothing makers dye the yarn first, weave it into fabric, and then cut and sew the fabric to create the finished garments. Under this traditional manufacturing system, the manufacturer must decide how much to make in each color six to nine months in advance of replenishing the stores.

In contrast, Benetton redesigned its manufacturing process to make some of its clothes—those with difficult-to-forecast demand for colors—in an undyed, generic state called *greige*. Benetton dyed a test batch of each new garment and sent it to a set of carefully chosen stores where its sales were monitored closely in order to discern consumers' preference for colors. With this information in hand, it was easier to forecast which colors would sell well during the rest of the season. Benetton then quickly dyed the greige garments and shipped the items to the retail outlets. It could dye and deliver the latest fashion apparel to all of its stores in only five weeks.[9]

Such postponement of the dying operation increased Benetton's manufacturing costs per garment by about 10 percent. On the other hand, it increased sales by reducing stock-outs of popular colors, and it decreased the cost of overstocking and the associated costs of discounts and merchandise liquidations. (Discounts can be well more than 50 percent of an item's list price; some retailers, such as Boston's Filene's Basement, will give their merchandise to charity when it fails to sell after successive rounds of discounting.)

The Principles of Postponement

Traditional garment manufacturing forces retailers like Marks & Spencer to forecast winter sales of each color before summer even starts; postponement lets Benetton make the color decision much closer to the selling season.

The postponement strategy had two major benefits for Benetton, both of which had increased its forecast accuracy and allowed it to manage the demand/supply imbalance:

- When deciding on the number and sizes of (griege) items that it needed to manufacture, Benetton had to forecast only the total number of items and sizes regardless of color. This forecast is more accurate than a forecast by color because it is an aggregate estimate.

- When deciding on how many items to dye each particular color, Benetton already had data of actual sales (from the test batches). In addition, the selling season with the current trends was already at hand. The result was that the mix of colors could be determined more accurately.

What and When to Postpone?

Products that can benefit from a postponement-based supply chain design are those characterized by a combination of uncertain demand, short customer lead times, high inventory carrying costs, and modular product design.

The first characteristic of such products is that they are facing uncertain demand for many product variants. The opening paragraph of this chapter described the varieties of toothpastes offered by two leading manufacturers. In other markets, the variety can be even more impressive. Nestlé's Purina offers eleven cat food brands (as distinct from its three cat *treats* brands), one of which—Fancy Feast—includes 50 varieties in 10 textures. Even if Purina could forecast the total demand for cat food, it is difficult to imagine that it could have the right mix of products at every store at all times.

The second characteristic is short customer lead time. If customers were willing to place their orders ahead of time and wait until their choice could be made to order, or at least shipped from a central warehouse, then postponement would have little benefit. Unfortunately, for the most part, retail customers will not wait, requiring retailers to carry inventory.

The third characteristic that makes a product a candidate for postponement is high inventory carrying costs. Products that are inexpensive to carry can be stocked with little penalty, giving customers instant buying gratification.

Last, postponement has to be technologically feasible. The company must have some means to convert a generic base product into any of the harder-to-forecast product variants. Some types of postponement—like postponing packaging or distribution decisions—can be exercised on most products. But form postponement requires a modular rather than integrated product design, so that the production process can be separated into two phases: manufacturing the base product first, and customizing it at a later time, given a more accurate demand forecast or an actual customer order.

The manufacturing of many small, inexpensive consumer products (such as most items sold in convenience stores) are typically *not* postponed, even though the variety of products is very large and customers are not willing to wait for special orders. The primary reason is that their inventory carrying costs are not too high. In addition, most of these products are not modular and would be hard to manufacture in stages. But sometimes the product *packaging* is delayed: Gillette manufactures its razor blades based on a long-term forecast of the total demand for blades, but their packaging is postponed in accordance with specific country and retail-chain orders and forecasts.

In most cases, when companies redesign products for postponement, the total manufacturing costs will go up, reflecting the two-stage manufacturing processes. This cost can be counterbalanced by lower inventory carrying costs, lower discounting, improved availability (higher sales), and better customer satisfaction. Postponement, when implemented with vulnerability in mind, can also increase supply chain resilience.

While the examples outlined in the following sections are not yet motivated by security or vulnerability considerations—because few firms have yet integrated such considerations into their product design—they are given here to demonstrate the basic notion of postponement. As new products requiring new supply chains are developed, and as the likelihood of high-impact disruptions grow, more companies are likely to use such postponement methods to increase their flexibility and resilience.

Customizing by Country

Hewlett-Packard manufactures its popular Deskjet and Deskwriter printers in its Vancouver and Singapore plants and distributes them to the United States, Europe, and Asia. Selling printers in Europe means following each country's requirements for printer configurations: different decals, a country-specific power plug, and language specific manuals. In the past, Hewlett-Packard forecasted demand for each European country and then manufactured the appropriate numbers of printers for each country. Unfortunately, the vagaries of forecast errors meant that HP might have had, for example, not enough printers for Denmark yet too many printers for Slovenia, without an easy way to convert Slovenian printers into Danish ones. Six printer models and 23 different country configurations meant that HP had 138 versions of the finished printers. The result was frequent shortages.

To increase product availability without increasing the retailers' inventory carrying costs, HP changed its processes, switching to a pan-European forecast and shipping generic printers to its European distribution center in Holland. As the printers arrive in Holland, an easily accessible side panel in the shipping carton lets HP quickly configure printers for each country once HP knows the local demand. This postponed customization operation turns a box with one of the six generic printer models into one of the 138 country-specific printers.

Of course, HP must still forecast the pan-European demand, but this aggregated forecast is more accurate than country-level forecasts. The result is a lower level of printer inventory required to achieve high service levels to the European customers.

Extending the same supply chain design worldwide, HP outfitted its five other regional distribution centers around the world for postponement. Using postponement, HP reduced inventories by 18 percent while maintaining service levels.[10] Overall, Hewlett-Packard cut printer supply costs by 25 percent.[11]

Building on its success, HP also extended the postponement concept to its packaging operation. In addition to configuring the printers, HP began shipping printers to the distribution centers in bulk and packaging them for distribution to retailers only once the orders were at hand. Postponing the packaging afforded HP several additional advantages:

- Shipping costs from the plants to the distribution centers dropped by millions of dollars. Because retail printer packaging includes a lot of cushioning, sending printers in bulk increased the shipments' density. That meant that HP could ship 250 percent more printers in a container-load from its plants to its distribution centers.

- Storage of the bulk-packed printers required 60 percent less space in the distribution centers.

- Dealing with unpacked generic printers simplified the basic postponement work at the distribution centers.

- HP was able to offer its customers language-specific packaging rather than multilanguage packages. In addition, the printer cartons were "fresh" when arriving at the customer location, with no soiling or scuffing from the extra handling on the long voyage across the Atlantic.

Build to Order

Dell's assembly operation uses several dozen parts to assemble a large number of possible computer configurations. Table 12.1 depicts the number of options available on a Dell Dimension 4600C desktop computer.[12] These options can be put together in almost 100 million combinations, not including the service and accessory options.

Table 12.1
Number of Dell Options

Parts	Options
Intel Pentium 4	5
Operating systems	5
Productivity software	6
Memory	8
Hard drive	4
Floppy/storage device	4
CD/DVD drive	6
CD/DVD software	4
Storage devices and media	2
Keyboards	3
Mouse	4
Monitors	9

Keeping all, or even a relatively small fraction, of these combinations in stock on retailers' shelves would mean forecasting what customers may want. With this large number of optional combinations, such a forecast would be challenging. Thus, facing a manufacturing process subject to uncertain demand (new components are coming to the market continuously, making old ones obsolete as customers demand the latest options) and high inventory carrying costs, Dell realized that the modular structure of desktop personal computers allows for postponement at the manufacturing phase. With efficient transportation, Dell could build and deliver computers to users within a few days. Indeed, Dell's success made it clear that most customers were willing to wait a few days in return for getting exactly the computer they wanted. The result is that Dell can operate with no finished goods inventory.[13]

Dell does not extend its "build-to-order" postponement strategy to many of its laptop computers. For example, its Inspiron 1000 laptop came in 2004 in three preconfigured combinations and allowed little customization. Many of Dell's lower-end laptops are pre-built by Taiwanese contract manufacturers. These laptops allow only a limited number of options. The reason is that laptops, in general, are much more integrated, less modular products than desktop PCs and therefore not as easy to customize as desktop computers. In addition, transportation and inventory carrying costs on laptops are lower since they take less space, and these inventory carrying costs are particularly low on the low-end laptop product lines. (Dell offers more configuration options on its high-end laptop, such as the Inspiron 9200.)

Last Minute Customization
Sherwin-Williams house paint comes in a number of varieties (such as interior/exterior, matte/semi-gloss/gloss, and seven different performance features) and an array of colors (more than 1,000 hues in the palette). Sherwin-Williams could never hope to forecast sales of each color, or to stock bulky cans of all the possible premixed colors in each of the 2,500 retail locations that sell its products. Thus, the company postpones coloring the paint.

Instead of carrying cans in every color, Sherwin-Williams retailers carry cans of white base paint and colorant dispensers. A database of recipes and mixing machinery lets the retailers blend the color in the store exactly to each customer's requirements. The strategy is similar to Benetton's delaying of dying its apparel, except that Sherwin-Williams pushes the customization point all the way out to the retailer, when the consumer is ready to buy.

Because of the low cost and compact size of colorants (a can of paint is only 2 percent colorant), postponement lets Sherwin-Williams dramatically reduce the costs of carrying inventory in its warehouses. It also reduces the transportation costs to its customers' retail outlets while letting the retailers reduce the floor space devoted to inventory. The result is low inventory carrying costs for both Sherwin-Williams and the retailers, and at the same time a virtually unlimited choice of colors for customers. As an added bonus, retailers can use the white base paint and colorants to customize colors to match samples brought in by customers— for example, creating a paint color that matches that of a treasured curtain, or a pre-existing wall color in the house.

Demand for the base paint (the component with the relatively high inventory carrying cost resulting from its bulkiness and relatively short shelf life) in each retail store can be forecast accurately because it represents the aggregate demand for all the colors. The demand for the various colorants can also be forecast with some accuracy because a modest number of colorants can be combined to make all the hues; and in any case their inventory carrying costs are low.[14]

Late Shipping

Birkenstock Shoes started manufacturing in 1774 when Johann Adam Birkenstock was registered as "subject and shoemaker" in the church archives of the small German village of Langenberg. In 1897 Johann's grandson, Konrad Birkenstock, developed the first shoe with a contoured insole, which together with his 1902 innovation—the flexible arch support—formed the basis for Birkenstock Shoes. The shoes were first exported to the United States in 1966 and became immensely popular in the 1970s. Today the company sells hundreds of styles, each in dozens of sizes and colors all over the world.

Such variety of styles, sizes, and colors implies that each model is sold in relatively small quantities, subject to significant variability. One of the main forecasting challenges is allocating the right mix of shoes to the right U.S. stores.

In 2004, UPS offered Birkenstock a postponement option as part of its international shipping service called Trade Direct. To cut down the distribution time from manufacturing until the shoes arrive at the U.S. stores, UPS took over the entire U.S. distribution of the shoes, allowing Birkenstock to eliminate several interim handling and repackaging steps.

More important, the arrangement allows Birkenstock to delay the point when store allocation decisions have to be made. Instead of making the allocations in the German factories, Birkenstock could now wait until the ocean shipments were received in Newark, New Jersey. This allowed Birkenstock to take advantage of the most recent retailer order updates, just days before delivery. "With Trade Direct, we've cut the time it takes to get shoes to stores in half," said Gene Kunde, chief operating officer of Birkenstock Footprint Sandals Inc. "Our spring fashion merchandise shipped 100 percent on time—for the first time in history."[15]

Postponement Creates Resilience

Supply chains that need to respond quickly to unpredictable customer demand, but cannot afford to build large inventories, can benefit from postponement-based design. Postponement provides flexibility in case the demand for one product variation is unexpectedly high while the demand for another is lower than expected. Such variations may, of course, be the result of a disruption. A generic product, prior to customization, can be redeployed or customized quickly to satisfy unexpected demand for a certain variant of the product or demand in an unexpected location. The reason is that undyed, undifferentiated, uncustomized products are fungible while fully finished ones are not.

Postponement also adds flexibility and resilience not only in responding to demand changes downstream in the supply chain, at the customer level, but also upstream. Specifically, one of the benefits of postponement is that the base product can be made in large quantities regardless of the number of final variants. This means that the materials can be made in more than a single plant or by a single supplier, creating both redundancy and flexibility in capacity and skills. For example, HP makes its generic "base" printers both in its Vancouver and its Singapore plants, allowing these plants to "cover" for each other.

Supply chains designed for postponement can also be helpful in cases of anticipated potential disruptions, such as deteriorating labor relationships at a critical supplier; seasonal material shortages resulting from expected high demand; or as a result of growing international tensions. In such cases, inventory of the base product can be accumulated without enduring the large carrying costs that would result from accumulating all the product variants.

13

Strategies for Flexible Supply

Over the last half century, supply chains have moved from the domain of a single company (such as the vertically integrated Ford River Rouge plant) to a web of suppliers and their suppliers. At the same time, the type of product bought from suppliers has changed—from commodity materials and parts to highly engineered specialized systems and subassemblies, requiring close cooperation between the trading partners. Outsourcing the manufacturing of complete products is only the next logical step in this progression, a step that has led to the rise of contract manufacturing companies in many industries. The result is that companies have become increasingly dependent on their suppliers' networks.

More and more processes that were traditionally performed by OEMs, have now been outsourced, many of them offshore. The original reasons for outsourcing were two-fold: first, to reduce costs and second to focus on core competencies. Outsourcing offers economies of scale and the expertise of the suppliers, while offshore manufacturing offers low labor costs and a flexible labor force. The focus on core competencies allows companies to increase their competitive advantage in the areas in which they are strong.

As more work was moved to suppliers, their manufacturing expertise and engineering prowess developed substantially. In fact, access to the suppliers' innovation in materials, products, and processes became one of the most important reasons for outsourcing.

This trend resulted in consolidation of the supply base. During the 1980s and 1990s most companies have cut significantly the number of suppliers they do business with. Maintaining close working relationships with suppliers meant that each supplier required significant management attention and resources. In addition, focusing a large part of a company's business on few suppliers meant that each supplier would get a large portion of the business, making the company's business more important for that supplier. This created incentives for the suppliers to invest in these relationships; an important consideration when companies depend more on their suppliers. For example, Lucent went from 1,700 transportation carriers to 167 carriers in 2000, while Sony spent 2003 weeding out nearly 80 percent of its 4,700 suppliers.[1]

The combination of outsourcing with supply base consolidation—which has been implemented, to varying degrees, by most companies in Europe and the United States—has, in many ways, altered the nature of competition. Instead of competing on the basis of their own capabilities, companies are now competing on the basis of their supply chain capabilities.[2] This new basis of competition has necessitated new types of contracts and relationships with suppliers, ranging from flexible contracts to risk-sharing arrangements to various types of partnerships.

Strong trading partnerships offer resilience when disaster strikes. In general, suppliers are likely to aid a customer in trouble because doing so will help solidify future markets. This is particularly true when the customer represents a large part of the business and the relationships are expected to last for a long time. These kinds of relationships are especially strong with the Japanese *keiretsu* and the Korean *chaebols*. Both structures involve supply chain "ecosystems," including groups of companies with cross-ownerships and long-term trading relationships.[3] Such ecosystems create resilience and accelerate disaster recovery.

Companies that are not part of a formal ecosystem can still create strong alliances with suppliers who will back them up when the need arises. In many cases, this results from single-sourcing and strong partnerships. Such partnerships, however, involve significant investment in the relationships, and single-sourcing creates its own vulnerabilities. Consequently, some companies choose to have multiple sources of supply. Both approaches: single- and multiple-sourcing, yield different costs and benefits, and either one is viable when implemented carefully.

Firing Up the Supply Base

Just after 4 A.M. on Saturday February 1, 1997, sparks from a broken drill ignited several wooden platforms at the Aisin Seiki Co. Factory No. 1 in Kariya, Japan. The fire spread quickly, swept through an air duct, and ignited the roof. As the fire swelled, it destroyed most of the 506 precision machine tools used by the company to manufacture P-valves—the small cigarette pack–sized proportioning valves used to prevent skidding on the rear brakes of cars. By 9 A.M. that day, much of the factory lay in smoking ruins.[4]

Although Aisin's P-valves cost only ¥770 to ¥1400 each (about $8 to $14), the brake systems of Toyota's cars depended on them. Aisin's ability to churn out the small precision-machined parts at low cost made the company a Toyota favorite. Over the years, Toyota had come to rely on Aisin for 99 percent of the P-valves used in Toyota's entire car production. Nisshin Kogyo Co., the second source supplier, could not boost production 100-fold to make up for the loss of Toyota's main supplier.[5]

Toyota Motor Corp. produces a quarter billion dollars' worth of cars per day. It is the largest company in Japan and the most valuable car maker in the world. Shutting down production would have idled tens of thousands of Toyota workers in Japan and hundreds of thousands of workers in Toyota's network of suppliers and suppliers' suppliers.

Early February 1997 was an especially bad time for a major disruption. Toyota expected a near-term sales boom in Japan, driven by an approaching increase in the Japanese sales tax from 3 to 5 percent, which was expected to spur consumers to buy cars ahead of the April 1 hike.[6] Thus, Toyota and its suppliers were already running at 115 percent of normal production volumes. Toyota had even taken the unusual step of hiring temporary workers in anticipation of the pre-hike boom in car sales. And then Aisin's plant caught fire.

As a just-in-time manufacturer, Toyota had assembly plants that held only a few hours' worth of P-valves. Toyota-bound P-valves, on board trucks dispatched before the fire, provided another couple of days' worth of stock. But on Tuesday, February 4, Toyota had to shut down 20 of its 30 Japanese assembly lines because it had no more P-valves.

The recovery of Aisin would take months; it required buying replacement machinery and creating alternative production sites. Salvaged and hastily acquired equipment let the company produce some P-valves about two weeks after the fire, but only 10 percent of the required amount. Six weeks after the fire, the company was still producing only 60 percent of demand. It would be two months before Aisin approached 100 percent production. Meanwhile, with too few P-valves, Toyota stood to lose the 15,500 vehicles per day that it had planned to make.

Rallying the Troops: Keiretsu in Action

Finding alternative suppliers meant mobilizing the supply base of Aisin and Toyota. Even as the fire raged, Aisin started this process, organizing an "emergency response unit" and alerting Toyota immediately. Aisin started calling suppliers for help, as did Toyota. The calls started with the Toyota keiretsu and the Aisin keiretsu. Sixty-five suppliers responded—22 Aisin suppliers and 36 Toyota suppliers, along with a few independent suppliers and suppliers belonging to other keiretsu groups.[7] By Saturday afternoon, Toyota and Aisin held a war-room conference with all potential P-valve makers and hurried engineers divvied up blueprints and valve-making assignments.[8]

Although conceptually simple, the P-valves contain precision-tapered holes and orifices that regulate the flow of brake fluid. To help the new suppliers, Aisin provided technical and engineering assistance; it also served as quality control for the impromptu supply chain of valve makers.

The backup suppliers ranged from a six-employee prototyping shop to Denso, the giant $24-billion a year Tier One supplier of automotive components, which ended up making thousands of P-valves per day. In fact, Denso outsourced manufacturing of some of its own products in order to focus its factories on making P-valves for Toyota.

Few companies had equipment similar to Aisin's specialized machinery. Because some of the makeshift suppliers used manufacturing techniques foreign to Aisin, Aisin could give them little technical assistance. These suppliers created their own collaborative processes to help each other learn how to make the valves. Denso helped translate Aisin's specs into designs suited to alternative machining practices. Suppliers also coordinated with each other on the purchasing of scarce equipment, ensuring that each supplier received what it needed.

Taiho, an engine parts manufacturer (and a Toyota supplier since 1944), involved eleven of its own suppliers in the effort, and Kayaba Industries, a manufacturer of hydraulic equipment, outsourced the P-valves to three of its suppliers. Brother Industries, the manufacturer of sewing and fax machines, spent 500 man-hours to convert a milling machine to make just 40 P-valves a day—its first experience with making auto parts. Some 150 other companies provided machinery and fixtures to help make P-valves and replace the equipment that Aisin had lost.

The effort entailed neither legal nor financial negotiations; suppliers simply went to work. Aisin provided engineering drawings and technical assistance to all participants, including more than 500 engineers from Toyota and Aisin's suppliers who were familiar with different machines and processes that could be used to make P-valves. Suppliers never asked Toyota or Aisin what they would be paid for rushing out the valves. "We trusted them," said Masakazu Ishikawa, executive vice president at Somic Ishikawa, a manufacturer of automobile parts and components who first became a Toyota supplier in 1937.[9]

The suppliers even turned the disaster into an informal race. The first prototype P-valves came from Kyoritsu Sangyo Okayama, a tiny welding equipment supplier to Aisin, and were delivered only two days after the fire. Aisin inspected the P-valves and gave Kyoritsu Sangyo approval to make more. The following day (Tuesday), Kyoritsu Sangyo shipped the first batch of P-valves. Dozens of other suppliers raced to provide prototypes and ramp up production in the days following the fire.[10]

The Aftermath

By Thursday, February 6, Toyota's Tahara plant was reopened. The other Toyota plants opened with a single shift each on the next day. Nine days after the fire started, on Monday, February 10, all Toyota-group Japanese assembly plants were back to normal with production volumes of 13,000 to 14,000 vehicles per day. Toyota reached its originally planned goal of making 15,500 cars per day about one week later.

In all, Toyota lost only four and a half days of production, even as Aisin lost at least five weeks of production. Without the self-organizing cooperation of its supply base, Toyota's lost production would have been much higher. Yet even these curtailed losses were high—Aisin lost ¥7.8 billion ($76 million) and Toyota lost ¥160 billion ($1.55 billion) in revenues. Although Toyota claims to have made up most of the lost production later, it did incur between ¥20 billion to ¥30 billion ($195 to $290 million) in extra costs.[11]

Eventually Aisin reimbursed all firms for the direct expenses incurred in P-valve production, including labor costs, special equipment, and material costs. Toyota settled the issue differently. It gave each of its participating Tier One suppliers a payment equivalent to 1 percent of their respective sales to Toyota from January to March 1997. This amounted to overall payments of more than ¥15 billion ($146 million). Many of the firms viewed the payment as a reward for cooperation rather than as compensation. Most of the Tier One firms receiving the payment followed Toyota's example and rewarded their Tier Two suppliers, who followed the example with their Tier Three suppliers.

Maybe the most surprising aspect of this corporate recovery story is that Toyota never exerted any pressure on Aisin to act, nor did it pressure Aisin to supply its P-valves at the expense of Aisin's other customers. Aisin had customers other than Toyota and Toyota respected Aisin's need to help everybody. Hino (a $7 billion Japanese heavy trucks manufacturer) had enough replacement P-valves coming on February 6 to reopen its own plant in Hamura.

Multiple Suppliers or Single-Sourcing

The case of Aisin and Toyota illustrates why many companies explicitly avoid sole source procurement, fearing the resulting exposure inherent in using a single supplier.

The fire and its aftermath, however, have left Toyota executives convinced that they have the right balance of efficiency and risk. "Many people say you might need to scatter production to different suppliers and plants, but then you have to think of the costs . . . of setting up expensive milling machines at each site," said Kosuke Ikebuchi, a Toyota senior managing director. "We relearned that our system works."

Working with its suppliers for many years and with cross-ownership and involvement in other businesses with its suppliers through the Keiretsu system, Toyota has very deep relationships with them. It is difficult, however, to develop such deep relationships with multiple suppliers of each part or raw material. The choices faced by most firms can, therefore, be summarized in figure 13.1.

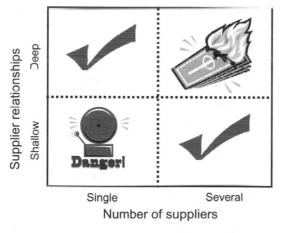

Figure 13.1
Procurement Alignment

The upper-right quadrant of this figure depicts the situation of deep relationships with multiple suppliers. This is too expensive and it is difficult to find examples of firms who practice such strategies. The relationship between Toyota and Aisin is an example of deep single sourcing belonging in the top left quadrant of figure 13.1. The next two sections give examples and discuss supplier relationships that fit in the two lower quadrants of the figure.

Multiple Suppliers

In late October 1998, the warm Caribbean waters off the coast of Central America brewed the fourth-largest Atlantic hurricane on record. A category 5 hurricane, Mitch lashed Honduras and its expansive banana plantations with sustained winds of 180 mph and dumped 2 to 4 feet of rain on parts of the country.[12]

Hurricane Mitch devastated much of Honduras, killing at least 6,500 people, destroying 70 to 80 percent of the country's transportation infrastructure, and causing more than $4 billion in damage. The banana plantations never had a chance. The fast-growing soft-stemmed banana plants, with their large leaves, were toppled by the winds or washed away in the floods. Honduras lost 80 percent of its banana crop to Mitch.[13] Other banana-producing countries, such as Nicaragua and Guatemala, also felt the fury of the storm. In total, Mitch destroyed 10 percent of the world's banana crop.

Both Dole and Chiquita relied on the tropical climate of Central American plantations for banana supplies, but they fared very differently. Dole lost 25 percent of its global banana supply. Chiquita suffered $200 million in damages but was less dependent on the affected region, losing only 15 percent of its capacity. In addition, Chiquita had secondary sources for Central American bananas in Mexico, Panama, and Colombia, which were less affected by the hurricane, as well as in the Ivory Coast, Martinique, and even Australia. Unlike Dole, it moved quickly to leverage its alternative sources, increasing production in other locales and purchasing the crops of associate producers.

In contrast, Dole had no plans for alternative sourcing and suffered more than one year of shortages in its banana supplies. The financial result was that Chiquita generated a 4 percent increase in revenues that year while Dole registered a 4 percent decline in revenues.

Many other companies also rely on multi-sourcing to moderate the consequences of supply disruptions. For example, following the 1999 Taiwan earthquake that disrupted the island's chip manufacturers, Motorola was planning to rely on second and third sources in case of a disruption. "We have a program called 1-2-3 for wafers and chips. If for some reason the primary supply is disrupted, we have secondary and tertiary sources," explained a Motorola spokeswoman. Even so, regional disruptions can affect multiple providers; Motorola was sourcing from TSMC and UMC in Taiwan when both suppliers were hit by the Taiwan earthquake, leaving Motorola with fewer supply alternatives than planned.

Shallow Single-Sourcing

Interviews by the MIT Center for Transportation and Logistics revealed that in the aftermath of the 9/11 attack, some firms started insisting on multiple sources of supply for everything they purchase. Other companies, however, decided to deepen their relationships with their main suppliers. One purchasing executive from a leading supplier to the aerospace industry summarized his company's approach this way: "We intend to put all our eggs in one basket and watch this basket very carefully."[14] The second part of the statement—watching the basket—is key to the success of the single-sourcing approach. Deep sourcing is more than just sole sourcing.

UPF Thompson has supplied chassis to Land Rover since the 1950s. As the sole chassis supplier for Land Rover's popular Discovery line of SUVs, it was selling Land Rover 70,000 chassis per year. Following Land Rover's acquisition by Ford in 2000, it completed the conversion of its planning and production processes to a modern just-in-time system in the third quarter of 2001. But then, on one Friday morning in December of that year, the chassis shipment from UPF Thompson failed to arrive at Land Rover's Solihull plant. When Land Rover managers called to inquire, they found out that as a result of losses suffered by UPF in an unrelated foreign venture, UPF Thompson was bankrupt and in receivership.[15]

The news got even worse.[16] The receiver assigned to manage the bankruptcy, KPMG, demanded that in return for continued supply of chassis, Land Rover should assume all of UPF Thompson's outstanding debt of £49 million. With only two days worth of inventory, Land Rover had its back to the wall. The Discovery line accounted for fully one-third of the company's revenues. Finding a new supplier would have suspended Discovery production for up to nine months while tooling was developed, and it would have led to 1,400 layoffs at the company's assembly plant. An additional 10,000 jobs among Land Rover's other suppliers would also have been severely threatened. Shortly thereafter, Land Rover received written notification from KPMG, asking them to buy the business or to agree to a long–term supply contract at higher prices. Land Rover, refusing to be strong-armed, rejected the offer and went to court to try to get a temporary injunction compelling UPF to keep supplying the chassis.

KPMG's hard-nosed stance received wide coverage in the British media. It even generated Motion 714, introduced on January 24, 2002, in the United Kingdom Parliament by Mark Tami, the labor MP representing the constituency of Alyn and Deeside. The motion called for Parliament to express its "deep concern" at the conduct of KPMG and called upon the government "to review all its department contracts with KPMG in light of their actions."[17] The dispute heated up when Land Rover chairman Robert Dover hinted in the media that if KPMG insisted on its demands, sourcing of the Discovery would move abroad.

Despite the hostile media reports, KPMG was simply doing its job in the competitive market culture of the U.K. Land Rover had no written supply agreement with UPF Thompson, and even though Land Rover paid for all the tooling that UPF Thompson installed in order to produce the chassis, it had no agreement as to ownership of the tools in case of bankruptcy. As receiver to

UPF Thompson, KPMG was, in fact, obliged to recover all the money it could on behalf of UPF Thompson's creditors, and a recent court ruling had held that in such situations receivers could exploit a customer's vulnerability to the benefit of the creditors.[18]

After weeks of failed negotiations and legal maneuvers, however, England's High Court found KPMG's demands to be "arguably illegal" and granted the injunction guaranteeing the flow of chassis on an interim basis. After a lengthy series of appeals and additional hearings, the two parties eventually came to an agreement. To settle the dispute, Land Rover paid £16M of UPF's £49M debt. Land Rover demanded, however, not only the continuing supply of chassis but also the replacement of KPMG as the receiver.[19]

The UPF Thompson bankruptcy almost stopped the production of the Discovery vehicle for many months and could have inflicted significant losses for Land Rover, as well as considerable job losses in the U.K. Land Rover clearly was not monitoring this supplier closely, despite its assertion that it had processes to "keep a careful and continuous financial reviews of all its suppliers, delving into order books and business and revenue plans."[20]

Single vs. Multiple Sourcing

But sole-source strategies do have their place. Firms cut down on their number of suppliers not only to consolidate buying power; the strong supplier relationships bring with them access to engineering prowess and innovation. This is particularly important as in many industries suppliers are providing more and more systems rather than simply parts. For example, Visteon, the $18 billion Tier One automotive supplier, offers complete all-wheel drive systems, entire climate control systems, integrated door modules, and entire audio systems, in addition to a full complement of parts and components. And Intel, the maker of processors and chips, builds complete chipsets and motherboards used by PC makers.

That sort of added value was one of the reasons Toyota made the decision, even after the Aisin fire, that its sole-sourcing system worked well and that it would stay with the same arrangements. It was also why Unilever decided to stick with a sole-source strategy even after the disruption it suffered when Hurricane Mitch swept through Central America in 1998. Unilever's Puerto Rico plant—a plant that produced roughly half of the North American supply of Q-Tip cotton swabs—was significantly damaged by Mitch; Unilever lost two weeks of production as a result of the hurricane and forced many of its customers into stock-out situations. But despite this experience, Unilever chose to relocate 100 percent of its Q-Tip production to the Puerto Rico facility after repairs were made.

To mitigate its exposure to similar disruptions, however, Unilever also increased inventory levels in North America by 10 percent and arranged contracts with barge shippers in the event that road or rail systems were made unavailable.[21] Likewise, many of Toyota's sole-source suppliers decided to increase their own resilience after the Aisin fire. Somic, which makes all of Toyota's steering linkages, revamped its system so that it could easily shift to another site if disaster struck its main plant. Toyota itself launched an effort after the fire to trim the number of its parts variations, realizing that most of the recovery difficulty was rooted in its use of hundreds of variations of the P-valve.

As Lucent moved to cut the number of suppliers and deepen the relationships with them as part of its Supply Chain Networks (SCN) organization, it has formally instituted the role of suppliers' relationship managers. These managers keep in close touch with all key suppliers, ensuring that information is flowing freely both ways and that neither Lucent nor its suppliers are caught unaware by the other party's actions.

Multi-sourcing, of course, provides built-in redundancy, and therefore flexibility to switch suppliers when disruptions occur. When, for instance, the Avon Rubber and Injected Plastics plant was destroyed by fire in 1999, all but one of the plant's customers were able to switch immediately to alternative sources for the rubber gaskets, door seals, and other automotive products made by the plant. The reason was that Avon was never the sole source supplier to any of them.

But even having multiple suppliers does not guarantee full continuity of supply, for at least three reasons:

First, regional disruptions can affect multiple suppliers. For example, the 2002 West Coast port lockout closed all Pacific ports. This motivates companies like GM to assess risks on a geographic level, not just a supplier facility level.

Second, the other suppliers may not always have available capacity; furthermore, suppliers who serve only as alternates may not be inclined to invest ahead of time or incur extraordinary costs in order to help out a customer who chose not to do business with them in the first place.

Third, the global connectedness of markets, especially for commodity materials, means that one supplier's disruption can create price and availability problems for all customers in that industry, even for customers who do not source from the disrupted supplier. For example, the September 1999 Taiwanese earthquake disrupted dozens of semiconductor makers accounting for 40 percent of the world's memory chip production during a period of tight supplies. As a result, the spot-price of memory chips climbed five-fold all over the world.[22]

Another risk associated with multi-sourcing is that second- and third-tier suppliers are often not as efficient as the first tier; Toyota sole-sourced from Aisin, for instance, largely because of Aisin's superior cost effectiveness. Some companies consider the extra costs needed to manage an additional supplier, and the incremental cost of the parts supplied, to be analogous to an insurance premium that the enterprise spends to ensure supply in an emergency. Toyota decided that such a premium was just too high.

Given the risk-spreading advantages of multi-sourcing, some companies further insist that their suppliers have other customers. To avoid suppliers depending on it completely, Wal-Mart usually specifies that its own business can represent no more than about 25 percent of a supplier's business (depending on the business in question). A portion of a supplier's business above that level, a Wal-Mart spokeswoman said, "makes us nervous," because "we don't want to be the sole source of survival for a company."[23] This stance gives Wal-Mart more flexibility to change suppliers with lower exposure to accusations that Wal-Mart uses its dominance to abuse a highly dependent supply base. And encouraging suppliers to have multiple customers can also provide a company with surge capacity, since it may be possible to use the capacity dedicated to another customer when that customer doesn't need it.

The question, then, is not whether to have one vs. many suppliers, but whether the sourcing strategy is internally consistent: Is the number of suppliers aligned with the nature of the relationships with those suppliers? When companies decide not to invest in close relationships with their suppliers, caution requires the use of multi-sourcing (unless the company uses commodity and off-the-shelf parts). Thus, the prudent combinations are either to have deep partnerships with a single supplier (or a small number of key suppliers) or to have multiple suppliers, as depicted in figure 13.1.

Watching the Suppliers

According to the U.S. Centers for Disease Control and Prevention (CDC), 36,000 American die annually as a result of the flu. In fact, the number of deaths attributed to the flu has risen four-fold between the late 1970s and the late 1990s.[24] During the 2000–2001 flu season, federal officials were caught unprepared when one of the four vaccine manufacturers had to cease production as a result of FDA concerns over plant conditions. Shortages, delays, and four-fold price gouging ensued. The situation was investigated by the General Accounting Office, which reported in May 2001 to the Department of Health and Human Services that "the circumstances that led to the delay and early shortage of flu vaccine during the 2000-01 flu season could repeat themselves in the future . . . Now, a production delay or shortfall experienced by even one of the three remaining manufacturers can significantly impact overall vaccine availability."[25]

A little over three years later, and despite continued warnings from public-health experts about the dangers of continued consolidation among pharmaceutical companies, the United States experienced another shortage. Chiron, one of the two companies relied on to manufacture the flu vaccine for the 2004–2005 season, had its sole vaccine plant in Bristol, U.K., shut down by British health authorities on October 5, 2004, because of contamination.

As a result, half of the 100 million doses of vaccines the United States needed were not available. Rationing, long lines, panic, and price gouging followed. And again, there was no easy and quick solution since the other manufacturer was already at 100 percent capacity and no manufacturer around the world had extra capability.[26]

Having a small number of suppliers, with no extra capacity to cover for each other, meant that the United States was, in fact, in a single sourcing situation. Despite that, the suppliers were not carefully monitored. In June 2003, a year before the 2004–2005 crisis took place, U.S. officials learned that Chiron had reprocessed contaminated batches of flu vaccine, but the problem was not investigated vigorously. As late as September 28, 2004, one week before his plant was shut down, Chiron CEO Howard Pien assured a U.S. senate committee that his company would deliver 48 million doses of the vaccine for the 2004–2005 flu season. They took his word for it.[27]

Chapter 10 argued that information technology should always be backed up and redundant sites prepared, since the cost of an IT disruption is high relative to the cost of back-ups. One can easily argue that when the cost of disruption is measured in lives, public policy should ensure redundancy through the use of more than a single supplier, or a supplier with more than a single plant. In any case, if the decision was made that two suppliers would suffice, the relationships with these suppliers had to be deep and they should have been monitored early and often.

Flexibility through Supplier Relationships

As companies depend more and more on their suppliers, it is important to examine the flexibility of the entire supply chain. Toyota's deep and trusting relationships with suppliers were instrumental in the company's recovery from the Aisin fire.

The MIT Supply Chain Response to Disruption study found that with sole-sourcing comes added engagement with the suppliers on the issue of resilience.[28] Suppliers get involved with the company's business continuity planning, and many companies require suppliers to develop and maintain comprehensive business continuity plans of their own. In some cases, industry groups set standards and provide security and resilience-related data—such as TAPA's guidelines regarding carrier selection and its distribution of carrier data to its hundreds of members. At the very least, resilience has become a factor in supplier selection. For example, Electra Ltd., an Israeli elevator installation and maintenance company, uses Otis Elevator Company as its sole source. Since Otis operates a worldwide network of more than three dozen plants, Electra decided not to develop a second source, effectively relying on Otis's network of multiple plants.[29]

Most companies treat suppliers of unique and/or complicated engineered parts—that is, parts that require significant supplier qualification for quality—very differently from the way they treat suppliers of near-commodities. P&G, for example, runs a training program for its top suppliers and conducts regular information exchange sessions with them. These suppliers are monitored for costs and can share in the success of the products they feed, but they generally do not have to compete annually for P&G's business. For the most part, these are the suppliers on which P&G relies for technology and innovation. Other suppliers, on which it relies mostly for capacity, do compete for the P&G business annually.

Nowhere is this strategy more evident than in Dell's procurement. Dell buys its processor chips and motherboards only from Intel,[30] and its operating system only from Microsoft, both of whom are very resilient. For all other components—such as disk drives, memory chips, modems, keyboards, and displays—Dell keeps multiple suppliers on hand, routinely whipsawing them against each other in its quest to reduce costs. Dell even outsources the manufacturing of its laptop computers to three contract manufacturers in Taiwan: Compal Electronics, Wistron, and Quanta (which also make laptops for HP, Apple, IBM, Sony, Sharp, Siemens, and Fujitsu).

Thus, aligning the procurement strategy with the supplier relationships can ensure resilience, either reducing the likelihood of an unexpected disruption with a single supplier or providing the resilience that comes with multiple supplier relationships.

14

Customer Relations Management

The main effort when recovering from a disruption is to isolate the firm's customers from the disruption's effects or otherwise to help them recover as quickly as possible. To this end, the firm's customer-facing functions—in particular sales, marketing, distribution, and public relations—can play a pivotal role in preserving customer relationships, by communicating with customers (and other stake holders), and prioritizing service during a disruption. Moreover, an effective response presents a chance for the firm to win customers' hearts with exceptional remediation and strong efforts.

Flexibility in the Face of Disaster: Dell vs. Apple

The Taiwan earthquake of September 21, 1999, struck near the heart of the country's high-tech manufacturing core. The Richter Scale magnitude 7.6 quake killed more than 2,300 people but did little structural damage to the 28 semiconductor fabrication plants concentrated in the Hsin-Chu Science-based Park, located about 80 miles north of the epicenter. Although the fabs seemed undamaged, they lost electrical power for nearly 24 hours, and when the lights went out on all the wafer-processing equipment, the fabs lost tens of thousands of wafers—wafers that were destined to provide chips for computers, communications gear, set-top boxes, and cellphones. It took weeks for the fabs to bring all the finely tuned systems back online, recheck the delicate equipment, and regain their pre-quake yields on chip making.

Taiwan accounted for 10 to 15 percent of the entire world's dynamic random access memory (DRAM) chips, 80 percent of graphics chips, and 60 percent of computer motherboards.[1] It also served as home to many liquid crystal display (LCD) suppliers and assemblers. With such a concentration, the disruption caused by the Taiwan quake rippled out quickly to the chip makers' customers. They included numerous leading computer makers, such as Hewlett-Packard, Compaq, IBM, Dell, Siemens, Fujitsu, and Apple. From there, disruptions in PC production and delivery affected end customers in different ways, depending on how each PC maker made its computers and how it structured its customer relations.

Hardest hit were computer companies using lean production systems—those carrying very little inventory and relying on last-minute supply of components such as memory chips, circuit boards, and laptop screens. Two of the leading firms in this business use lean build-to-order systems, but they fared very differently. The company that perfected the build-to-order business model is Dell, which takes possession of standardized components at the last minute, assembles them, and ships out completed computers. Less well known is that Apple Computer Inc. runs a similar build-to-order supply and manufacturing operation. "Last quarter, we ended with less than a day of inventory—15 hours. As a matter of fact, we've beat Dell now for the last four quarters," declared Steve Jobs at the August 31, 1999, Seybold conference keynote speech.

The Perils of Preorders

Dell and Apple run similar lean supply and manufacturing operations. They differ, however, in the sales and distribution side of their supply chains. Apple emphasizes leading-edge design and a narrow portfolio of models. Apple's launch of the new iBook and G4 Power Macintosh followed a characteristic pattern for the company. It announced the eagerly awaited products at the New York Macworld Expo on July 21, 1999, published the configurations and prices, and allowed customers to preorder the machines with expected shipment dates starting in mid-September.

The much-anticipated iBook was intended to be like a mobile version of Apple's popular iMac—stylish, inexpensive, and available in multiple colors. Knowing that some early adopters would jump at being the first to get the new machine, Apple used preorders to gauge market interest. These data helped Apple estimate demand and commit appropriate resources to manufacturing. Apple received orders for more than 160,000 iBooks before it began shipping them on September 15, 1999.

Apple had delivered only a tiny fraction of the preordered iBooks before the quake halted production in Taiwan and disrupted component supplies only a week later. "We lost one week of production on both PowerBooks and iBooks during the September quarter. Some component supplies were also impacted," said Fred Anderson, Apple's chief financial officer.[2] Frustrated customers saw weeks added to the expected delivery dates.

Adding to Apple's woes, another supplier disruption hit the company at the same time as the earthquake. On the same day that the earthquake hit, Apple announced that Motorola had not been shipping the needed volumes of the speediest G4 processors that Apple used in its just-announced high-end desktop machines. The shortage of high-end chips from Motorola—it was having problems with new chip-making technologies licensed from IBM—meant that Apple would have to downgrade customers (send them a slower-than-ordered computer) or have an indefinitely delayed shipping date for the faster processor.

Apple chose to ship computers with a less powerful chip (but the fastest available from Motorola) without lowering prices.[3] Only after an avalanche of customer complaints did the company relent and offer price reductions.[4] Because Apple could not modify preordered computers, the problem persisted into the fourth quarter of 1999. Many customers responded by either ordering lower-margin machines or canceling their Apple orders altogether.[5]

Managing Demand during Disruption at Dell
Dell also faced component shortages, such as memory and laptop computer screens.[6] And like Apple, Dell had a second, simultaneous supply disruption that exacerbated the consequences of the Taiwan earthquake. Dell was backing a new memory technology supported by new chips from Intel. On September 24,

1999, three days before the official launch of the chip, Intel canceled the production release because of serious performance defects in the design. Dell had expected to use the new technology on one-third of its computers in the fourth quarter of 1999. The indefinite delay from Intel forced Dell to switch back to the old memory standard and scramble to buy older-technology memory chips in the quake-constricted market.

Dell's sales process, which is part of its supply chain design, afforded it much more flexibility compared to Apple. While Apple was locked into rigid preordered commitments, Dell used a much shorter order-to-ship cycle. Apple had months of pent-up demand in its preorder backlog, but Dell usually operates with only three days of orders in the pipeline, and consequently had no commitment to specific models, configurations, and prices beyond these three days. Dell sold only what it could make based on components on hand.

Dell's basic build-to-order model of postponed assembly means that it orders components based on forecast and then assembles the computers based on its customers' orders. This supply chain design affords Dell unique day-to-day flexibility. Since Dell is dealing with the customers directly through its web site and telephone, it can use a "sell–what–you–have" strategy.[7] The company steers its customers toward configurations that it can supply easily and profitably. It raises prices on configurations that are based on components in short supply and lowers the prices on configurations based on components in excess supply. It also bundles certain available components with popular configurations and runs promotions on them, highlighting these configurations on its web site. Dell's normal operations include continuous adjustments of prices and promotions daily and sometimes even hourly, based on component availability and prices, competitors' pricing, and expected market conditions.[8]

Apple, on the other hand, can be locked into agreements with retailers and into customers' preorders that hamper its ability to manipulate the demand for its products. Consequently, Apple does not change configurations and prices frequently. When memory chip prices spiked after the quake, Dell announced that it would halve the amount of memory in base configurations to hold prices constant and charge customers who wanted more memory.[9] On the web and on the phone, Dell guided customers toward configurations that it could build and ship.

In spite of the disruption, Dell increased its market share and increased its third-quarter earnings over the previous year by 41 percent. In contrast, Apple lost market share.[10]

Flexible Redistribution at Caterpillar

Caterpillar Inc. is the world's leading manufacturer of construction and mining equipment. It has created a unique flexibility in its relationships with its dealers in order to increase its resilience: To respond to an emergency order from a customer, Caterpillar can buy back and resell parts that have already been sold to dealers, and are in those dealers' warehouses.

Customers pay $50,000 to $1 million per piece of Caterpillar equipment for use at mining sites, putting out oil fires, digging foundations for skyscrapers, building roads, and moving earth for dam projects all over the world. Not only is the equipment expensive, but downtime can halt a multimillion-dollar construction project, significantly increasing customers' costs. For example, mine operators depend on massive Caterpillar earthmovers and trucks to extract valuable ore. "If a truck isn't available to a mine, it could cost that mine anywhere from $20,000 to $30,000 per hour," said Larry Newbanks.[11] As head of inventory research management for Caterpillar, Newbanks understands the costs of downtime to Caterpillar's customers. Consequently, one of Caterpillar's main selling points is the reliability of its products and the speed with which it can get spare parts to a stranded piece of equipment anywhere around the globe.

To minimize disruption to its customers, Caterpillar must stock copious quantities of spare parts, ready at a moment's notice. Because Caterpillar supports both its new equipment and its older models, it has over half a million different kinds of spare parts (stock keeping units or SKUs) that it could carry, and over 25 parts distribution warehouses in which to carry them. The problem is that most of these parts—more than 350,000 of them—sell in very low volumes of less than one per month worldwide.

Parts Exchange

In order to minimize spare parts inventory and maximize level of service, Caterpillar created a unique partnership with its 220 independently owned dealers. Caterpillar's dealers have nearly 2,000 outlets and are, collectively, larger than Caterpillar itself. The partnership focuses on joint management of Caterpillar's and its dealers' inventories of parts, providing flexibility both to the company and to its dealers.

Caterpillar's Dealer Parts Inventory Search (DPIS) system features an automated search-and-fill capability that finds spare parts anywhere within Caterpillar or its dealer network. Every day, dealers inform Caterpillar how many parts they have and how many they are willing to share. Caterpillar feeds that information into its order management system, so that the system knows the inventory level, by part number, at every dealer store. (This jointly managed spare parts inventory includes only the inventory that each dealer is willing to share, not the dealer's entire inventory.)[12]

A request for a spare part usually comes from a dealer who is notified by a customer of a stranded piece of equipment. If the dealer does not have the part in its own inventory, it can turn to the DPIS. The system first looks at the nearest Caterpillar-owned distribution facility. If the needed part is not there, it searches dealers in that region and then expands the search to Caterpillar locations outside the region. If DPIS finds the part at a dealer store, it routes the orders for that part to the dealer. "We treat that inventory as our own, no matter where it is," Newbanks said. "That allows us to direct orders to wherever the inventory is, out in the world."[13]

Caterpillar buys the part back from the dealer who has it, at the original (wholesale) price plus 10 percent. Caterpillar pays for the transport and sells the part at the regular (wholesale) price to the dealer who needs it. (All of this is done automatically by the DPIS system.) Caterpillar absorbs the 10 percent charge in the name of service and avoids the costs of excessive inventories on rarely needed spare parts.[14]

DPIS provides inventory risk pooling that helps both Caterpillar and its dealers reduce inventories; at the same time Caterpillar maintains high availability of emergency spare parts. Many companies pool the risks of finished goods inventory by having a single replenishment system with access to their entire inventory in all of their warehouses. Similarly, many retail outlets can direct consumers to a different store of the same retailer, where a wanted item can be found. But what is unique about Caterpillar's system is that it takes such inventory risk pooling a step further by creating a single virtual inventory *involving its customers*—the independent network of dealers—in order to serve the ultimate customer, the equipment owner. The result: "We operate 24 hours a day, every day of the year. We'll ship 99.7 percent of all those items the same day," Newbanks said.[15]

Caterpillar and its dealers' inventory risk pooling strategy does not only offer flexibility in responding to emergency orders; it also means that its parts inventory is physically decentralized, and is therefore less vulnerable to regional disruptions.

Communicating with Customers after a Disruption

One of the most important elements in helping customers recover from a disruption is giving them as much information as possible. The inevitable confusion and uncertainty that is part of most large-scale disruptions can be mitigated by open and proactive communications with trading partners and, in particular, customers. Such communications help trading partners focus their own recovery efforts based on up-to-date and accurate information.

As a supplier to the fast-paced electronics industry, Taiwan Semiconductor Manufacturing Company (TSMC) needed to inform its customers of the impact of the 1999 Taiwan earthquake on production and shipment of chips. Within minutes of the quake, the company reestablished communications between TSMC in Taiwan and its sales and marketing headquarters in the

United States and immediately contacted major customers with the latest information. By 9:00 A.M. local time, seven hours after the quake struck, the company had set up a 24-hour hotline for customer inquiries. Top executives broadcast two letters within 48 hours of the earthquake. Twelve press releases rounded out the stream of customer communications.[16]

To avoid negative reports on the company's post-quake health or its progress in combating the disruption, TSMC's post-quake customer relations initiative also focused on the press and analysts. The company conducted more than 100 interviews in the first five days.

As a result of its dominant position in the industry, TSMC knew that it would receive more than its share of media and analyst attention. Deadline-obsessed reporters often tell the story of only one or two leading companies. Thus, TSMC received 57 percent more coverage than its largest competitor. The challenge facing TSMC was that more obscure competitors, who were not covered in these press reports, could easily have manipulated any negative news on TSMC to their own advantage.[17]

With an audience that spanned 15 time zones and four languages, TSMC hosted events for the press and analysts in both Asia and North America so that it could provide accurate information and avoid morbid speculations. As a result, 86 percent of reports that mentioned TSMC did so in a favorable or neutral light. Finally, TSMC used the event as an opportunity to talk about other, nonquake-related issues, and 85 percent of the reports mentioned these issues. TSMC won a Silver Anvil Award from the Public Relations Society of America for its exemplary communications campaign.

The first stage in communicating with customers and trading partners is to collect accurate information to feed the communications campaign. Many disasters strike core infrastructure and disrupt communications, especially in low-cost producer nations where the infrastructure is limited to begin with. The vulnerability of power, phone, and data lines adds to the vulnerability of the company because it disrupts management communications.

Lacking contact with the affected facility means managers cannot assess the situation, implement business continuity plans, or provide reassuring status information to customers. For this reason, Intel built a regional emergency operation center in each region in which it operates, and it equipped these facilities with layers of backup communications. Landline telephones, cell-phones, SSB[18] communications, satellite phones, Internet connections, and even globe-spanning ham radios ensure that the company can be in continuous contact with its entire international network of facilities. Periodic drills ensure that each regional emergency operation center knows how to regain contact with headquarters and the facilities in its region. Timely communications ensure that customers do not fear the worst when news of a disruption reaches them.

Johnson & Johnson has always earned high marks for living up to its credo of highly ethical corporate behavior. After the 1982 Chicago Tylenol poisoning (see chapter 2), J&J launched an immediate nationwide recall of all Tylenol, redesigned the product's packaging, and reintroduced the product. Using nationwide media, the company ensured both the safety and the peace-of-mind of its customers. J&J's actions in this case remain the gold standard of corporate disruption response and responsibility. Similarly, in 2002, when someone counterfeited J&J's anemia drug Procrit (see chapter 7), the company launched an intensive direct mail campaign that targeted health care professionals (who are the de facto customers and administrators of the injected medicine). J&J sent out more than one and a half million letters in eight mailings. The letters informed distributors, doctors, and hospital workers how to spot the counterfeit drugs, what J&J was doing about the problems, and how to recognize the new anti-counterfeit features.

As these examples demonstrate, one of the most important requirements after a disruption occurs is to communicate. Communications to the public can be based on press conferences, but it is important to have a direct line of communication with stakeholders. To this end, Martin-Lockheed maintains, in a central location, all the supplies needed to communicate in writing with each of its 170,000 employees and 45,000 shareholders within two to three days.[19]

An Opportunity to Shine

Disruptions can in many cases offer companies the opportunity to make a positive impression with a quick and ready response, thus enhancing the brand.

In 1992 Lexus, the luxury division of Toyota, was just getting a foothold in the United States. In April of that year it recalled its flagship LS400 model for some minor brake and hydraulic system defects. Owners of the car were initially upset, given that they had just bought an expensive luxury car from a company known for its reliability. On the phone, customer service representatives were reassuring; they asked each customer to leave the car outside the home where it would be picked up. On the appointed day, Lexus representatives left an identical car in the driveway—a loaner for the day. The owner's car was returned by evening, fixed and cleaned, with a full tank of gas and a voucher for a free oil change.

By comparison, Audi reacted angrily to a November 1986 television exposé (aired on CBS's popular program *60 Minutes*) that documented drivers' claims that their Audi 5000 had "sudden acceleration" problems. VW, Audi's parent company, issued press releases of engineering explanations that demonstrated that the problem was with American drivers, not the cars (the problem was never reported in Europe). While government studies in the United States, Canada, and Japan proved conclusively that VW was right and the cause was driver error, the damage was done. As VW continued to blame its customers, Audi's U.S. sales shrank from 74,061 units in 1985 to 12,283 units in 1991, with dealers dropping the franchise and VW considering leaving the U.S. market.

The point of this comparison is not the fairness of the allegations but rather the realization by Lexus that a problem can offer an opportunity for impressing its customers with excellent customer service. Audi "went to war" against its customers[20] while Lexus looked at the recall as an opportunity to increase customer loyalty. In the final analysis, Audi management did not understand the disruption they were facing: They thought it was a technical problem that their engineers could prove did not exist. In reality, they had a customer relations problem that they hardly addressed at all and they were duly punished by the market.

Similarly, in late 1994, Intel did not understand that a problem with the floating-point operations of its Pentium 486DX chip was not a technical issue (for the vast majority of users) but a customer relations issue. In mid-1999 Thomas Nicely, a mathematics professor at Lynchburg College in Virginia, was computing the sum of the reciprocals of a large collection of prime numbers on his 486DX Pentium computer. Finding an error in comparison to theoretical values, he traced the error to the chip and notified Intel. After getting no answer he posted the problem on The MathWork Worldwide, a mathematics web site. Magazine and TV interviews followed.[21]

Intel first did not acknowledge the problem and then tried to minimize it and belittle those who complained. It announced that "an average spreadsheet user could encounter this subtle flaw once in every 27,000 years of use." This response generated an avalanche of headlines such as "Intel . . . the Exxon of the Chip Industry," as well as Internet board messages such as "It's close enough . . . we say so" and "You don't need to know what's inside." As a result of the problem IBM stopped shipping computers with 486DX chips.[22] When Intel finally acknowledged the problem, it announced that it would replace the chip only if users could demonstrate their *need* for floating point operations. It took a strong public outcry for Intel to relent and recall all the 486DX chips[23]—however grudgingly—and as a result, Intel took not only a $475 million charge to earning, but also tarnished its reputation and lost customer confidence.

Intel's problem was, in a sense, more similar to Audi's than to Lexus's. The floating-point-operation defect of the 486DX almost never showed up, and affected a very small fraction of the customers a very small fraction of the time. Intel, however, had a customer-relations problem that it took too long to acknowledge and correct.

Good long-standing customer and community relationships can help a company recover from a disruption by making customers willing to help the company directly or to be flexible in accommodating the company's needs during the recovery. The story of Cantor Fitzgerald is a case in point.

Rebounding from a Crisis: Cantor Fitzgerald

The 105th floor of the World Trade Center in New York City was an enviable office location. More than 1,200 feet above the bustling financial capital of the world, it was an excellent aerie for running a financial trading powerhouse. Cantor Fitzgerald, with more than 1,000 employees in its New York offices, occupied the 101st, 103rd, 104th, and 105th floors of the North Tower of the WTC.

Cantor brokered trades worth a staggering $1 trillion every week. The company played an important role in the U.S. Government Treasuries market, specializing in brokering billion-dollar trades between major Wall Street institutions. Because of Cantor's massive trading volumes, the company also supplied valuable pricing information to Wall Street firms, selling real-time data on the latest prices of the financial instruments that Cantor handled. The events of September 11, 2001, would severely test the company's ability to survive a major disruption.

At 8:45 A.M. on that Tuesday morning, nearly two-thirds of Cantor's New York contingent of traders, analysts, and other employees were already at the top of the North Tower, at their desks. They were busy checking the latest financial news, analyzing the overnight numbers from the European and Asian markets, talking to customers, and getting ready for another hectic day on Wall Street. Howard Lutnick, the firm's CEO, was late to work because he was dropping his son off on his first day in kindergarten. At 8:45 A.M., a time-stamped photograph shows the CEO with his son at the school.

At 8:46 A.M., a hijacked fuel-laden wide-body Boeing 767 struck the WTC about 10 floors below Cantor's offices in the North Tower. While at his son's school, Howard Lutnick heard the news that a plane had hit the WTC.[24] A second plane struck the South Tower at 9:03. Lutnick rushed to the site and tried to find Cantor employees among those streaming from the burning skyscraper, but nobody above the 91st floor ever came out. When the South Tower collapsed at 10:05, Lutnick fled and was knocked down by the enveloping tornado of debris and choking dust. At that moment, he was convinced his company and his life were over. As the dust started clearing, Lutnick realized he was not dead. But he couldn't be sure about his company.

At 10:28 A.M., the North Tower of the WTC collapsed, killing 658 of Cantor's 1,050 U.S. workers—everyone who was in Cantor's offices when the first plane hit. The dead included most of the superstar traders who had made the company successful, most of the people who had hard-won personal relationships with Cantor's customers, and most of the support personnel who kept the high-energy operation going. The dead even included Howard Lutnick's younger brother, Gary.

Without computers, phones, and a place to work, Cantor could not survive. Despite the emotional devastation, the remaining employees in the United States, as well as employees from Cantor's European offices, worked around the clock to recreate its systems in temporary offices in New York, New Jersey, and Connecticut.

Less than 48 hours after the first plane struck the WTC, Cantor was ready to trade. Its eSpeed electronic trading systems were back online in time for the September 17 reopening of the U.S. Treasuries markets.[25]

Less than two months later, Cantor was handling its usual volume of bond trading and 80 percent of its usual level of stock trading, ramping back up to its previous $1 trillion-a-week rate. The company also continued its recovery process, looking for permanent space on the lower floors of another office building.

"We played the cards the terrorists dealt us," said CEO Lutnick.[26] Fortunately, Cantor had redundant systems that allowed it to recover. Its backbone trading system, eSpeed, was built on a dual architecture that replicated all machines, connections, and functionality at the World Trade Center and at a Rochelle Park, New Jersey, site, with a third facility in London.

In addition to data, the backup systems stored critical corporate knowledge, including customer relationship information. Systems redundancy was crucial to Cantor's recovery. Just as crucial was the external support it got from suppliers, competitors, regulators, and customers.

It is not surprising that suppliers would help. Lending a hand to a customer in distress is good business. Thus, Compaq delivered 100 desktop computers at 2 A.M. on Wednesday, September 12, and Verizon expedited the installation of voice lines and the transfer of some of eSpeed's digital circuits. Cisco provided a phone system based on Internet protocols and Microsoft had a Windows operating system team continuously on hand, as eSpeed's server and desktop maintenance group had been especially hard hit. (Some of the systems' passwords were lost with the lost people.)

Competitors helped too. ICI/ADP, another electronic trading company, offered to take care of eSpeed's clearing and settling of transactions through its own connection to banks, and UBS PaineWebber provided temporary office space in Manhattan.

Regulators also wanted Cantor and other afflicted market participants to survive. Cantor had hundreds of billions of dollars of pre-9/11 trades that were awaiting settlement—the final exchange of the money and securities that is legally required to occur within a specified number of business days after the trade is logged. Chaos in closing these trades could have affected liquidity for financial institutions in all areas of commerce, reverberating throughout the world economy. Regulators kept the equities markets closed for four days, in part to allow companies like Cantor to recover.

But the most important help came from customers. Major financial institutions relied on Cantor as a discrete middleman. For example, when financial giants like Goldman Sachs or Merrill Lynch want to sell a billion dollars in U.S. Treasury securities based on a bet on changes in interest rates, they do not want their competitors to know that they are bearish on the bonds. Trading houses, like Cantor, broker these mega-deals, helping financial institutions keep their trading strategies private.

When asked, immediately following the 9/11 attack, what it would take for Cantor to survive, Lutnick had suggested that "if every money manager of a pension fund just gave us a little bit of business, then maybe we'll survive."[27] Lutnick discovered that Cantor's customers really wanted the company to survive.

When the equity markets reopened on September 17, Cantor was unsure that its systems would operate, much less handle the normal volume of trades. To ensure a "soft start," the company instituted a rule of one trade per customer to avoid stressing the system. The response from customers to this conservative restart surprised Cantor. When Cantor's head of equities took his first client call on the 17th, he explained to the fund manager of a large mutual fund, "We are open for business, but we're not here to impress anyone, we just want to do one trade—as a test." But that wasn't enough for the client. "Our management committee got together and we're giving you all our business today and you have to do all of our trades," she said. The Cantor employee replied, "We're not sure we can handle it," to which the fund manager said, "You don't understand. If you don't take these trades, I'm going to lose my job. I'm faxing them to you, you do the best you can," and then she hung up.[28] Cantor used customers' bursts of goodwill and willingness to deal with "the best you can do" to get back on its feet and worked hard to justify customers' willingness to help the company.

While cases of customers helping suppliers may be less common in Western business, some East Asian systems are, in a sense, built on corporate mutual assistance. The Japanese keiretsu system of cross-holdings creates bi-directional support as suppliers help their customers and customers help their suppliers. Similarly, the Korean chaebols, such as Samsung, Daewoo, Goldstar and Hyundai, involve groups of companies with cross-holdings and cross-commitment to the other members of the group.

Prioritizing Customers

Even if a company has strong and flexible customer and distribution relationships, it may not be able to satisfy all customers during a disruption. Although no company wants its disruption to propagate to the company's customers, limited resources can force a firm to make difficult decisions during severe disruptions.

Setting customer service priorities for post-disruption activities involves a decision process similar to the emergency medical practice of triage. In the realm of emergency medical care, doctors divide patients into three groups: those who have minor injuries not needing immediate medical attention, those who will die regardless of any medical attention, and those who will live only if they receive prompt attention. When resources are scarce, doctors treat the last group first, because that is where the incremental ounce of medical intervention can make the maximum difference.

In the immediate aftermath of a disruption, managers face a triage-like choice about which customers to serve first. Such decisions can be based on customer vulnerability or on more internally focused criteria such as how profitable the customer is, how costly would it be to serve it, or how important the customer is in the long term. Which criterion is used may be less important than having a coherent process for setting priorities during the time-sensitive post-disruption period. The company has to be seen as using a fair allocation process so long-term relationships are damaged as little as possible.

Continental Teves, a supplier of automotive, industrial, and agricultural products, had to make tough decisions when 9/11 shut down all U.S. air freight traffic and disrupted cross-border freight flows. On the afternoon of 9/11, the company assembled a list of all outstanding customer, part, and supplier orders. Most important, it collected data on its North American customers' inventory levels. Knowing these customers' production rates from past order patterns, it calculated the number of days of parts supplies each customer had before their operations would run out of parts. This statistic—days of supply—was the one on which Continental Teves based its priorities.

By late afternoon on 9/11, Continental knew which shipments were the most critical to its customers and required immediate action, and it expedited many of these by rerouting them via ground transportation, leveraging its relationships with transport firms such as Emery Ground to supplement air cargo delivery.[29] In emphasizing customer needs in mitigating the disruption, the company did incur some added costs, but "Cost is not the question," said James Gill, a spokesman for Continental Teves. "It's keeping the customers happy and making them feel comfortable."[30]

Most Taiwanese semiconductor manufacturers also considered customer vulnerability to set priorities in the aftermath of the Taiwan quake. A month after the earthquake hit the island, Richard Chang, president of Worldwide Semiconductor Manufacturing Corp., reported that "certain customers are asking us for some parts that they very urgently need to be delivered. Those things we are going to hurry and ship out to them, and in one case, we'll do it two weeks ahead of time. I think the key is to work with the customers to find which is the most urgent and support them."[31]

Deciding which customer is vulnerable, and to what extent, requires a qualitative assessment of which customers' situations are more critical than others. Practically, in many cases it will be the customers who exert the most pressure. This was the case with the Philips chip plant fire. Originally Philips chose to focus all of its efforts on serving its two highest-volume customers, Nokia and Ericsson. But Nokia's aggressive pressure and immediate attention to the problem, including the involvement of the highest levels of the company, forced Philips's hand. Nokia actually monopolized the limited recovery resources of Philips (in fact, overriding Philips's allocation decisions), leaving Ericsson with a severe parts shortage.

When producing for the consumer market, companies can prioritize on more internally focused metrics. For example, when New United Motor Manufacturing, Inc., ran out of parts in the midst of the 2002 West Coast port lockout (see chapter 4), it decided to airfreight parts from Japan. But at $50,000 of added costs per container, airfreight "would increase production costs of the cars by $300 to $600 each and the trucks by $2,000 apiece," said a NUMMI spokesman,[32] because truck parts were heavier and larger than car parts. NUMMI chose to airfreight only car parts[33]

In effect, NUMMI has set its priorities on the basis of cost and profitability impacts. Consequently, its car customers were not disrupted, but truck customers experienced delays.

Public agencies prioritize on effectiveness, measured by helping the largest number of people in the shortest period of time. For example, snow removal after a storm is focused on major arteries and mass-transit routes first, while local streets are plowed only later. Health authorities also prioritize based on effectiveness (and vulnerability), offering limited influenza vaccines to the most vulnerable members of society first: the old, the very young, and pregnant women first, as well as to health workers and caregivers.[34]

Flexible Customer-Facing Processes

Downstream processes can help flexibility in many ways. Dell achieved flexibility by structuring its entire supply chain around its make-to-order system, thus avoiding difficult-to-change long-term customer commitments.

Risk pooling provides flexibility for sending products or parts from customers who do not have an immediate need for them to customers who do. Caterpillar's parts distribution system uses the inventory already delivered to dealers as if it were still available to be sold to other dealers, thus increasing its ability to respond to demands for rare parts anywhere in the world. Similar systems are used by retailers to move merchandise from one store to another where the merchandise is needed to fill outstanding orders.

Strong partnerships with customers are likely to help secure both help and leeway when disasters strikes. Customer reactions can be the difference between a company rebounding or not, because signs of confidence from a major customer are likely to signal to other customers, suppliers, financial institutions, and investors that the company is likely to survive.

15

Building a Culture of Flexibility

Much of this book deals with supply chain designs for increasing security and resilience. Some organizations respond to disruption better than others not because their supply chain designs are fundamentally different, but because there is something "in their DNA" that is conducive to fast response. Both Ericsson and Nokia received the same warning from Philips on March 17, 2000—yet one acted swiftly and the other did not. Following the 1999 Taiwan earthquake, Dell quickly adjusted its offering to balance supply and demand and continued its growth despite the parts shortage. And Toyota and its suppliers sprung immediately into action following the fire in Aisin's P-valve factory, demonstrating extraordinary flexibility in reconfiguring production lines, thus minimizing the disruption to Toyota.

What makes some organizations so flexible? What makes them contain disruptions quickly and bounce back from disruptions before they become catastrophes and possibly drive the organization out of business? Some of the answers lie in superior supply chain designs. But MIT interviews with dozens of companies, along with prior research, point to another element common to most resilient companies—*culture*.[1]

Culture is elusive, difficult to define, and even more difficult to change and manage. What is an organizational culture? How is it created and sustained? How is it articulated? What role does it play in the business?

The culture of an organization can be defined as the pattern of beliefs and expectations shared by the organization's members; these beliefs and expectations produce norms that shape the behavior of individuals and groups.[2] In a sense, culture is "the way we do things around here." The tangible elements of culture are the artifacts and the espoused values that one can find in any organization. The artifacts are the visible organizational structures and processes such as language, dress code, rituals, office layout, and the way that meetings are conducted. The espoused values include strategies, goals, philosophies, credos, and mission statements.[3]

Company culture can play a defining role in the firm's competitive advantage. 3M has a strong culture of innovation, leading to highly successful products such as Post-it Notes, Scotchgard fabric protector, and cellophane tapes, as well as hundreds of other innovations. To encourage innovation, 3M allows its engineers to spend 15 percent of their time on projects of their own choosing.[4]

The immense pride engendered at the U.S. Marine Corps feeds its warrior culture, which is a crucial element in one of the world's most effective fighting forces. Its members believe they are superior as a result of their selection and training, and can perform tasks that other forces cannot. Its basic task is to be "the most ready when the nation is least ready" and consequently it is always in training.

Toyota's respect for people is the most important tenet of the "Toyota Way." Cars have to be reliable (since this is what the customers want) and Toyota respects that, creating fierce customer loyalty; respect for suppliers leads to true partnerships, encouraging suppliers to share their innovations with Toyota and to stand by them when needed; and respect for employees means that they are empowered to take unilateral actions, suggest improvements, and support each other rather than act as interchangeable automatons.[5]

The essence of resilience is the containment of disruption and recovery from it. Culture contributes to resilience by endowing employees with a set of principles regarding the proper response when the unexpected does occur, and when the formal organization's policy does not cover the situation at hand or is too slow to react. It suggests the course of action to take.

The elements of culture that contribute to resilience and flexibility can be found in widely diverse organizations.

Dell

Dell[6] epitomizes the fast-moving culture of a high-tech company. Founded as recently as 1984, with its much-admired founder still in control twenty-one years later, the company pioneered high-throughput, low-inventory manufacturing with its direct sales, build-to-order PC manufacturing. The speed of its operations is evident in Dell's cash-to-cash cycle of negative 37 days; in 2004 Dell got paid by customers more than a month before it had to pay its suppliers.

Dell's competitive advantage is based, in part, on its ability to adjust quickly to changing conditions, including part availability, new product and component introduction/phase-out, product line mix, volume fluctuation, market demands and trends, and delivery requirements. This flexibility-oriented culture is based on four tenets:

(i)   obsession with results,

(ii) teamwork and communications,

(iii) value of personal relationships, and

(iv) leadership at all levels.

Obsession with Results

The first tenet of the Dell culture is the obsession with execution. "Dellocity" is the company's term for its fast-paced operations and working environment. Dell employees spend most of their time working on projects that will produce immediate results. One company senior manager summed it up when he said that "about 80 percent of employees work on a time horizon of one-to-two weeks, and the maximum time horizon for most employees is twelve weeks." Officially, Dell requires ROI of twelve months or less on any project. Dell employees do not over-analyze and the company prefers experimentation to lengthy study. A Dell executive described it as a "see the hill—take the hill" mentality.

The short-term mentality and the fast pace are created, in part, by setting "stretch" goals. It is common practice for a goal to be set and accepted, even when the individual or team responsible for it is not exactly sure how it will meet the goal. Once they agree to goals, teams get great latitude to figure out how to accomplish them.

Fueling this focus on execution and fast problem solving is an emphasis on personal accountability. Dell runs a strong meritocracy based on ranking individual performance, not team performance. Top performers can expect generous rewards, a policy that has created an estimated 3,500 "Dellionaires" as of 2004. Dell pressures the 5 to 10 percent that receive the lowest rating to change jobs inside Dell or leave. Although teams are essential to the coordination-intensive tasks inside Dell, teams are not rated by any formal process; they are simply understood as necessary to get things done.

Teamwork and Communications

The second tenet of Dell's culture is teamwork and communications. The process of creating and disbanding teams at Dell is fluid and ongoing—much more so than at other companies. At any one point, managers can be part of three to five teams working on diverse issues. In the space of a few years, a person might shift multiple times from production to marketing, from PCs to printers, or from consumer to government sales. As people change positions they shift teams, causing managers to "own" their resources for only a short time. This way, employees learn all aspects of Dell's business, tend to share resources with those who need them most, and develop broad social networks with others in the company in a relatively short period.

Like other organizations, the company also runs formal cross-training programs where certain higher-level employees learn all of the different parts of the production process. They spend part of their time on the production line and part of their time working on special issues.

Frequent, widely attended meetings are required to keep everyone up to date. These meetings follow many rules to help them run smoothly. While the meetings take time, they are crucial in such a fast and open environment to get everybody coordinated.

For example, one of the ironclad rules is that no new information can be brought into a meeting; all information has to be distributed at least an hour beforehand. This avoids knee-jerk, nondata-based decisions and unfocused meetings. While meetings are a fact of life in most organizations, Dell's high frequency and effective management of meetings set the company apart.

To support this environment, Dell sends out a production report hourly to hundreds of operations people. This report, sent via pagers or e-mail, creates a fast "cadence" of organizational activity.

Informal Networks Based on Personal Relationships

While Dell has a formal escalation process for dealing with manufacturing problems, these processes are rarely followed because the informal networks are quicker. Bypassing a supervisor and going directly to the person who can solve a problem is an accepted practice because it gets results. The use of such personal networks is the third tenet of Dell's culture.

To encourage the development of the informal networks, Dell maintains an open-door policy, meaning that anyone can schedule a one-on-one meeting with anyone else in the organization, regardless of title and position.

The fast process of making up and disbanding teams also ensures that information flows freely and is not hoarded. Any teammate may be tomorrow's team leader. In addition, the fast movement of people throughout the organization ensures that no "fiefdoms" develop, as any employee is likely to find himself on the "other side" at any point.

Leadership at All Levels

Dell empowers workers to lead efforts, no matter what position they hold in the organization. One practical manifestation of this belief is seen in the design of Dell's Six Sigma program[7] (called BPI, or Business Process Improvement). Instead of emphasizing high-level ("black belt") training of executives and highly skilled employees—like GE's original version of Six Sigma—Dell's program puts more emphasis on training and engaging a larger number of lower-level employees. Thus, it trained thousands of employees in the basic program ("yellow belts" and "green belts").

"Leadership at all levels" means that all team members are expected to be innovative and enterprising in solving problems. This egalitarian culture is supported by visible artifacts (which is not unique to Dell but fits its culture well): Almost everyone at Dell has cubicles, and walls are kept to a minimum. Directors and VPs have larger cubicles, but they are located with everyone else in the functions they manage. This use of space sends signals of both equality and access to the organization.

These four tenets mean that employees are empowered and expected to solve problems continuously. Through the personal networks and the wide knowledge of the organization, they can call on resources throughout the company and tap expertise quickly without "going through channels." At the same time, continuous stretch goals and the emphasis on short-term performance, coupled with the ever-changing environment of high-technology manufacturing, mean that Dell employees are accustomed to a hectic and constantly changing environment. In such an environment they have to make decisions on the spot without much case-specific guidance, based only on the cultural underpinning of the organization. Such traits, naturally, serve the organization well when disruptions strike.

The "usual" disruptions and challenges at Dell condition the organization for flexibility. When Steve Herrington, a second-shift production control manager, arrived at work one day in October 2003, he was told that the factory had to build and ship 9,000 PCs that day (the usual run was 4,500 and the maximum capacity was only 8,000). As the second shift started, less than 50 percent of the commitment had been met, with 5,600 machines to go.

In a quick meeting, the team decided to reconfigure the printer production lines to make PCs instead, and to modify the shipping lanes for the added volume that night. The production control manager called on people to create a team that he knew could help, even if those people weren't officially responsible for the problem. After only an hour into the second shift, Dell's printer line was making PCs, and trucks were loading and driving out of the reorganized loading dock. After a long night of managing and monitoring the situation every 15 minutes, the factory more than met the goal, building 9,100 PCs. "We achieved this goal by challenging our assumptions, working together as a team, and being flexible as individuals," said Steve Herrington.

The changes required to meet the goal, including trading off printer manufacturing against PC manufacturing, were made at the local level without consultation with top management and with single-minded resolve to meet the goal.

United Parcel Service

UPS moves packages "pony express style," riding on a series of trucks, airplanes, and rail cars. Each package moves from a collection point to a local package center, and then through a series of break-bulk-and-consolidation hubs across the country, to the destination package center, and finally to the delivery truck and the destination. Once handed over to a driver, or dropped at a UPS collection facility, a long-haul package is likely to be unloaded, sorted, and loaded four times at various terminals. It is likely to be hauled by up to eight drivers on the individual segments that make up its journey.

To offer the high service demanded by its customers at a low cost, these handoffs have to be highly coordinated with regimented procedures. But delivery processes are subject to bad weather conditions, missed schedules, personnel problems, and mechanical troubles. And any disruption or delay typically ripples throughout the UPS network, creating downstream scheduling disturbances and displaced volumes of activity.

At the same time that UPS insists on a set of tight procedures, it also empowers its local managers to solve local problems in novel ways. In fact, industrial engineers work every morning in every region of the company to adjust the day's operations to whatever disruptions are in the making—downed equipment, driver problems, road construction, weather delays, anything that means the daily assignments of the delivery center may have to change. Some of these changes are substantial and require re-planning of package sorting patterns and delivery routes as some centers have to take the work load of others.

Delivery drivers follow the "340 Methods" in the process of delivering packages. The methods cover everything from a 57-point pre-trip checklist, to strategies for thinking ahead in traffic, and to highly choreographed movements while delivering pack-ages. Once trained, however, delivery drivers get very little super-vision. They are supposed to solve problems such as late starts, congestion, flat tires, and adverse weather as they encounter them. This approach is not limited to the front lines; even with man-agement "by the book," managers are expected to improvise. The *UPS Management Policy Book* details 89 policies regarding the UPS's people, customers, shareholders, and communities. Yet managers are expected to solve problems whether there is a pro-cedure for it or not; the company expects managers not to use the policy as a crutch in explaining their actions.

For the most part, UPS recruits full-time employees from its pool of part-time workers, allowing it to conduct, in essence, a long on-the-job interview. This screening, on top of the require-ments to get into the part-time positions, allows UPS to hire service-oriented employees. Managers are typically promoted from within. "Once you understand the package cycle, you understand how to deal with any of the instances," said Dan Silvernale, a UPS manager. All UPS employees understand the process.

The company communicates constantly with its employees. A publication called *The Big Idea* informs employees about UPS national and district news. The management committee meets every Monday with representatives of all departments to assess the state of the company; the meeting's minutes are disseminated to all UPS managers. The results of the company's annual strat-egy meetings are disseminated to all districts. A short morning meeting is held daily in each hub and package delivery center. In addition, UPS is the biggest user of cellular communications in the world; more than a million messages a day help the company stay synchronized.

Such intensive communications mean that when a disruption takes place, drivers, terminal operators, and local managers are all aware of what are the important issues of the day, what is happening around the company that week, and what is the current state of the system as a whole. With this knowledge, and with the ingrained culture that gives them the general guide, employees can take fast actions in response to disruptions without specific instructions.

Since disruptions are daily occurrences at UPS, it uses a likelihood/severity framework to manage the responses.[8] As shown in figure 15.1, high-frequency disruptions are mitigated mostly through redundant capacity, regardless of their magnitude. Such redundant capacity include fueled planes and crew ready to go on 30 minutes notice, and extra drivers and package cars. Lower probability events are managed through contingency planning. Every belt in every sorting facility has a failure plan: The center workers know how to reroute the packages if any of the belts fail. Similarly, if a center is closed, there are plans for other centers in the region to shoulder its load. Low-frequency/high-impact events require a special crisis management operation that can be set up in short order.

The long history of UPS includes many folklore stories about exceptional customer service and recovery from disruptions. For

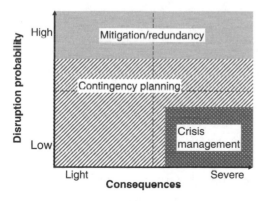

Figure 15.1
UPS Disruption Management

example, Ray Chezna, a weekend maintenance supervisor, took a call from a panicked customer in Alabama, whose suit for a funeral was in the system and scheduled for delivery too late. Ray was able to locate the suit and expedite it in time for the funeral. His manager did not even know of the event until a grateful letter from the family told the story.

In another case, a UPS public relations employee got a call informing him that a crucial part needed for the NASA mission to fix the Hubble telescope was mistakenly shipped via ground service and would delay the launch. The employee tracked the part down to a train, contacted the railroad to intercept the train, and had local UPS employees identify the right rail car and container. The local employees opened the container, found the small package inside, and air-freighted it to the Kennedy Space Center.

In both of these examples, the people who solved the problems took personal responsibility for seeing the whole operation through. They did not transfer responsibility either when they got the call or anytime through the process of solving the problem, even though they were not dispatchers and such problem-solving was not normally part of their jobs. UPS has numerous cases of service calls like these (many of them seem to be about wedding dresses, according to dispatchers) and the culture is such that the dispatchers try to do their utmost to get the packages delivered. This is possible, in part, because of the extensive information technology infrastructure that supports nonstandard operations (such as expediting a single package out of the daily flood of shipments).

A culture artifact that emphasizes the service orientation, according to Albert Wright, a UPS corporate engineering manager, is UPS's insistence that "no one goes home until all the packages are delivered." Such mentality underscores the importance of customer service and fosters cross-functional team orientation.

The main problem-solving mentality at UPS is probably rooted in the decentralized nature of the operations in which managers are expected to "do whatever it takes" to solve the problems they encounter daily. The ultimate manifestation of this is the lone driver who has to deal with daily problems on his or her own.

Aircraft Carrier Operations

Military organizations are designed to expect the unexpected. But whether in wartime or during training operations, few environments are less predictable and less forgiving than an aircraft carrier's flight deck. A Nimitz-class carrier, the newest in the American fleet, is home to 6,200 sailors. It is propelled by twin nuclear reactors and carries 80 combat aircraft, which it can launch at a rate of up to four aircrafts a minute.

On the deck, the carrier catapults jets laden with fuel and bombs and retrieves these jets on a short, slanted, rocking, and moving runway—day and night, rain or shine. At the same time, the carrier has to coordinate the actions of about ten support vessels in the battle group while possibly engaged in combat, and with radar and radios shut down to conceal the carrier's location.

During day-to-day operations, the carrier operates along its hierarchical structure of command, with discipline strictly enforced and procedures done "by the book." But during hectic times, such as during flight operations, the entire organization seems to follow a different mode of operation.[9] The command and control structure gives way to collegial cooperation based on extensive communications between experts, rather than on the basis of orders handed down from above.

For example, several teams are involved in bringing a jet in to land on the carrier. These include the command team on the bridge, the air controllers, the arresting wire team, the on deck emergency teams, the search and rescue team, and the operators— the pilot and the landing signal officer (LSO) who guides the pilot on the final approach. These teams communicate constantly among themselves while the jet is approaching, making sure that the approach is open, the arresting wire is set, the deck is all clear, and emergency teams are standing by. At the same time, the LSO communicates with the pilot regarding the approach, while the flight controller communicates with the pilot from the tower regarding the environment on the deck and in the air.

To the uninitiated, these conversations sound like a lot of unnecessary chatter. Yet listening officers and team personnel know what to expect; the first sign of trouble is a phrase, a tone, or a response not according to expectation. This allows all involved—from the captain to the air wing commander to the team members on the deck—to be aware immediately of a developing dangerous situation. Officers and enlisted men on the deck can take corrective actions without the delay associated with going through channels, explaining the situation, and getting instructions.

The deck environment during flight operations illustrates the value of continuous communications in challenging situations; the "listening network" provides all involved with a context regarding the general situation (planes in the air, mission, and deck status). When a problem starts to develop, the listening network makes sure that all the people who could do something about it are informed not only about the developing problem but also about the status of the environment, and it allows for monitoring corrective actions. Such communications are in addition to the provision of general context. Day in and day out, carrier personnel are kept informed about the ship, its mission, the battle group status, and conditions in the outside world through continuous briefing and debriefing, as well as through daily meetings and announcements throughout the ship.

Critical decisions made during flight operations on the deck are also characterized by "deference to expertise" rather than rank or seniority; team members on the deck defer to experienced petty officers and veteran enlisted men. This environment is reminiscent of Dell's reliance on personal networks and teamwork to meet stretch goals in a short time.

It may be surprising to some who view the navy as a "Yes Sir/No Sir" environment to realize that even the person with the lowest rating on the deck has not only the authority but the obligation to suspend flight operations immediately, when circumstances demand it, without first clearing it with superiors. Flight operations are the carrier's reason for being, and stopping it means stopping dead in its tracks the mission of a multibillion-dollar plant and its more than 6,000 highly trained workers. Events on the flight deck, however, unfold too quickly to use the normal chain of command, so individual acts to avert a disruption are encouraged. Most important, the person halting the operations will not be penalized for being wrong and will often be publicly congratulated if the stoppage avoided or prevented a significant problem.[10]

Other operations also condition the crew for flexibility. To this end, the air wing combat or training assignments are frequently reconfigured in response to actual or simulated change in conditions. Each reconfiguration may involve different ordinance, different departure sequences, and/or different approaches, requiring fast coordinated actions by many teams. Such reconfigurations, performed under pressure, condition the planning and execution team to work closely and fast, preparing the system for response to unfamiliar and stressful situations that may rise as a result of a large-scale disruption.

Common Cultural Traits

On the face of it, the free flow of ideas and activities at Dell, the regimented efficiency of UPS, and the command and control structure of a U.S. Navy carrier may seem to have little in common. Yet all three organizations are flexible and resilient—they respond quickly to disruptions, making sure that small disruptions are not allowed to become large ones. The main cultural traits that lead these organizations to respond quickly and flexibly can be characterized by

(i)   continuous communications among informed employees,

(ii) distributed power,

(iii) passion for the work, and

(iv) conditioning for disruption.

Continuous Communications among Informed Employees

Fast and flexible organizations continuously transmit information throughout. Toyota displays continuous production reports in all its plants; Dell updates all its managers hourly on production; UPS keeps the vast reaches of its network in constant cellphone communications; and aircraft carrier deck operations are conducted in view of the air wing commander and through constant communications in several interconnected listening networks. When a disruption occurs, such communications provide employees with the knowledge of the immediate state of the system so they can respond intelligently and immediately.

Very intensive communications also have a negative aspect: People may "tune out" if a high portion of the data is irrelevant, if they do not trust that the senders of the information understands their job, and if they are not empowered to act on it.

The information regarding "how do we do things around here?" is transmitted in formal learning, job descriptions, and standard operating procedures. Since the organizations described here are large, no one person can fathom the complexity of the entire operation. Consequently, people are moved around from job to job in order to build a comprehensive and deep understanding of the entire operation.

Examples include the ever-forming and ever-disbanding project teams at Dell; the constant movement between jobs on an aircraft carrier and between navy ships and shore duties; and UPS's reshuffling of managers across functions and territories. Southwest Airlines achieves this through their "Walk a Mile" program, in which any employee can do another employee's job for a day. The operations agents cannot fly the planes, but the pilots can—and do—work as operations agents. Seventy-five percent of Southwest's 20,000 employees have participated in the job-swapping program.[11]

High intensity of communication yields benefits only if managers have a deep knowledge of operations, so they "know what they are talking about." The leaders of the organizations mentioned here are perfect illustrations of such managers. Mike Eskew, UPS's CEO and chairman, has been with the company since 1972; he started with the company as an engineering trainee. His predecessor, Jim Kelly, started out washing package cars then graduated to driving. Michael Dell founded the company and is still very much involved in daily operations. And the pool of chief petty officers, who basically run any navy ship, rotate in and out of similar ships in the fleet; these officers have long service records in their specialty and are a source of the "navy way" to new recruits and new officers alike.

All the organizations mentioned here have to train new operators continuously and they have developed processes to ensure they hire the right people. In that sense, having to hire a large number of people is not looked upon as a problem but rather as an opportunity to hire the type of individual who is likely to fit with the company and then indoctrinate him or her into the corporate culture.

Between 1984 and 2004, Dell grew from a single entrepreneur in a Texas dorm room to a worldwide manufacturer with 50,000 employees. UPS grew from a bicycle messenger service in Seattle (it was founded in 1907) to the world's largest package delivery company, then adapted to being a technology company, a supply chain management company, an international operator, and an airline. Each phase required the hiring of thousands of people and acculturating them.

When Toyota expanded to the United States it hired thousands of American workers to turn out cars with quality comparable to their Japanese counterparts. Toyota avoided hiring former American auto industry workers and preferred hiring employees with no previous manufacturing experience, so it could train them in its own processes and culture. Their success demonstrated that it was the processes and culture that make Toyota succeed, not the work of Japanese "automatons."

The U.S. Navy may represent the most impressive success of hiring and indoctrinating people into an organization. The navy continuously brings new recruits onto its carriers, training them and giving them significant responsibilities at a young age. (The average age of the 9,000 sailors in the Theodore Roosevelt battle group, and the 5,000 marines in its Amphibious Ready Group, is 22 to 23 years old.[12])

All of these organizations transfer knowledge and cultural norms to new and new-on-the-job people continuously. This knowledge transfer sustains the organization's culture and ways.

It takes place through the espoused values (such as mission statements), artifacts (such as dress codes and employee benefits), employee training and, most important, the continuous communications sent formally and through examples of the leaders' actions and behavior.[13]

At the same time, senior managers understand operations and are attuned to them. It is difficult to imagine a carrier captain promoted from the accounting department or from an armored brigade; they accumulate vast operational experience before assuming command. The same is true of Mike Eskew at UPS, with his engineering background, and Michael Dell, who still calls on production line supervisors when there is a problem. This is also the case with other companies known for their operational excellence; Fred Smith founded FedEx and is still active at the company; Herb Kelleher cofounded Southwest Airlines and ran it for 30 years, creating and sustaining its winning culture; Hiroshi Okuda, Toyota's chairman (with Toyota since 1955), was familiar with almost every aspect of his company's operations before assuming his leadership role; and Sam Walton started as a management trainee at J. C. Penny and founded several successful retail stores before starting Wal-Mart.

Distributed Power

In situations that require immediate action, flexible organizations allow for and empower individual actions by "first responders." These are the people who are on the front line and close to the action; they are the most likely to spot a problem first and their immediate reaction can prevent it from growing.

A culture of distributed power and empowerment can be found in many successful and flexible organizations. Any worker can sound an alarm on the Toyota production line by pulling an *andon* cord if he or she sees a quality problem. Within seconds, supervisors and specialists will descend on the manufacturing station in question and try to fix the problem. If the problem cannot be fixed within 60 seconds, the production line will stop and the problem will be solved before the line can be restarted. Giving this kind of responsibility to lower levels of the organization is one of the ingredients in Toyota's success; it allows the system to react quickly before a large number of defective cars move down the line, creating an expensive "rework" challenge.

Some retailers are much more flexible and faster than others in responding to the fickle demand of fashion clothing consumers. The Japanese retailer World and Spain's Zara need only three weeks' production lead time (vs. the industry standard of six to eleven months); they take six weeks to introduce a new product (vs. the industry standard of one to two years); their markdowns are only 15 percent of sales (vs. the industry standard of 33 percent); and they turn their inventory ten times a year (vs. the industry standard of six).[14] A critical ingredient in their success is the empowerment of the product development, production, and marketing teams to tackle challenges immediately and without headquarters approval. Managers from these departments meet every day to plan reaction to daily sales figures from the stores. They have the power to change product designs in order to respond to sales trends and solve component shortages.

At one point Southwest Airlines faced a problem. Its competitors, the large airlines who own most international and national reservation systems, began demanding payments of tens of millions of dollars a year from Southwest for use of their computerized reservations systems by travel agents. In response, Herb Kelleher decided to embark on an electronic, ticket-less system. It turned out that people from several departments had already gotten together, anticipated such a contingency, and begun work on a system, unbeknownst to Kelleher or the rest of Southwest's top executives. That kind of initiative exemplifies most of the empowerment principles mentioned above—anticipating the crisis, taking action without asking for permission, cobbling together a group of experts, and working toward a solution. The Southwest Airlines culture encourages and celebrates such an attitude.[15]

To be successful, such employees have to "internalize" what is the general mission of the organization and what is its current state so they can take the correct action. They must have the authority and the orientation to take such action in the first place, and they must be rewarded for the initiative and not disciplined for mistaken calls under pressure.

In his book chronicling the World War II European campaign, *Citizen Soldiers*,[16] the historian and popular writer Stephen Ambrose makes the point that part of the superiority of the U.S. Army was rooted in its soldiers' local decision-making power. In the fog of battle, senior officers had no clear picture of the battlefield and neither the Americans nor the Germans were prepared for several contingencies. The difference was made up by the tendency of American local unit commanders to take initiative and improvise. His argument is that, by and large, the German army was more command-and-control oriented and as a result reacted too late or inappropriately to changing battlefield conditions and requirements.

Passion

Flexible organizations have one more element in common, an element that the artifacts and the espoused values try to instill and that the training and acculturation try to implant in new members of the organization. This element is a personal, deeply felt concern and responsibility to serve the objective of the firm, or simply *passion*. Others call it "urgency," "mindfulness,"[17] or "alignment" quality.

The difference between the accepting-and-trusting Ericsson and the apprehensive-and-fast-responding Nokia in the face of the Philips plant fire can, in part, be explained by their respective cultures. Nokia's response can be captured by the Finnish term *sisu*, which translates loosely into "curtness under pressure." Nokia took swift action because its culture included two critical elements: (i) deep relationships and extensive communications with suppliers and (ii) broad and fast internal communications. It was able to recognize immediately the severity of the disruption and it had the implements in place to communicate critical information broadly and quickly. Nokia always encouraged quick escalation of bad news within the company. Ericsson, by contrast, with a more laid-back culture, did not spring into action the moment employees detected the disruption. Ericsson's employees lacked the urgency, mindfulness, and passion that helped Nokia react quickly.

When asked about Southwest Airlines's culture, Herb Kelleher commented, "Well, first of all, it starts with hiring. We are zealous about hiring. We are looking for a particular type of person, regardless of which job category it is. We are looking for attitudes that are positive and for people who can lend themselves to causes."[18] In a *Business Week* interview,[19] Kelleher gave the following example: "A guy calls our Dallas reservation center from St. Louis, and he tells the reservation agent that TWA has canceled its flight out of Dallas/Fort Worth Airport to St. Louis on which his 85-year-old mother was supposed to fly, and that he's very concerned about her coming over to Love Field after having to make an intermediate connection in Tulsa. So the reservation agent says, 'I'm going to be off in five minutes. I'll pick her up at Dallas/Fort Worth, drive her to Love Field, and fly with her to St. Louis to make sure that she gets there okay.' That's the kind of devotion I'm talking about."

In the private sector, such "passion" and alignment with corporate goals is often encouraged through stock options and other success-sharing mechanisms that align the financial success of the organization and the individual. The 3,500 "Dellionaires," and the thousands of UPS managers who own UPS stock, have an incentive to see the company succeed. (UPS insiders own 90 percent of its stock and 99 percent of the voting rights.) Southwest officers' salaries are about 30 percent less then the norm in their industry, but Southwest offers more generous incentive compensation in the form of a substantial amount of stock options. Cash or stock incentives, however, are not the only or even the most effective way to breed passion. Many companies give stock options without such results, while others do not give options at all but are very flexible and resilient with employees who are loyal to a fault. Neither Toyota nor the U.S. Navy uses stock options to motivate employees.

Flexible and fast-responding companies align the employees' interests with the organization's. They seem to succeed in this at a fundamental level—their employees *identify* deeply with their company. Such employees fulfill their personal needs when the company succeeds, reaching self-actualization in the process.[20]

While employees of most organizations care about doing their job well, members of flexible organizations are truly passionate about it, thereby creating the flexibility and resilience of the organization. This passion is typically shown in a combination of pride and humility. The pride is part of a belief that the company's business is a cause, not only a commercial enterprise: UPS drivers and managers understand deeply that the packages they deliver are part of their customers' fabric of life and consequently the packages *have* to be delivered on time.

Don Schneider, chairman of Schneider National, the largest truckload company in the United States, motivates his employees by stressing that Schneider National is not really in the trucking business. According to him, Schneider is in the business of raising the standards of living of its customers and the nation by providing a low-cost freight transportation service. Since transportation is imbedded in the cost of all products, the company contributes to the nation's access to affordable goods.

As a Southwest executive put it: "The important thing is to take the bricklayer and make him understand that he's building a home, not just laying bricks." Clearly, officers and sailors in the navy think about what they do not in terms of driving big ships but in terms of serving the nation and defending freedom.

The other part of the passion exhibited by flexible organizations is humility. Firms with passionate employees are never satisfied, always recognizing they could do better. When a Dell organization gets great results, Michael Dell says he is "pleased . . . but not satisfied" because they can do more and better. While such senior managers are proud of their organizations, they are also humble about what they have not yet achieved, knowing they could and should improve.

Andrew Grove, former CEO of Intel, popularized the notion of a "paranoid" culture—one that is constantly looking out for threats and potential disruptions. He advocated a certain mindset that continuously questions existing common wisdom and beliefs to maintain a vigilant watch for new and evolving threats. Instead of viewing itself as the dominant market leader that it is, Intel scrutinizes its competitors' and customers' every move and privately bemoans its own future, apprehensive of new competition from unanticipated parties and cynical about its ability to succeed. And perhaps because of this arguably healthy skepticism, Intel continues to dominate the industry.

At Toyota, any form of waste creates dissatisfaction.[21] The company's continuous effort to improve itself is focused on seven categories of waste that add cost without adding value:[22] over-producing; wasting time; unnecessary transportation; over-processing; excess inventory; excess motion of operations and workers; and scrap and rework. The company broadcasts its wasteful ways internally so that employees and managers will focus on what is wrong rather than on the company's spectacular results in the marketplace.

UPS's founder, Jim Casey, called it "constructive dissatisfaction"—the drive to improve constantly. He believed that "once you make up your mind that you are pretty good, you will no longer feel the urge to do any better."

Conditioning for Disruption

Resilient organizations appear to be regularly conditioned to be innovative and flexible in the face of low-probability/high-impact disruptions through frequent and continuous "small" challenges. UPS, like FedEx and other transportation carriers, operates a vast network subject to weather, traffic congestion, city construction, and many other daily disruptions. Dell operates in the high-technology industry, subject to widely changing demand patterns, continuous new component introductions, and a global supply chain where something goes wrong daily. Intel is not satisfied with the daily ebbs and flows of its business; it introduces added uncertainty into its processes by conducting simulated disruptions and exercising response, preparing the firm for a broad range of possibilities.

Conditioning drives the firm's culture and how it responds to the cards it is dealt; the frequency and broad range of "normal" disruptions (or exercises) builds a "get ready for anything" mentality that permeates the ranks of the firm. UPS's Albert Wright captured the quality that comes with conditioning through response to daily disruptions by saying "disruptions are really normal [at UPS]."

Flexibility through Culture

Company culture may be the real secret to the business success of the companies discussed in this book. The cultural traits mentioned also provide these companies with a flexibility that breeds resilience to high-impact disruptions. Day in and day out, this culture allows them to respond quickly and effectively to fluctuations in demand, small supply disruptions, and manufacturing woes. Dell's build-to-order system is no secret; Wal-Mart's use of cross-dock operations instead of traditional distribution centers is well known; and Toyota is willing to teach anybody its methods and to take competitors for tours of its plants. Yet competitors are not able to duplicate the less tangible element of these organizations' success—their culture.

The cultural elements mentioned in the previous section complement each other and, by virtue of this, they constitute a self-perpetuating system. Understanding the interrelationships of these activities and principles unlocks the secrets of success of these systems.

First: Continuous communications provide workers with both a general "state of the company" and with real-time situation reports so actions can be taken quickly and in context.

Second: In time-constrained situations, there is deference to expertise (whether or not the expertise comes with a title)[23] and strong teamwork, helping to identify the right response without delay.

Third: Distributed power allows employees to take timely action.

Fourth: Management is very much involved with the operations and is knowledgeable and experienced. In fact, it is management's knowledge of the operational environment that makes it confident enough to let underlings respond with no supervision in cases in which a fast action is called for. It also lets management lead by example.

Fifth: Hiring and training practices lead to passionate employees who can be entrusted with the power to act when called upon by special situations.

Sixth: These organizations are conditioned to be innovative and flexible in the face of low-probability/high-impact disruptions through frequent and continuous "small" challenges.

Instilling passion is a long and difficult process. Changing an existing culture is even more difficult. Examples of massive culture changes—indicated by changes to attitudes and beliefs—include the antismoking campaign in the United States and the antidrinking-and-driving movement. The first resulted in a decrease in the U.S. population that smokes from 43 percent in 1966 to 25 percent in 1997. The second resulted in a decrease in the percentage of U.S. highway deaths because of drunk driving from 55 percent in 1980 to 38 percent in 1999.[24]

Corporate turnarounds are invariably based on changing the corporate culture. In just one year, Continental Airlines went from being the last U.S. airline, in terms of on-time performance, to being the first. Gordon Bethune, the CEO who led the change, described the process in his book *From Worst to First*. Most of the book is devoted to the many ways in which Bethune was able to change the culture at Continental Airlines—in particular improving the trust and respect between labor and management.[25]

In the late 1980s, Magma Copper went from being beset by violent confrontations between labor and management, teetering on the verge of bankruptcy, to the cover of *Industry Week* in about two years. Its CEO, J. Burgess Winter, used the same approach—focusing on changing the culture first—to change the fundamental relationship between the company and its (unionized) workforce.[26]

The literature on corporate culture change is vast. The process is extremely difficult, but the few examples mentioned here demonstrate that it can be done.

V

Resilience for Competitive Advantage

16
Moving Ahead

For many companies in North America, Europe, and Japan, September 11 did not "change everything." In fact, it changed very little. The MIT study of corporate response to the potential of large-scale disruptions found that most companies are still not thinking systematically about managing supply chain risks and vulnerabilities. The exceptions (which was true even before 9/11) are companies that have suffered disruptions in the past, ranging from kidnapped executives to sabotage at their overseas plants. While these companies were taking steps to increase their security and resilience, many companies that have not suffered from past attacks were, at best, just "going through the motions."

And, for the most part, that holds true not only for intentional disruptions, such as terrorist attacks, but also for large-scale accidents and random disruptions caused by weather or earthquakes. Companies that have experienced high-impact disruptions of any kind are more likely to invest in avoiding and mitigating future disruptions.

A case in point is Nokia, whose response to the Philips fire was chronicled in chapter 1. In 1995, five years before the Philips fire, Nokia was experiencing a supply-demand imbalance resulting from the combination of poor delivery performance and a relatively weak product line. Inventory was piling up and the company was hemorrhaging cash at a dangerous rate. Fixing the problems entailed linking production control to demand fulfillment, as well as launching a collaborative planning process involving key suppliers. Just as important, the company installed a monitoring process that could move from weekly to daily frequency when the system was stressed.[1] These processes served Nokia well in March 2000, as it responded to the Philips fire.

This book is a call for action. It is not, however, a call to start spending large amounts of resources on turning every plant into a fortress and stockpiling mountains of inventory. Instead, it is a call for systematic analysis of vulnerability, for learning from other people's experience, for increasing supply chain flexibility, for focusing on resilience as much as on security, and for effective use of resources designed to get business benefits out of investments in security and resilience.

Steps to Reduced Vulnerability

One of the most important lessons of this book is that by reducing vulnerability to high-impact/low-probability disruptions, a company will reduce its vulnerability to day-to-day market fluctuations as well, and therefore improve its general performance. To reduce vulnerability, companies should consider the following:

• organizing for action,

• assessing the vulnerabilities,

• reducing the likelihood of disruptions,

• collaborating for security,

• building in redundancies,

• designing resilient supply chains, and

• investing in training and culture.

Organizing for Action

Companies that are risk-aware have a chief security officer to coordinate the company's defenses. In that action they mirror the government, focusing on security. But such an approach tackles only one part of the problem—avoiding (or reducing the likelihood of) a disruption. It does not consider resilience—increasing the ability of the enterprise to bounce back from disruptions. To this end companies should be thinking not of a chief security officer but of a chief risk management officer. This officer's responsibility should include not only security but also the continuing effort to build in the flexibility to recover quickly and to isolate the company's customers as much as possible from a disruption.

The standard approach to resilience is to have a "business continuity plan." Often, this plan is a document collecting dust in a backroom in headquarters. At best, it is a plan that is occasionally updated and used to guide employee training in disruption response. While business continuity plans are an important element in the approach advocated in this book, they are but a small part of it. Security and resilience considerations have to be taken into account in designing the supply chain and woven into the fabric of business decision making.

An ongoing effort to build flexibility may involve redesign of operational processes, transformation of corporate culture, changes in product design, organizational changes within the company, and different relationships with customers, suppliers, and other stakeholders. The chief risk management officer should be a business person who is intimately familiar with the company's operations, since risk factors should be considered whenever strategic decisions are taken. Decisions involving centralizing operations, using offshore suppliers, entering foreign markets, labor negotiations, mergers and acquisitions, new infrastructure investments, new product introductions, new organizational structures, and many other strategic decisions should pass through the filter of vulnerability assessment: Which risks increase and which decrease? Can the risks be quantified? Can processes for early detection of specific risks be developed? Can the risks be mitigated? Do the business benefits of a planned course of action outweigh the increased risks?

Some companies are already moving in this direction. IBM's security executive is a member of its Global Trade Council and Gillette's security executive is represented on its Executive Operating Committee. Nike uses cross-functional leadership teams to evaluate security and business continuity best practices. Furthermore, in many companies security is becoming part of the responsibility of each process owner, rather than the security personnel.

Given the day-to-day pressures of running any modern business, the ultimate responsibility for asking the tough vulnerability questions lies with the board of directors. Most metrics used to motivate senior management, such as stock options and grants based on economic value added (EVA),[2] reward executives for economic gains, without taking into account the level of risk the firm takes on to realize these gains.[3] Consequently, it is the board that should insist on proper analysis of risk when undertaking strategic projects.[4]

Assessing Vulnerabilities

To assess business unit vulnerability, the three basic questions are:

1. What can go wrong?
2. What is the likelihood that it will happen?
3. How severe is the possible impact likely to be?

The use of vulnerability maps lets managers place possible disruptions in a likelihood/consequences framework that focuses on the disruptions with the highest likelihood and the most severe potential consequences. Such vulnerability maps should be updated continuously because each significant company action may introduce or eliminate vulnerabilities and change their overall likelihood or potential severity. The risk management team should also update vulnerability maps in response to decisions taken by other companies (including trading partners and competitors) and general external conditions (such as the geopolitical climate, new laws and regulations, or long-range weather forecasts).

Assessing the likelihood of a disruption differs according to its nature, be it a random event, an accident, or an intentional attack. The probability of an earthquake, flood, or tornado can be estimated from publicly available data. The probability of large-scale accidents can be developed and updated from incidences of near misses, coupled with industry-wide data about the relationships between near misses and significant disruptions. Intentional disruptions require a different type of assessment, since corporate actions may affect the likelihood of occurrence; "hardening" one area of operations may increase the probability of a disruption elsewhere. The assessment of such a threat requires imagination (often best accomplished by simulations and "war games") and monitoring of relevant events at other companies.

Assessing the severity of accidents and random events can be based on statistics and industry experience. Low-probability/high-impact events also involve public fear, that may lead to two phenomena that exacerbate the disruption: The first is hording of critical resources, be it gasoline during a fuel shortage or antibiotics during an Anthrax scare; the second is government overreaction, motivated by the need to show a firm hand and restore confidence. Both phenomena should be regarded as part of the disruption and companies should account for them in estimating severity.

An important element to remember when assessing either security or resilience is that no company lives alone—it is a citizen of its supply chain. Consequently, each member of the supply chain is only as secure and as resilient as the chain's weakest link. In order to understand their own vulnerability, many companies therefore audit their suppliers' security on an ongoing basis.

Standard accounting practices highlight another potentially risky situation: when a large part of a company's output is sold to a single customer. This situation is disclosed in financial statements in order to alert investors that such a customer may exert undue price pressure or even abandon the company for a competitor. Another danger, however, is that such a customer may experience a disruption of its own, which will reverberate immediately to its supplier.

Once the various threats have been prioritized, effort should be focused both on reducing the likelihood of a disruption and on improving the organization's ability to bounce back, thus reducing the severity of a disruption, should one take place.

Reducing the Likelihood of Disruptions
Many companies have long been working to increase safety, thereby reducing the likelihood of accidents and the impacts of

random events. Intentional disruptions, which get an increasing level of attention at many firms, call for an additional set of tools and approaches.

The first challenge is to detect a disruption quickly and recognize it for what it is. The focus should be on separating the "abnormal" activity from the "normal" baseline activity—deciding which containers should be checked; which employees warrant special attention; which passengers should be searched before entering an airline terminal; what concentration of doctor visits indicates a possible spread of a biological agent; or how many product failures per period may indicate sabotage. The tools to develop such "sensing" are based on statistical process control, a well-developed body of knowledge. But when dealing with the potential for an intentional disruption, such as terrorism or sabotage, detection must be complemented by trained human screeners who can review suspicious outliers.

Security and safety measures should be "layered," since the alternative may be prohibitively expensive. A single defensive mechanism guaranteed to prevent a disruption, if possible at all, may cost more than the value of the asset being protected. Properly layered security measures, woven together, reduce the combined probability of all of them failing to very low levels. Furthermore, early detection and layered defenses may also increase the company's resilience, as they may help keep any disruption that does occur contained and relatively small.

In general, there is no "bright line" separating security and resilience. Reducing the probability of a disruption may be considered a security activity, while keeping a small disruption from becoming a devastating one may be considered resilience. Many of the other methods for increasing security, such as collaboration, cultural changes, and training, are also effective at increasing resilience.

Collaborating for Security
Collaboration allows companies to reduce their vulnerability before they suffer from a disruption that "brings home the message," since they learn from others' experience. Industry bodies

such as TAPA, the American Chemistry Council, the Toy Industry Association, and many others have developed standards of safety and security. Such groups allow participants to exchange know-how and enable cross-company benchmarking of processes.

Collaboration has many other dimensions. Companies can collaborate with their own employees, making sure that they are motivated and trained to watch for anomalies in the environment and report them. Such a "citizen watch" approach can be extended to the surrounding community, whose members know who belongs in the vicinity of a facility and who does not.

Collaboration also extends to cooperation with the government on two fronts: complying with security requirements, even when they are voluntary; and advising the government on the proper application of security standards so that the cost to commerce is not too high. Some companies, such as FedEx, are even encouraging their employees to spot would-be terrorists and report them directly to the DHS via a special computer link.

Building in Redundancies

One of the most straightforward methods for creating resilience is building in redundancy. Clearly, multiple suppliers, extra inventory, spare capacity, added workers, and low utilization can help a company recover quickly from a disruption. But the enormous productivity gains of the last quarter of the twentieth century were based, in large part, on lean manufacturing and lean supply chain operations—doing more with less. Just-in-time inventory management freed capital tied up in safety stock; outsourcing of manufacturing was used to create flexibility to ramp production up and down; auction methods were used to whipsaw suppliers against each other in pursuit of the lowest costs; and employment rolls were cut as information technology fueled a surge in productivity.

Such lean operations, however, also created brittleness in supply chains. With no redundancy to fall back on, operations can shut down quickly once a disruption takes place. Hence, a tight supply chain, by itself, may be an indication of danger; when too many "redundant" employees are let go, when capacity utilization is "too high," and when procurement is focused on a single supplier, risk management alarms should go off. This does not mean that the processes should change or that decisions should be reversed, just that the company should be aware of the risk and plan for it.

In many cases, limited operational redundancies, or surpluses, make sense, since they give a disrupted company some "breathing room" to keep operating while looking for a permanent solution. As a long-term strategy, however, surpluses are expensive. Their cost, in fact, is higher than the straightforward direct expense; the major insight from the adoption of lean manufacturing and supply chain methods is that product quality and service to customers are all significantly higher under lean operations. The real hidden cost of abandoning lean business processes is that quality and service are likely to deteriorate, leading to lost sales.

In one area of operations, however—information technology—there is little doubt that redundancy is the preferred approach. Most modern corporations depend on their information technology infrastructure. Fortunately, once that infrastructure is built, the cost of redundancy, including back-up sites, back-up data, and back-up applications, is relatively small.

Designing Resilient Supply Chains

Instead of relying solely on supply chain redundancy and its inevitable costs, a well-managed firm should develop resilience, by building flexibility that can be used to "bounce back" from disruptions, even with limited redundancy. Instead of being a dead weight on the company,[5] flexibility is a clear and present asset when managing daily problems of matching supply and demand. To this end, one should look for relevant ideas at companies in highly uncertain demand industries such as computers, consumer electronics, and fashion.

Because short component and product life cycles, as well as fickle consumers, make for difficult forecasting challenges, leading companies in these industries adopt agile supply chain designs. They use risk pooling, so that parts, subassemblies, and products can be moved from surplus areas to deficit areas. They shorten the time to the market by using postponement and build-to-order methods, thus committing to a specific product only when the demand is better known or even certain (in the case of build-to order). They share data and collaborate extensively in times of product introduction and promotions (when demand is most difficult to predict). They engineer their products so that each part can be used in many products, creating parts interchangeability and reducing the total number of different parts. And they maximize the use of standard parts, rather than custom-made and engineered-to-order parts, so that these parts can be procured from many sources.

On a basic level, supply chain design involves relationships with suppliers on one hand and customers on the other. When choosing vendors, companies have to align their procurement strategy with their choice of suppliers. Many companies believe in working with a single supplier for each part or family of parts. Such "single sourcing" strategy is viable if it is accompanied by deep partnership with that supplier, since that supplier becomes as crucial to the company as its own manufacturing capacity. Staying away from close relationships and continuous monitoring of suppliers is also a viable approach, but it requires multiple vendors and the ability to move the procurement from one to another.

Clearly, strong relationships with customers are an important asset in terms of managing disruption risk. If major customers "stick with the company" during a disruption, that can send a vote of confidence to other customers and the financial markets and give the company more time to recover.

Investing in People and Culture
Sometimes the trite is true: The most important assets of most companies are their employees. Cross-training and shifting assignments help people understand the operations of large organizations. It also means that there are many employees who can perform each job—a capability that can be used both during disruptions and during peak times.

Communicating with employees on a strategic level (regarding the mission and the strategy of the company), a tactical level (the main hurdles and main initiatives this quarter and this month), and an operational level (the current status of the production, shipments, cash flow, inventories, and commitments) keeps everybody "on the same page." Coupled with empowering employees to take actions when necessary, such extensive communications allow them to contribute efficiently to flexible operations.

A large part of investment in people involves training. Teams trained to morph quickly as the rules of the game change respond better not only to demand fluctuations, but also to unexpected disruptions. In the context of disruption management, hectic environments may actually condition an organization to manage disruptions well. Examples include Zara's continuously changing product designs, Dell's stretch goals, and UPS's continuously exposed operations. These environments help "sensitize" employees to the demands imposed by high-impact disruptions.

In addition, many companies invest significant amounts in specific disruption training—developing and practicing emergency processes as well as simulating disruptions so that employees can learn to react. Repeated exercises are hardly popular, but they can make a difference. Rick Rescorla, the vice president of corporate security at Morgan Stanley, was a decorated Vietnam veteran. After the 1993 World Trade Center bombing, he created an evacuation plan for the company that was exercised, often begrudgingly, many times by its employees. The plan was put into action on September 11, 2001, with Rick Rescorla helping 2,700 well-trained Morgan Stanley employees evacuate the towers. As a result, only six Morgan Stanley employees perished that day. Unfortunately, Rick Rescorla was one of them.

In addition, such training aims to "socialize" security and resilience so that all employees are conditioned to notice and respond to threatening situations. It also brings security and resilience to managers' attention so they are a part of any decision-making process.

Finally, highly flexible organizations seem to exhibit a culture characterized by passion for the work and the company. Such culture means that employees are treated with respect and are given information and training, yet they are expected to go beyond the call of duty and "go through walls" to achieve corporate goals.

Such attitudes not only characterize high-performing organizations in general, they are likely to be the difference between making it or not making it during a disruption.

Building the Business Case

This book does not suggest a new fundamental terminology, original algorithms, or new processes. Rather, its primary message is a two-sided coin: The best way to achieve supply chain resilience is to create flexibility; flexible companies are top marketplace performers on a day-to-day basis.

The good news is that this introduces a framework for creating the business case for change. One of the difficulties in dealing with the risks of disruptions is that it is not easy to measure the economic benefits of cost avoidance, since avoided disruptions do not show up as revenues, costs, profits, assets, or in any other form on the company's financial statements; only the costs associated with disruption avoidance show up. Consequently, it is difficult to develop and justify the business case for avoiding and mitigating disruptions—particularly those that are difficult to pinpoint—even though there is a definite likelihood that they will occur.

The approach for justifying such investments should be twofold:

Security investments should be justified both by their contribution to *avoiding* disruptions (even when not all the benefits can be quantified) and by the collateral benefits they provide.

Resilience investments should be primarily justified by their contribution to flexibility—creating a competitive advantage for the company.

Security Investment Justification

The return on security investments comes from the following separate but inter-related sources:

Insurance Security investments constitute true insurance. First, they are there to prevent a loss rather than compensate for it. Second, while insurance payments may cover financial losses, they rarely cover the loss of customer confidence and tarnished reputations. Furthermore, many insurers have raised substantially the costs of terror insurance and in some markets it is not available at all. Consequently, it may be more cost-effective to invest in avoidance than in financial insurance.[6]

Cost Avoidance   To demonstrate the value of investments in security and disruption avoidance, companies should benchmark others in their industry and related industries. While such benchmarking may not be relevant to low-probability/high-impact disruptions, detection and security measures are likely to deter or minimize even minor, more common disruptions such as pilfering, counterfeiting, gray market diversions, warranty fraud, and minor embezzlements. A cross-company comparison of security investments vs. disruption frequency will often demonstrate that security investments do yield benefits that outweigh the investments' costs. At the same time such benchmarking can provide a gauge of how much should be invested.

Operational Speed   With the United States and other countries instituting stringent security measures, companies that choose not to upgrade their security and not comply with voluntary standards are likely to find their shipments spending more time going through ports and customs. Companies operating time-sensitive supply chains, such as The Limited and Seagate, do not require any other justification for joining C-TPAT, certifying their suppliers for security, and upgrading their own.[7]

Public Responsibility   With most of the infrastructure in the United States, and more and more in Europe and Japan, now held in private hands, companies have a societal responsibility to protect their assets and operations, not only for their own sake, but for society's sake—avoiding the loss of products, services, and jobs that people depend on. As disruptions and terrorism may become more prevalent throughout the world, companies are likely to be required to demonstrate that they have taken every reasonable precaution to avoid a disruption, even if it is the result of a terrorist act. The public and the political desire to find scapegoats after the fact—already evident in product failure cases, the 9/11 commission, and medical malpractice suits—is likely to assert itself in the aftermath of terrorist acts as well; executives may have to answer to orphans, grieving spouses, ruined investors, and their lawyers regarding the actions taken and actions not taken.[8]

Some companies consider their safety and security processes as a competitive advantage, and will not share them. Alan Fletcher, group manager of global operations and investigations for Target Stores said: "You can't help but realize that this [security] is a competitive advantage. It's not a lead weight around somebody's neck. It actually does give us some advantage over our competition."[9] According to Rick Dufour, GM's associate administrator for Executive Protection and member of its Global Security Staff, General Motors has developed a set of metrics for use in managing security. Despite outside interest GM does not sell those metrics to companies who learn about it through benchmarking, since GM regards its security management practices as a competitive advantage.[10]

Resilience Investment Justification

Some investments in preparedness should be taken because their cost is relatively low and they can provide immense benefit in case of disruptions. Most companies already invest in redundant information technology infrastructure and back up their data, applications, and processes frequently.

Going beyond business continuity planning, this book argues that security has to be built into the enterprise, following the practices used for safety and quality management, rather than added after the fact. The point is even more compelling when the challenge is to build in resilience, since that requires building flexibility (rather than increased redundancy) into the organization.

Building flexibility not only requires participation from all parts of the firm, it may require fundamental changes in the ways the firm conducts its business. These include product and process redesign, as well as a certain style of leadership and culture. But even more modest changes such as standardization of parts or a reduction in the number of elements used in products will increase the firm's resilience.

The value of increased resilience may be difficult to measure directly. But the general business benefits of flexibility show up in better matching of product availability with demand patterns, leading to lower costs and higher customer service at the same time. Similarly, operational improvements such as production monitoring and shipment visibility systems increase detection sensitivity, allowing managers to anticipate and even avoid disruptions. They also improve day-to-day flexibility to respond to demand changes.

The need to build more flexibility into supply chain operations has been increasing continuously over the last decade or two, mainly because of the increased uncertainty about demand for products. Some of the reasons for the increased uncertainty, which makes forecasting so challenging, include:

- the explosion in the varieties of most products—meaning that each is sold in relatively low quantities, not allowing for risk pooling

- the shortening of product life-cycles—so that new products with little history are continuously introduced into the marketplace

- increasing customer expectations—requiring high availability of product, while tougher competition in most markets drives prices down

- globalization—leading to increased supply lead times and long distribution networks

- information and communications connectivity, which introduces positive correlations across global markets.

Businesses constantly explore the building of supply chains that can respond to such uncertainty. U.S. automobile companies, for example, have benchmarked their operations against Dell, rather than against each other, in their quest to move to a build-to-order system for automobiles.

The volatility of demand is not the only reason to build in flexibility. Supply (and other) disruptions are also becoming more common as a result of the increased length and complexity of global supply chains, coupled with geopolitical tensions. But as companies move to build flexibility in order to respond to demand and supply volatility, they are also building in resilience.

Because of the dual nature of such investments, specific resilience projects should be made with an eye toward increasing flexibility and agility. For example, when considering an extra supplier in order to mitigate the risk inherent in sole-sourcing, it is advantageous to add a different *type* of supplier, creating a "portfolio" of different suppliers rather than just duplicating capabilities. A low-cost offshore supplier may be supplemented with a local supplier that has reactive capacity and can respond quickly to market changes. Such capacity can supplement the offshore supplier not only when that supplier is disrupted but also during volatile periods such as new product introduction and during the phasing out of products.

Thus, important investments in security and resilience are often the same investments that companies should be making in any case. Putting an emphasis on increasing resilience may simply accelerate investments in projects that would be beneficial for reducing costs and improving customer service.

Getting Ready

An important activity that should allow companies to respond quickly and even benefit from a disruption (in the sense that they may be able to respond before their competitors do and control the information flows) is the preparation of disruption response centers. Companies such as Intel and General Motors operate central as well as regional "crisis centers" or "emergency centers" whose function is to collect intelligence for disruption avoidance and to coordinate the response in case a disruption takes place. A large part of these centers' function, in case of a disruption, is to find out the facts and to be able to communicate to the outside world the company's version of events and its recovery actions. Having accurate, up-to-date information and being ready to communicate it will increase the confidence of customers and suppliers that the company is on top of events.

Making Lemonade

Many of the characteristics that make for successful firms in today's uncertain marketplace are the same characteristics that make them resilient. The same advanced supply chain designs that let companies respond flexibly to demand and supply fluctuations also help them react decisively to disruptions. The same corporate culture that allows them to succeed in a tightly competitive environment can be counted on to encourage employees to rise to the challenge posed by a disruption. And the same collaborative, risk-sharing relationships with trading partners that allow companies to move faster into new markets and introduce new products ahead of the competition are likely to be the source of strength and recovery resources in the aftermath of a disruption.

Security and resilience efforts can generate significant "collateral benefits," helping avoid pilferage, tightening processes, and increasing flexibility. In a different realm, discussions about security and resilience can serve as a common ground between labor and management, among competitors, and between the private and public sectors. Such discussions can bring about benefits in cooperative relationships that extend beyond safety and security.

But even when a disruption takes place, prepared and resilient companies may be in a position to take advantage of the situation and turn the disruption into an opportunity. Such companies can use a disruption to demonstrate to their stakeholders (in particular their customers and the financial community) their resilience and ability to bounce back quickly. When a disruption hits many companies at once, or affects a whole region, prepared companies may be able to take advantage of the reduction in market capacity to enter new markets and serve new customers; they may be able to help other companies in trouble, thereby cementing long-term partnerships; and they can use the opportunity to demonstrate to the communities in which they operate their commitment and good will.

* * *

Thinking about what can go wrong is unpleasant for most people. In particular, mulling the idea that others would want to harm and destroy the place they work for, the communities they live in, and the society they are part of, is no one's idea of fun. The normal human tendency to see the world as we want it to be, rather than as it is, stands in the way of preparedness.

But thinking about disasters as opportunities and using disaster preparedness to increase resilience are the essence of making lemonade from lemons. Enhanced security measures that lead to tightened processes, and the advantages of flexible supply chains, create the case for directing corporate attention to and investing in resilience. The advantage of creating resilience is that unlike the important activities of security enhancements and business continuity planning, resilience does not start with analysis of specific threats. Instead, it is a characteristic that gives enterprise buoyancy in the wake of *any* disruption, increasing its day-to-day flexibility to respond to a world that is changing fast and becoming ever less certain.

Notes

Chapter One

1. Shea Andersen, "Fire Costs Company Millions," *New Mexico Business Weekly*, August 4, 2000.

2. Ibid.

3. Cleanrooms are categorized into six classes. These classes are specified in the Federal Standard 209E, *Airborne Particulate Cleanliness Classes in Clean Rooms and Clean Zones*, September 11, 1992. Retrieved October 8, 2004, from www.aeg-idea.com/Federal_Standard_209.pdf

4. A. Latour, "Trial by Fire: A Blaze in Albuquerque Sets off Major Crisis for Cell-Phone Giants," *Wall Street Journal*, January 29, 2001, p. A1.

5. Andersen, "Fire Costs Company Millions."

6. Latour, "Trial by Fire."

7. Randy Starr, Jim Newfrock and Michael Delurey, "Enterprise Resilience: Managing Risk in the Networked Economy," Booz Allen and Hamilton's Consultant Briefing, CIO.com. Retrieved September 10, 2004, from www2.cio.com/consultant/report2349.html

8. Amit Mukherjee, "Planning for an Ambiguous World," A Forrester Case Study, Forrester Research, March 2003.

9. Latour, "Trial by Fire."

10. Mukherjee, "Planning for an Ambiguous World."

11. Latour, "Trial by Fire."

12. A Philips senior executive described the flavor of the meeting to the author by saying that his CEO "was summoned" by Nokia executives and was told how things will progress from that point on.

13. Latour, "Trial by Fire."

14. Ibid.

15. Ibid.

16. Ibid.

17. Ibid.

18. Ibid.

19. Ibid.

20. Ibid.

21. Andersen, "Fire Costs Company Millions."

22. Royal Philips Electronics, *Annual Report 2001*. Retrieved October 8, 2004, from www.investor.philips.com/reports/01_AR/profile/semicond.htm

23. Andersen, "Fire Costs Company Millions."

24. Mukherjee, "Planning for an Ambiguous World."

25. Andersen, "Fire Costs Company Millions."

26. Ibid.

27. Latour, "Trial by Fire."

28. The company first announced on January 26, 2001, that it will no longer manufacture handsets and outsourced all its manufacturing to Flextronics Inc. and then announced the Sony joint venture three months later. See Martyn Williams, "Sony, Ericsson Eye Cell Phone Joint Venture," *CNN.com SCI-TECH*, April 20, 2001. Retrieved October 8, 2004, from www.cnn.com/2001/TECH/industry/04/20/sony.ericsson.headsets.idg/

29. Latour, "Trial by Fire."

30. Dan Gearino, "Telephone Line Damage in Eagan Shuts Down Northwest Airlines," *Dakota County Tribune, Thisweek Online*. Posted 3/24/00. Retrieved October 12, 2004, from www.thisweek-online.com/index.html

31. stats.bls.gov/cpi/

32. Tom Andel, "Material Handling in Troubled Times: Will Logistics Save the Day?" *Material Handling & Warehousing*, December 1, 2002.

33. Greg Ip, "As Security Worries Intensify, Companies See Efficiencies Erode," *Wall Street Journal*, September 24, 2001, pp. A1, A14.

Chapter Two

1. "Earthquake Facts and Statistics," *Earthquake Hazards Program, U.S. Geological Survey*. Retrieved September 13, 2004, from neic.usgs.gov/neis/eqlists/eqstats.html

2. Richard L. Arnold, "The Kobe Quake," *Disaster Recovery Journal, Special Report*, 1995. Retrieved September 13, 2004, from www.drj.com/special/quake95.html

3. "The January 17, 1995 Kobe Earthquake: An EQE Summary Report, April 1995." Retrieved September 13, 2004, from www.eqe.com/publications/kobe/lifeline.htm

4. Paul Somerville, "The January 17, 1995 Hyogo Ken Nanbu (Kobe) Earthquake, Geoscience and Geotechnical Aspects." Retrieved September 13, 2004, from www.ce.berkeley.edu/Programs/Geoengineering/research/Kobe/Somerville/qnews.html

5. John N. Louie, "What Is Richter Magnitude?" Nevada Seismology Center, 1996. Retrieved September 13, 2004, from www.seismo.unr.edu/ftp/pub/louie/class/100/magnitude.html

6. Nick Cumming-Bruce and Campbell Robertson, "Most Powerful Quake in 40 Years Triggers Death and Destruction," *New York Times*, December 26, 2004. Retrieved December 30, 2004, from www.nytimes.com/2004/12/26/international/asia/26cnd-quak.html?oref=login

7. quake.wr.usgs.gov/info/1906/intensity.html, retrieved April 17, 2004.

8. neic.usgs.gov/neis/eq_depot/usa/1964_03_28.html, retrieved April 17, 2004.

9. Linda Lynton, "Capacity Planning for the 21st Century," SupplyChainBrain.com, 1997. Retrieved September 13, 2004, from www.glscs.com/archives/8.97.capacity.htm?adcode=75

10. John Nevola, "The Shock Heard 'Round the World,'" *Disaster Recovery Journal, Special Report*, 1995. Retrieved September 13, 2004, from www.drj.com/special/quake95.html

11. "Kobe Port's April Imports Top ¥200 billion," *Kansai Window* 3, no. 90 (May 28, 1996). Retrieved September 13, 2004, from www.kippo.or.jp/KansaiWindowHtml/News/1996–e/19960528_NEWS.HTML

12. Cole H. Emerson, "The Kobe Earthquake: Assessing Your Risk," DisasterResource.com, 2003. Retrieved September 13, 2004, from www.disasterresource.com/articles/kobe_eq_emerson.shtml

13. Christopher B. Pickett, "Strategies for Maximizing Supply Chain Resilience: Learning From the Past to Prepare for the Future," Master of Engineering in Logistics thesis, Massachusetts Institute of Technology, Cambridge, Mass., June 2003.

14. Nevola, "The Shock Heard 'Round The World.'"

15. Emerson, "The Kobe Earthquake."

16. This is much less of an issue today as Limited Brands routes a smaller fraction of the shipments through its central distribution center.

17. Debra Elkins, "Managing Uncertainty for High-Impact/Low-Probability Disruptions," a presentation in *The New Frontier for Managing Supply Network Uncertainty*, A Conference sponsored by the Stanford GSM Forum and MIT Center for Transportation and Logistics, Cambridge, Mass., December 3–4, 2003. The chart also appears in Debra Elkins, "A Framework for Business

Interruption Risk Analysis," an unpublished GM Research lab paper. There, the author refers to a related chart in a paper by Michael Zea, "Is Airline Industry Risk Unmanageable?" *Mercer on Travel and Transport*, Fall 2002/Winter 2003, pp. 21–26.

18. Elkins interview with the MIT project team, May 2004.

19. "Steel Shortage Hits Nissan Plants," BBC News, November 25, 2004. Retrieved November 26, 2004, from news.bbc.co.uk/2/hi/business/4041031.stm

20. R. O'Harrow, Jr., and A. E Cha, "Internet Worm Unearths New Holes," *Washington Post*, p. A01, January 29, 2003. A detailed description of the virus and many more references are given in Reshma Lensing, "Historical Events and Supply Chain Disruption: Chemical, Biological, Radiological and Cyber Events," Master of Engineering in Logistics thesis, June 2003, Massachusetts Institute of Technology, Cambridge, Mass.

21. Nancy Giges, "New Tylenol Package in National Press Debut," *Advertising Age Magazine*, November 15, 1982.

22. See the twin articles in the *New York Times*: Tamar Lewin, "Tylenol Posts an Apparent Recovery," *New York Times*, December 24, 1982; and Tamar Lewin, "Tylenol Maker Finding New Crisis Less Severe," *New York Times*, February 12, 1986.

23. Mark L. Mitchell, "The Impact of External Parties on Brand-Name Capital: The 1982 Tylenol Poisonings and Subsequent Cases," *Economic-Inquiry* 27, no. 4 (October 1989): 601–618.

24. Dan Ackman, "Tire Trouble: The Ford-Firestone Blowout," Forbes.com, June 6, 2001. Retrieved October 6, 2004, from www.forbes.com/2001/06/20/tireindex.html

25. Elkins interview with the MIT project team, May 2004.

Chapter Three

1. MIC is a colorless liquid in temperatures up to 44°C (111°F). It reacts violently with water and is highly flammable. It decomposes upon heating and produces toxic gases like hydrogen cyanide, nitrogen oxides, and carbon monoxides. See, for example: www.chm.bris.ac.uk/webprojects2002/tan/methyl_isocyanate.htm

2. "Bhopal Accident," *Corrosion Doctor*. Retrieved October 4, 2004, from www.corrosion-doctors.org/Pollution/bhopal.htm.

3. "Bhopal Disaster," *The Trade & Environment Database Case Studies*. Retrieved October 4, 2004, from www.american.edu/TED/bhopal.htm

4. David Weir, *The Bhopal Syndrome: Pesticides, Environment, and Health* (San Francisco: Sierra Club Books, 1987).

5. Jamie Cassels, *The Uncertain Promise of Law: Lessons From Bhopal* (Toronto: University of Toronto Press, 1993).

6. James R. Phimister, Ulku Oktem, Paul R. Kleindorfer, and Howard Kunreuther, "Near-Miss Incident Management in the Chemical Process Industry," *Risk Analysis* 23, no. 3 (2003): 445–459.

7. Diane Vaughan, *The Challenger Launch Decision: Risk Technology, Culture and Deviance at NASA* (Chicago: University of Chicago Press, 1996).

8. "The Columbia Accident Investigation Report," *Columbia Accident Investigation Board*. 2003. Retrieved October 4, 2004, from www.caib.us/news/report/default.html

9. "The Train Collision at Landbroke Grove 5 October 1999," A report of the HSE investigation, Health and Safety Executive, 2000. Retrieved October 4, 2004, from www.hse.gov.uk/railways/ladbrokegrove.htm

10. Lord W. D. Cullen, "The Ladbroke Grove Mail Inquiry," Her Majesty's Stationary Office, Norwich, UK. 2000.

11. "The Morton International Explosion," *Investigation Digest*, U.S. Chemical Safety and Hazard Investigation Board, August 2000. Retrieved October 4, 2004, from www.csb.gov/completed_investigations/docs/mortondigest.pdf

12. "Firestone and Ford Place Blame," December 19, 2000, CBS News. Retrieved October 16, 2004, from www.cbsnews.com/stories/2000/12/06/national/main255111.shtml

13. Sara Nathan, "More People Die Despite Recall," *USA Today*, 11/03/00. Retrieved October 15, 2004, from www.usatoday.com/money/consumer/autos/mauto774.htm

14. The Decatur plant was subsequently closed in July 2001. See "Firestone Closing Decatur Plant," *CBSNews.com*, July 27, 2001. Retrieved October 4, 2004, from cbsnews.cbs.com/stories/2001/06/27/national/main298685.shtml

15. The shoulder pocket is the spot where the tread and wall of the tire meet. The design of the pocket caused tires to be prone to cracking, which may have led to tread failure.

16. See, for example, www.ibiblio.org/expo/soviet.exhibit/chernobyl.html

17. An account of the accident and many sources are given by The Wikipedia. Retrieved December 1, 2004, from en.wikipedia.org/wiki/Chernobyl_accident

18. Reactor Bolshoi Moschnosti Kanalynyi, which means "Channelized Large Power Reactor." Seventeen of them were built throughout the Soviet union.

19. Ross Visscher maintains a web site shedding light on the accident, the factors leading to it and its aftermath. The site was accessed on December 1, 2004, at www.chernobyl.co.uk/

20. This letter can be accessed from the site maintained by Ross Visscher (see prior note).

21. "Near Miss (Aircraft)." Definition retrieved October 4, 2004, from usmilitary.about.com/library/glossary/n/bldef04276.htm

22. This figure follows approximately the safety pyramid suggested by Frank E. Bird, George L. Germain, and F. E. Bird Jr., *Loss Control Management: Practical Loss Control Leadership*, rev. ed., Det Norske Veritas (U.S.A.), Inc., 4th ed., August 1996. The lowest stratum in the figure was suggested by Phimister et al. (see note 6).

23. Phimister et al., "Near-Miss Incident Management in the Chemical Process Industry."

24. The NTSB database can be publicly accesses at www.ntsb.gov/ntsb/query.asp

25. Investigation reports are publicly available at www.csb.gov/index.cfm

26. See, for example, www.epa.gov/region08/community_resources/ppt/pptrmp.html

27. This figure is taken from Michael L. Branick, "Tornadoes in the Oklahoma City, Oklahoma Area Since 1890," National Weather Service Forecast Office, Norman, Oklahoma, February 2000. Retrieved on October 5, 2004, from www.nwsnorman.noaa.gov/tornadodata/okc_main.html

28. Tornado strength in figure 3.3 is depicted on the Fujita ("F") scale which is based on damage intensity (with F=0 being negligible damage and F=6 "inconceiveable" damage). See, for example, www.tornadoproject.com/fscale/fscale.htm (retrieved February, 7, 2005).

29. Michael L. Branick, "Tornadoes in the Oklahoma City, Oklahoma Area Since 1890."

30. The best known of these rank-size rules was first popularized for cities, word frequencies, and income distributions by G. K. Zipf, "Human Behavior and The Principles of Least Effort" (Reading, Mass.: Addison Wesley, 1949).

31. H.W. Heinrich, "Industrial Accident Prevention: A Scientific Approach" (New York: McGraw-Hill, 1959).

32. Bird, Germain, and Bird, *Loss Control Management.*

33. The U.S Occupational Safety and Health Administration (OHSA) has issued PSM regulations and the Environmental Protection Agency has issued requirements for accident prevention. Many companies, such as DuPont, go beyond the minimum required in the regulations when setting their processes and procedures.

34. Copyright 2004, E. I. Du Pont de Nemours & Company.

35. "Could a Dock Strike Cripple Britain?" *Independent*, August 10, 2004. Retrieved October 4, 2004, from news.independent.co.uk/business/analysis_and_features/story.jsp?story=549894

36. "When Employees Strike Public Relations Must Have a Strong Message: Picket Line Turmoil, Political Pressure, as Hospital Negotiated with 1199," *Medical News*, Special Report, 2004. Retrieved November 4, 2004, from www.medicalnewsreport.com/xstrikes.htm#ri

37. "Greenpeace Activists Sabotage GE Wheat Trial in Germany," *Reuters Securities News (Eng)*, April 9, 2003. Retrieved October 4, 2004, from www.organicconsumers.org/ge/germany041103.cfm

38. A general report on the strike was retrieved October 5, 2004, from: www.cnn.com/WORLD/9511/france_strike/. The site of the International Workers Bulletin (retrieved October 5, 2004) mentions some of the tactics employed, www.wsws.org/public_html/prioriss/iwb12–4/france.htm

39. Mike Allen, "President to Drop Tariffs on Steel," *Washington Post*, December 1, 2003.

40. The material in this subsection follows R. Lensig, "Historical Events and Supply Chain Disruption: Chemical, Biological, Radiological and Cyber Events," Master of Engineering in Logistics thesis, May 9, 2003, Massachusetts Institute of Technology, Cambridge, Mass.

41. F. Caldwell, R. Hunter, and J. Bace, "'Digital Pearl Harbor' War Game Explores 'Cyber-terrorism,'" Gartner Research, E-17-6580. August 2002.

Chapter Four

1. "EU Bans British Meat," *BBC NEWS*, February 21, 2001. Retrieved October 6, 2004, from news.bbc.co.uk/1/hi/uk/1181444.stm

2. "Big Rise in New Cases of Foot-and-Mouth," BBC News *On This Day*, March 11, 2001.

3. The information is included in numerous reports issued by the Country Side Agency of the British government regarding the effects of the Foot and Mouth Disease on the British economy. See, for example, www.countryside.gov.uk/WhoWeAreAndWhatWeDo/pressCentre/state_aug_2001.asp (retrieved October 14, 2004) and many other related reports on the site: www.countryside.gov.uk/index.htm

4. "Travel Firms Hit by Farm Disease," *BBC News Online*, April 12, 2001. Retrieved October 6, 2004, from news.bbc.co.uk/1/hi/business/1273482.stm

5. "FMD Report: Outbreak's Economic Impact," *BBC News*, August 29, 2001.

6. "Farm Crisis 'Body Blow' to Tourist Industry," *Ananova*, June 8, 2001. Retrieved October 6, 2004, from www.ananova.com/business/story/sm_320820.html

7. Iain Anderson, "Foot and Mouth 2001: Lessons to Be Learned Inquiry Report," *Inquiry Report HC888*, July 22, 2002. Retrieved October 6, 2004, from http://213.121.214.218/fmd/report/index.htm

8. Guna Selvaduray, "Effect of the Kobe Earthquake on Manufacturing Industries," SEMI (the high technology forum for material suppliers), San Jose State University, March 2003. Retrieved September 13, 2004, from www2.sjsu.edu/faculty/selvaduray/page/recent/EffectOfTheKobeEarthquake.pdf

9. The Pacific Maritime Association (PMA) negotiates and administers maritime labor agreements with the International Longshore and Warehouse Union (ILWU). The membership of the PMA consists of American flag operators, foreign flag operators, and stevedore and terminal companies that operate in California, Oregon, and Washington ports.

10. Andrea Shalal-Esa, "U.S.A: Bush Intervenes in Port Lockout," *Corp Watch*, October 7, 2002. Retrieved October 6, 2004, from www.corpwatch.org/news/PND.jsp?articleid=4308

11. Doug Desjardins, "Effects of West Coast Port Lockout Expected to Linger," *DSN Retailing Today*, October 28, 2002. Retrieved October 5, 2004, from www.findarticles.com/cf_dls/m0FNP/20_41/93917318/p1/article.jhtml

12. Gary Gentile, "Retailers' Christmas Wish: End Import Backlog at Ports," *Times Herald-Record*, October 28, 2002. Retrieved October 5, 2004, from www.recordonline.com/archive/2002/10/28/portbusy.htm

13. Gary Gentile, "Backlog at West Coast Ports Still Maddens Merchants, Exporters," AP Business wire, retrieved October 18, 2004, from: www.detnews.com/2002/business/0210/28/business-622769.htm

14. Chris Isidore, "Bite of Port Lockout to Be Felt Soon," *CNN/Money*, September 30, 2002. Retrieved October 5, 2004, from money.cnn.com/2002/09/30/news/economy/port_impact/

15. Pia Sarkar, Matthew Yi, and *Chronicle* Staff Writers, "Export Industry Fears Disaster/Port Lockout Comes at Peak Shipping Season," *San Francisco Chronicle*. October 1, 2002. Retrieved October 5, 2004, from www.sfgate.com/cgi-bin/article.cgi?file=/chronicle/archive/2002/10/01/BU125656.DTL

16. For example, Dole lost at least $2.4 million from spoilage and higher transportation costs as of October 8.

17. The World Series is the American baseball championship which is decided by a series of the "best of seven games" between the two contenders: the pennant winner of the American League and the pennant winner of the National League. (The Boston Red Sox won it in 2004 after trying unsuccessfully for 86 years.)

18. Matthew Crowley, "Railroad Tackles Backlog of West Coast Cargo," *Las Vegas Review-Journal*. October 15, 2002.

19. "Bush Gives Board 24 Hours to Assess Lockout," *American City Business Journals Inc.*, October 7, 2002. Retrieved October 5, 2004, from www.labournet.net/docks2/0210/lockbush1.htm

20. CNN Saturday Morning News Show aired October 5, 2002. Transcript can be found at cnnstudentnews.cnn.com/TRANSCRIPTS/0210/05/smn.11.html. Last retrieved October 7, 2004.

21. A Morgan Stanley report estimated that if the lockout would have lasted a month, East Asia would have plunged into a recession. See: www.morganstanley.com/GEFdata/digests/20021003–thu.html.

22. B. Bower, "9/11's Fatal Road Toll: Terror Attacks Presaged Rise in U.S. Car Deaths," *Science News*, January 17, 2004. Retrieved October 5, 2004, from www.findarticles.com/p/articles/mi_m1200/is_3_165/ai_112943643.

23. Robert J. Lineback "Anadigics Expects Sales Drop Due to Fire Disrupting Wireless Customer," *Silicon Strategies*, September 15, 2000. Retrieved October 6, 2004, from www.siliconstrategies.com/showArticle.jhtml?articleID=10813843&_requested=87229

24. "Foot-and-Mouth Hits McDonald's," *BBC News*. April 19, 2001.

25. A special issue of the *Journal of Transportation and Statistics* was dedicated to the transportation effects of the Northridge earthquake. It was volume 1 number 2, May 1988, ISSN 1094–8848, published by the Bureau of Transportation Statistics at the U.S. Department of Transportation.

26. "Effects of Catastrophic Events on Transportation System Management and Operations, Northridge Earthquake, January 17, 1994," U.S. Department of Transportation, John A. Volpe National, Transportation Systems Center, Cambridge, Mass. Retrieved October 21, 2004, from www.itsdocs.fhwa.dot.gov/JPODOCS/REPTS_TE/13775.html

27. Steven Debban, "Innovative Traffic Management Following the 1994 Northridge Earthquake," Intelligent Transportation Systems Joint Program Office, August 9, 1995. Retrieved October 16, 2004, from www.itsdocs.fhwa.dot.gov/JPODOCS/REPTS_TE/1BJ01!

28. "Simi Valley Resident Named Metrolink's 35 Millionth Rider," *Metrolink News Update*, October 26, 1999. www.Metrolinktrains.com/news_update/detail.php?news_id=117565

29. "FedEx Announces Return to Normal Services," FedEx Archives—1997 Press Releases, August 2, 1997. Retrieved August 2004 from www.fedex.com/us/about/news/pressreleases/archives/pressrelease457076.html

30. Tim Ruel, "Isle Drivers Lining up for New Tires," *Honolulu Star-Bulletin*. September 1, 2000.

31. Jeff Plungis and Joe Miller, "Firestone Fires New Salvo at Ford," *The Detroit News*, May 24, 2001. Retrieved October 30, 2004, from www.detnews.com/2001/autos/0105/25/b01–227749.htm

32. Christine Tierney, "Goodyear: Still Spinning Its Wheels," *BusinessWeek*, May 28, 2003.

33. Timothy Aeppel, "How Goodyear Blew Its Chance to Capitalize on a Rival's Woes," *Wall Street Journal*, February 19, 2003, p. A1.

34. K. B. Hendricks, and V. R. Singhal, "How Supply Chain Glitches Torpedo Sharcholder Value," *Supply Chain Management Review* 6, no. 1 (January/February 2002): 18–24.

35. James B. Rice, Jr., and Federico Caniato, "Building a Secure and Resilient Supply Network," *Supply Chain Management Review*, September/October 2003.

Chapter Five

1. Vivian Baulch and Patricia Zacharias, "The Rouge Plant—The Art of Industry," *Detroit News*. Retrieved October 6, 2004, from info.detnews.com/history/story/index.cfm?id=189&category=business.

2. This example was suggested by Dr. George Kocur of the Civil and Environmental Engineering Department at MIT (personal communication).

3. John Magretta, "Fast, Global and Entrepreneurial: Supply Chain Management, Hong Kong Style," *Harvard Business Review*, September-October 1998.

4. Modern supply chain management includes the flow of returned and recycled goods, in which case the directions of the product and cash flows in figure 5.3 are reversed.

5. The January 31 issue of the *Economist* has credited Professor Hau Lee of Stanford University with this story in an article titled "Chain Reaction."

6. Hau L. Lee, V. Padmanabhan, and Seungjin Whang, "The Bullwhip Effect in Supply Chains," *Sloan Management Review* 38, no. 3 (Spring 1997): 93–102.

7. Janice Hammond, "Barilla SpA (A)," *Harvard Business School Case #9-694-046*, June 1994.

8. Ibid.

9. Melanie Ann Porter and Lance Dixon, *JIT II Revolution in Buying & Selling* (Newton, Mass.: Cahners, October 1, 1994).

Chapter Six

1. P. Kotler, *Marketing Management: Millennium Edition*, 10th ed. (Englewood Cliffs, N.J.: Prentice Hall, July 19, 1999).

2. Linda Loyd, "Wyeth to Close Lancaster County Plant," *Philadelphia Inquirer*, March 26, 2004. Retrieved October 10, 2004, from www.philly.com/mld/inquirer/business/8278698.htm

3. Flu vaccines have to be formulated anew every year because the flu strains change from year to year.

4. Michael Barbaro, "FluMist Offered Free to Public Health Agencies." *Washington Post*, January 21, 2004. Retrieved November 10, 2004, from www.washingtonpost.com/ac2/wp-dyn/A33882–2004Jan21

5. Oral testimony of Jim Young, president of research and development at Med-Immune, at the U.S. congressional hearing on government reform on October 8, 2004. Retrieved January 10, 2005, from reform.house.gov/UploadedFiles/MedImmune%20-%20Young%20Vaccine%20Testimony.pdf

6. Point forecasts are forecasts constituting a single number, such as the future sales of a given product in a region during a given month.

7. This statement assumes that the errors are independent of each other. When the errors are positively correlated the effect is diminished; when they are negatively correlated the effect is strong.

8. Jim Rice, "Supply Chain Response to Terrorism: Creating Resilient and Secure Supply Chains," Interim Report of Progress and Learning, Supply Chain Response to Terrorism Project, MIT Center for Transportation and Logistics, Cambridge, Mass., August 8, 2003.

9. Ibid.

10. Corey Billington and Blake Johnson, "Creating and Leveraging Options in the High Technology Supply Chain," *Journal of Applied Corporate Finance*, Winter 2003.

11. Customers of Volkswagen in Germany, where about 80 percent of new cars sold are built to the buyer's specification, would wait eight months or more for hot models.

12. Interestingly, while the system achieved Cadillac's goals for increased service and reduced costs, GM discontinued the program. GM's larger volume dealers did not support it because it leveled the playing field with small dealers; the main advantage of large dealers was the large on-hand inventory.

13. David Anderson, *Build-to-Order & Mass Customization, the Ultimate Supply Chain and Lean Manufacturing Strategy for Low-Cost On-Demand Production without Forecasts or Inventory* (Cambria, Calif.: CIM Press, 2002).

14. Peter Roberts, *Any Color so Long as It's Black: The First Fifty Years of Automobile Advertising* (New York: William Morrow and Co., 1976).

15. See, for example, Rajan Suri, *Quick Response Manufacturing: A Companywide Approach to Reducing Lead Times* (University Park, Ill.: Productivity Press, June 1, 1998).

16. A. Raman, M. Fisher, J. Hammond, and W. Obermeyer, "Making Supply Meet Demand in an Uncertain World," *Harvard Business Review*, May-June 1994.

17. Patrick Pawling, "Wal-Mart: Internet Business Leaders 2002," *iQ Magazine*. November/December 2002. Retrieved October 10, 2004, from www.pawling. net/walmart.html

18. The process was developed by the Voluntary Inter-industry Commerce Standards (VICS) Association (see www.vics.org).

19. The software engine used was the one developed by Syncra Systems Inc. of Watertown, Massachusetts. Syncra was acquired in 2004 by Retek Inc. of Minneapolis, Minnesota.

20. In practice, publishers credit book sellers for unsold books upon receiving proof of destruction of the merchandise. Typically, book sellers simply tear the front cover and send it to the publisher in order to get the credit.

21. Gerard Cachon and Martin Lariviere, "Turning the Supply Chain into a Revenue Chain," *Harvard Business Review*, March 2001.

22. The independent retailers did not participate in the revenue sharing arrangement mainly because many of them were not computerized and the studios had difficulties verifying the number of units rented.

Chapter Seven

1. For example, in October 2004 the retail price of a 3.4 gigabyte Pentium IV chip was $1,005–$1,379 on Shopping.com. The prices were retrieved October 9, 2004, from www.shopping.com/xPP-Processors-Pentium_4_Prices-price_range_600_30801

2. "Computer Chips Heist at Depot," *BBC*, January 13, 2003. Retrieved October 10, 2004, from news.bbc.co.uk/1/hi/england/2651297.stm

3. See articles:
- Robin Ajello, "Watch Out for Fishy Chips," *AsiaWeek*, October 25, 1996. Retrieved October 10, 2004, from www.asiaweek.com/asiaweek/96/1025/feat1.html
- Franck Moecke and Christine Persson, "Pentiums in the Baggage," *c't 1/97*. July 22, 1999, p. 18. Retrieved October 10, 2004, from www.heise.de/ct/english/97/01/018/
- Erich Luening, "Intel Files Counterfeit Chip Suit," *CNET News.com*, May 28, 1998. Retrieved October 10, 2004, from www.news.com/News/Item/0,4,22522,00.html
- "U.S. Customs Cracks Multi-Million Dollar Counterfeit Computer Components Smuggling Operation in Miami," U.S. Customs and Border Protection, pres release. October 22, 2002. Retrieved October 10, 2004, from www.cbp.gov/xp/cgov/newsroom/press_releases/archives/legacy/2002/102002/counterfeit_computer_1022.xml

4. Marcia Savage, "Software Tool to Check Processor Speeds," *Computer Reseller New*, March 15, 1999, pp. 6(1).

5. Andrew S. Grove, *Only the Paranoid Survive* (New York: Currency, 1996).

6. Many of the details in this section are taken from Stephen Flynn, *America the Vulnerable: How Our Government is Failing to protect us from Terrorism* (New York: Harper Collins, 2004). This section is also based on discussions with and the work of Lieutenant Abby Benson, of the Massachusetts Coast Guard, who was a student at the MIT logistics program from 2003 to 2005.

7. To understand the pre-9/11 mindset, note that Mohamed Atta, the commander of the group that took over the American Airlines flight out of Boston, was flagged for additional screening on the morning of 9/11 in Boston by a computerized prescreening system, but that meant only that the airline had to ensure that his checked bags were held off until it was confirmed that he boarded the

plane. In addition, two of the five attackers that boarded the United Airlines flight in Boston had trouble understanding the usual security questions asked by the ticket agent, who had to repeat the questions several times until the terrorists came up with the correct answers.

8. Megan Scott, Associated Press, "Fan Gets Jail Time for Airport Showdown." Retrieved December 1, 2004, from www.cbsnews.com/stories/2002/03/06/national/main503151.shtml

9. "Security Concerns Prompt LAX Showdown," Associated Press report. Retrieved on December 1 from www.foxnews.com/story/0,2933,131476,00.html

10. "Modeling Terrorism Risk for Business," Business Week Online, February 20, 2003. Retrieved October 20, 2005, from www.businessweek.com/bwdaily/dntflash/feb2003/nf20030220_5472_db049.htm

11. Reshma Lensing. "Historical Events and Supply Chain Disruption: Chemical, Biological, Radiological and Cyber Events," Master of Engineering in Logistics thesis, June 2003, Massachusetts Institute of Technology, Cambridge, Mass.

12. From the testimony of Diana Dean before the U.S. Senate Judiciary Subcommittee. Retrieved October 20, 2005, from judiciary.senate.gov/oldsite/21020dd.htm

13. For articles about El Al security, see for example:
- "Model for Air Travel Security May Be El Al," *CNN*, September 26, 2001. Retrieved October 10, 2004, from www.cnn.com/2001/WORLD/meast/09/26/rec.el.al.security/
- "El AL to Test Missile Defense System," *FOXnews.com*, April 22, 2004.
- "El Al Airlines Success," *Sanctum*, August 2002. Retrieved October 10, 2004, from www.sanctuminc.com/pdf/SuccessStory_ElAl.pdf
- "El Al 'Planted Gun on Passenger,'" *BBC News*, March 16, 2004. Retrieved February 27, 2005, from news.bbc.co.uk/2/hi/middle east/3517570.stm

14. Examples of how resources can be wasted rather than concentrated on the most threatening factors include pulling out former vice president Al Gore at Reagan National Airport in Washington in June 2002 for a random check. In fact, Midwest Express Airlines did it twice in one week. Furthermore, in March 2004, Senator Edward Kennedy of Massachusetts was stopped and questioned at American airports at least five times because his name appeared on the government's secret "no fly" list. It is safe to assume that even most Republicans do not consider the former vice president and the senior senator from Massachusetts, whose faces are familiar to most Americans, a security threat to airline operations.

15. At times young overzealous Israeli security officers invent their own procedures with questionable results. One young officer asked a visiting British priest to recite selected passages from the Old Testament by heart in order to prove his genuineness. As Nissim Malchi, Chief Financial Officer of El Al related the story to the author in June 2002, he sighed and said "There is another customer we lost for ever."

16. In essence, the fund placed bets that tiny deviations in the traditional relationships between the prices of various securities would eventually return to normal. What they did not fully appreciate was the liquidity risks involved—in other words, while the strategy was bound to work in the long term, short term market fluctuations could create losses which were larger than the company's reserves, which is what happened. The event was covered extensively—see for example a series of articles in the *New York Times* and the *Wall Street Journal*, September 25 through October 1, 1998.

17. Sarah Fister Gale, "Quaker Food and Beverage: Fighting Terrorism through Training," *Chief Learning Officer Magazine*, May 2003. Retrieved October 12, 2004, from www.clomedia.com/content/templates/clo_casestudies.asp?articleid=179&zoneid=9

18. Ibid.

19. MIT interview, September 21, 2004.

20. Personal communication with Dennis Lucket in November 2002.

21. Even from 1973 to 2001, the rate of industrial accidents (as reported in OSHA's Incident Rate of Occupational Injuries) in the United States fell from 10.5 per 100 workers per year to 5.4 per 100 workers.

22. Marv Foss, Joshua Williams, and Steve Roberts, "Case Study: Koch Refining uses Total Safety Culture Principles to Improve Safety." Retrieved December 3, 2004, from www.safetyperformance.com/kochcase.doc

23. Readers interested in safety culture can consult the excellent book by Karl Weick and Kathleen Sutcliff, *Managing the Unexpected: Assuring High Performance in the Age of Complexity*, University of Michigan Business School Management Series (San Francisco, Calif.: Jossey-Bass, 2001).

24. James Womack, Daniel Jones, and Daniel Roos, *The Machine That Changed the World: The Story of Lean Production* (New York: HarperCollins, 1991).

25. Bill Crosby, *Quality Is Free* (New York: McGraw-Hill, 1979).

26. The notion was suggested in Yossi Sheffi, "Supply Chain Management under the Threat of International Terrorism," *International Journal of logistics Management* 12, no. 2 (2002): 1–11. It was expanded on by Hau Lee and Michael Wolfe in "Supply Chain Security without Tears," *Supply Chain Management Review*, January/February 2003. Further expansion was offered by Hau Lee and Seungjim Whang Later in "Higher Supply Chain Security with Lower Costs: Lessons from Total Quality Management," research paper #1824, Stanford Graduate School of Business, 2003. Retrieved October 12, 2004, from gobi.stanford.edu/ResearchPapers/Library/RP1824.pdf

27. David Schwab, "Drug Industry Fights Back against Counterfeiters," *Newhouse News Service*, 2003.

28. Ibid.

29. This comment was made during a presentation at MIT in November 2001.

30. Jonathan Littman, "Thwarting the Perfect Crime," *Electronic Business*, April 4, 2003.

31. James N. Dertouzos, Eric V. Larson, and Patricia A. Ebener, *The Economic Costs and Implications of High-Technology Hardware Theft* (RAND, 1999). The report is available at www.rand.org/publications/MR/MR1070/

Chapter Eight

1. See www.tapaonline.org

2. "FSR Certification Requirements & Documents," Technology Asset Protection Agency. Retrieved October 10, 2004, from www.tapaonline.org/new/engl/fsr_certification.html

3. "Incident Information Service: TAPA EMEA Technology Asset Protection Association Europe (TAPA-EMEA)." Retrieved January 20, 2005, from www.tapaemea.com/engl/incident_information_service.html

4. See TAPA EMEA press release at www.tapaemea.com/download/news/press_releasemay2004.pdf

5. Ben Mezrich, *Bringing Down the House: The Inside Story of Six M.I.T. Students Who Took Vegas for Millions* (Free Press, September 9, 2003).

6. Adam Goldman. "Detective Firm for Casinos Uses Database to Net Cheats, Card Counters," *Associated Press*, January 11, 2004.

7. "Borgata Hotel Casino & Spa Turns to Visage to Enhance Gaming Security," *Business Wire*, September 23, 2003.

8. Paul Eng, "Keying in on Faces," *ABCNews.com*, July 6, 2001. Retrieved October 11, 2004, from www.saddleback.cc.ca.us/faculty/jclark/Computer/Prelim%20Face%20Articles/ABC%20news.doc

9. The story was related to the MIT research team by Don Patch of Gillette. It was uncovered during a transportation security benchmarking effort performed by Gillette.

10. Neil V. Gayle and Dave Anderson, "Materials Supply Chain Management Efforts at ISMT," *Semiconductor International*, March 1, 2003.

11. Now the Democratic Republic of Congo.

12. Interview with the MIT research team on October 1, 2004.

13. Markle Foundation, Task Force on National Security in the Information Age, "Creating a Trusted Network for Homeland Security," Second Report, December 2, 2003. Retrieved December 10, 2003, from www.markletaskforce.org/ This excellent report continues to outline a framework for sustainable information sharing between the government and the private sector.

14. Philip W. Spayd, "U.S. Customs Perspective," *Conference Report: Supply Chain Response to Terrorism-Planning for the Unexpected*, MIT Center for Transportation and Logistics, Cambridge, Mass., December 5, 2002.

15. To this day, the city of Halifax sends an annual Christmas tree to the city of Boston in gratitude for Massachusetts's help in money and volunteers after the explosion. The tree is lighted in a public ceremony on the Boston Common every Christmas evening with representatives of the Nova Scotia government present.

16. C-TPAT web site, www.customs.gov/xp/cgov/import/commercial_enforcement/ctpat/

17. Vivien S. Crea, "Maritime Supply Chain Safety-Operation Safe Commerce." *Conference Report: Supply Chain Response to Terrorism-Planning for the Unexpected*, MIT Center for Transportation and Logistics, Cambridge, Mass., December 5, 2002.

18. Deena Disreally, "Public-Private Partnerships: Security and Emergency Response Collaboration in a New Threat Environment," Master of Engineering in Logistics thesis, June 2004, Massachusetts Institute of Technology, Cambridge, Mass.

19. Fermin Cuza, "Business and Customs Partnership against Narcotics Smuggling," World Customs Organization, WCO Business Partnership, 1999. Retrieved October 3 from www.wcoomd.org/ie/En/Topics_Issues/WCOBusinessPartnership/1999/wco-eng.htm

20. Sarah D. Scalet, "Four Slow Steps to the Fast Lane," *CSO Magazine*, September 2003.

21. Spayd, "U.S. Customs Perspective."

22. Comments of CBP Commissioner Robert C. Bonner at the Center for Strategic and International Studies (CSIS), Transnational Threats Audit Conference on February 11, 2004. Retrieved February 9, 2005, from: www.customs.gov/xp/cgov/newsroom/commissioner/speeches_statements/mar03 2004.xml

23. FAST allows C-TPAT-qualified importers and carriers who use prescreened drivers to freely move low-risk cargos at selected border crossings between the United States and Canada and Mexico. Paperless customs forms and cargo release mechanisms in conjunction with border-side transponders let the importer receive pre-approval before the trucks even leave Canada or Mexico. They can then breeze through a special lane on the U.S. side.

24. "SST Smart and Secure Tradelanes to Extend Network Footprint to 5th Continent, Linking Africa with Europe, U.S., Asia, S. America," Strategic Council on Security Technology- Press Release, February 11, 2004. Retrieved October 10, 2004, from www.scst.info/releases/feb11.b_04.html

25. In 2004, the program involved over 65 partners such as terminal operators, carriers, service providers and shippers in a global information network for inter-

modal container security, covering 70 percent of the world's container port operations. SST uses the U.S. Department of Defense Total Asset Visibility (TAV) network for automatic data collection to aid tracking of containers, detection of potential threats, and identification of high-risk containers. The system is based on INMARSAT, which is a private operator of a constellation of geostationary satellites that extend mobile phone, fax and data communications to every part of the inhabited world. Support for this industry effort is also provided by the U.S. Trade and Development Agency, which aims to work with private trading partners to ensure that improved supply chain security facilitates, rather than hinders, global commerce.

26. The original SOLAS convention was developed in an international conference in London in 1914, following the Titanic disaster in 1912, in which 1,503 people lost their lives. It focused on means for avoiding collisions with icebergs and post-accident assistance. The convention was amended many times since then as new considerations, threats and technologies have evolved.

27. K. Linebaugh, R. Hindrati, S. Moffett, G. Parker, and C. Conkey, "Why Quake Warnings Failed. Hours After Indonesia Was Hit, Victims in Africa Had No Inkling," *Wall Street Journal*, December 29, 2004, p. B1.

28. P. McGeehan, "On Security Panel, Executives Think the Unthinkable," *New York Times*, September 22, 2002.

29. Compañía Sudamericana de Vapores (CSAV) is a Chilean publicly traded ocean carrier. In 2004 it was the largest ocean carrier in Latin America.

30. R. G. Edmonson, "If the Unthinkable Happens," *Journal of Commerce*, September 27, 2004, pp. 12–14.

31. Steve Flynn, *America the Vulnerable: How Our Government Is Failing to Protect Us from Terrorism* (New York: HarperCollins, 2004).

Chapter Nine

1. Ann H. Reid and Jeffery K Taubenberger, "The Origin of the 1918 Pandemic Influenza Virus: a Continuing Enigma," *Journal of general Virology Online*, no. 6, June 2003, www.socgenmicrobiol.org.uk/JGVDirect/19302/19302ft.htm

2. See several sources regarding the 1918 "Spanish Influenza" in dir.yahoo.com/Arts/Humanities/History/By_Time_Period/20th_Century/1918_Influenza_Pandemic/

3. Jim Duffy, "The Blue Death," Johns Hopkins Public Health, Fall 2004, www.jhsph.edu/PublicHealthNews/Magazine/prologues/index.html

4. Emma Young, "Dozens of Dialysis Deaths across Europe," *New Scientist*, October 16, 2001.

5. Keith H. Hammonds, "Harry Kraemer's Moment of Truth." *Fast Company*, no. 64, November 2002, p. 93. Retrieved October 11, 2004, from www.fastcompany.com/magazine/64/kraemer.html

6. "Baxter Sends Nephrologists to Croatia Following Reports of Hemodialysis Deaths." *RAPS, RA News*. Retrieved October 11, 2004, from www.raps.org/ s_raps/view.asp?CID=116&DID=18254

7. Young, "Dozens of Dialysis Deaths across Europe."

8. "Croatia Links Kidney Deaths to Machines. " *BBC News*, October 15, 2001. Retrieved October 11, 2004, from news.bbc.co.uk/1/hi/world/Europe/ 1600667.stm

9. Hammonds, "Harry Kraemer's Moment of Truth."

10. "Kidney and Urologic Diseases Statistics for the United States," National Kidney and Urologic Diseases Information Clearinghouse (NKUDIC). Retrieved October 11, 2004, from kidney.niddk.nih.gov/kudiseases/pubs/kustats/index.htm

11. The number of deaths in the United States from End Stage Renal Disease (ENRD) in 2001 was 76,584 (see, for example, kidney.niddk.nih.gov/ kudiseases/pubs/kustats/index.htm#5). Assuming four percent total population growth, no change in the disease and 365 days per year, the average daily death rate in 2005 will be around 218.

12. For purposes of exposition, these calculations assume that the death rate follows a Poisson process.

13. ISO 10993 is a set of harmonized standards that address the biological evaluation of medical devices, developed by the International Standards Organization (ISO). Cytotoxicity is the quality of being poisonous to cells; intracutaneous reactivity test is the standard protocol for determining a medical device's potential for causing irritation; hemolysis refers to the breakdown of red blood cells— some diseases and toxin (and some treatments) can cause premature breakdown of red blood cells.

14. "Baxter Urges Comprehensive Scientific Analysis of Hemodialysis Treatment Safety," *Baxter, News Releases*, October 15, 2001. Retrieved October 11, 2004, from   www.baxter.com/about_Baxter/news_room/news_releases/2001/10–15 croatia.html

15. Statement of Julie L. Gerberding, director of the Centers for Disease Control and Prevention in testimony Before the Subcommittee on Labor, Health, and Human Services, Education, and Related Agencies, Committee on Appropriations, United States House of Representatives, April 28, 2004.

16. Diedtra Henderson, "CDC to Watch Flu Remedy Sales for Spike," AP News. Retrieved December 12, 2004, from news.orb6.com/stories/ap/20041107/ flu_season.php

17. See, for example, "DNA fingerprint techniques may help identify bioterror agents—Pathogen Detection," OBGYN.net, Reprieved October 10th from www.obgyn.net/newsheadlines/headline_medical_news-Pathogen_Detection-20030331–8.asp. A detection algorithm was announced by researchers at the University of Pittsburgh and Carnegie Mellon University. See, for example, www.bizuournals.com/pittsburgh/stories/2002/12/02/daily10.html, retrieved in

October 2004. There are numerous similar announcements of hardware and software detection tools for bioterror.

18. "9/11 Commission: The FAA Got 52 Warnings in 6 Months," The Associated Press, February 10, 2005. Retrieved February 10, 2005, from www.nytimes.com/aponline/national/AP-Sept-11-FAA.html

19. "Stored Value Systems/COMDATA Case Study," *Insession Technologies*, November 2003. Retrieved October 11, 2004, from www.insession.com/casestudies/SVS_CaseStudy.pdf

20. "Hibernia National Bank Survives Hurricane Lili," *Continuity Insights*, March/April 2003, p. 50.

21. Christopher B. Pickett, "Strategies for Maximizing Supply Chain Resilience: Learning From the Past to Prepare for the Future," Master of Engineering in Logistics thesis, June 2003, Massachusetts Institute of Technology, Cambridge, Mass.

22. "Blair Moves to End Growing UK Fuel Crisis," *CNN.com*, September 12, 2000. Retrieved October 11, 2004, from edition.cnn.com/2000/WORLD/europe/09/12/london.fuel.02/

23. Following the tsunami in the Southeast Asia, there was a wide coverage of the various tsunami warning systems around the world. See, for example, Sharon Begley, "Tsunami Warnings Would Have Spared Lives Scientists Say," *Wall Street Journal*, December 28, 2004, p. B1.

24. For a review of supply chain applications of RFID tags, see, for example, Duncan McFarlane and Yossi Sheffi, "The Impact of Automatic Identification on Supply Chain Operations," *International Journal of Logistics Management* 14, no. 1 (2003): 1–17.

25. "Testing Begins on Anti-Terror Detection Methods," U.S. Water News Online, February 2003. Retrieved October 8, 2004, from www.uswaternews.com/archives/arcquality/3tesbeg2.html. This article contains the phrase "Is it anthrax or flour? Cyanide or almond paste?," which is used at the first paragraph of this section.

26. Barton Gellmon, "Fears Prompt U.S. to Beef Up Nuclear Terror Detection Sensors Deployed near D.C., Borders; Delta Force on Standby," *Washington Post*, March 3, 2002.

Chapter Ten

1. Robert Redding, Jr., "Brentwood Reopens after Anthrax Cases," *Washington Times,* December 23, 2003.

2. "Cleanup Set for Anthrax Post Office," *USA Today,* June 14, 2002.

3. Paul Schwartzman, "Postal Workers 'Edgy,' but Still Delivering," *Washington Post,* October 23, 2001, p. B01.

4. Marie Beaudette, "Maryland Post Office Gets Mail, After Anthrax Closes Facility in Washington, "*Capital News Service,* October 23, 2001.

5. "Fact Sheet: President Bush Signs Biodefense for the 21st Century," retrieved October 6, 2004, from www.dhs.gov/dhspublic/display?theme=43&content=3522&print=true

6. Yossi Sheffi, "Supply Chain Management under the Threat of International Terrorism," *International Journal of Logistics Management* 12, no. 2 (2001):1–11.

7. It was released after the 9/11 attack.

8. Such practice parallels "just in case" inventory management regime and can lead to sloppy processes and quality problems in the long run. To protect against high-impact events, it is generally better to keep separate redundant resources. That practice, however, may be too expensive for some companies.

9. Demand Flow Technology is a commercial version of lean enterprise principles. A general explanation can be found, for example in www.camstar.com/solutions/industries/popups/demand-flow-technology.html% (retrieved December 10, 2004.)

10. Claudia H. Deutsch, "Planes, Trucks and 7.5 Million Packages: FedEx's Big Night," *New York Times,* December 21, 2003.

11. J. Ballman, "Merrill Lynch Resumes Business Critical Functions within Minutes of Attack," *Disaster Recovery Journal* 4, no. 4 (2001). Retrieved October 12, 2004, from www.drj.com/special/wtc/1404–04.html

12. Six Sigma is a statistics-based methodology to measure and improve a company's operational performance. It is based on systematic identification and elimination of "defects" in manufacturing and service-related processes. The metric, Sigma = NORMSINV(1–(Defects/Cases)) + 1.5. Thus, Six Sigma equals 3.4 defects in a million cases. Six Sigma, however, is more than a metric; it entails an entire philosophy and methodology. See, for example, Peter S. Pande, Lawrence Holpp, Pete Pande and Larry Holpp, *What Is Six Sigma?* (New York: McGraw-Hill, 2001), or George Eckes, *Six Sigma for Everyone* (Hoboken, N.J.: Wiley, January 2003).

Chapter Eleven

1. Robert Ristelhueber, "SARS Virus Casts Pall over Electronics Supply Chain," *Electronic Supply & Manufacturing,* April 4, 2003.

2. The company does keep a single plant were experimentation is carried out and innovation tested, but the results are then implemented across the globe in the same way.

3. Chris J. McDonald, "The Evolution of Intel's Copy Exactly! Technology Transfer Method," *Intel Technology Journal,* 1998.

4. Ristelhueber, "SARS Virus Casts Pall over Electronics Supply Chain."

5. Based on an MIT CTL research team interview with Steve Lund on February 7, 2003.

6. "To Cut Costs, GM Is Adding Four Near-Identical Facilities," *Wall Street Journal,* August 4, 1997.

7. Marjorie Sorge, "GM Manufacturing Wants to Be Common." *Automotive Industries,* February 2000. Retrieved December 12, 2004, from www.findarticles.com/p/articles/mi_m3012/is_2_180/ai_59966980

8. Martin Piszczalski, "Thailand Tales: Profits Still Elusive," *Automotive Design & Production,* April 2002.

9. Drew Winter and David Zoia, *Ward Auto World,* March 1, 2001.

10. Hau L. Lee and Michael Wolfe, "Supply Chain Security without Tears." *Supply Chain Management Review* 7, no. 1 (January 1, 2003): 12.

11. Ken Cottrill, "Out of a 'Black Hole'; Lucent's Supply-Chain Networks Team Helped Charter the Way Back to Profitability by Connecting the Dots," *Traffic World,* November 10, 2003

12. Jim Carbone, "Lucent's Supply Chain Focus Fattens Margins," *Purchasing Magazine,* September 19, 2002.

13. Douglas Smock, "Lucent's Bright New Idea: Supply Chain Power," *Purchasing Magazine,* September 19, 2002.

14. UPS September 27, 2002, press release. Retrieved October 10, 2004, from www.pressroom.ups.com/pressreleases/archives/archive/0,1363,4170,00.html

15. Joseph Gerth, "Epic Storm Taught Area a Chilling Lesson." *Courier-Journal* (Louisville, Ky.), January 16, 2004.

16. Ibid.

17. Ibid.

18. Helix Technology Corporation, Form 10-K, December 31, 2003.

19. David Jensen, "Airlines as Jugglers," *Aviation Today,* January 2000.

20. "Easyjet Ditches Boeing for Airbus," BBC News, October 14, 2002. Retrieved October 20, 2004, from news.bbc.co.uk/2/hi/business/2325679.stm

21. Assuming the demands for the four computers are i.i.d.—independent and identically distributed. In other words, the demand for the four computers follow the same distribution and these demands are independent of each other.

Chapter Twelve

1. Postponement does not necessarily involve either outsourcing or off-shoring but these strategies accentuate the opportunity for postponement.

2. *1997 Annual Report*, Marks & Spencer, 1997. Retrieved September 10, 2004, from www2.marksandspencer.com/thecompany/investorrelations/pastannualreports/1997.shtml

3. Jane Simms, "Top Marks," *Marketing Business*, July/August 1998, pp. 26–30.

4. Martin Christopher and Helen Peck, "Moving Mountains at Marks & Spencer," Council of Logistics Management, Case Studies, 2001. Retrieved October 12, 2004, from clm1.org/Downloads/CaseStudy/ms.pdf.

5. Tom Buerkle, "Marks & Spencer Plans to Brighten Its Image," *International Herald Tribune*, May 19, 1999.

6. *1999 Annual Report*, Marks & Spencer, 1999.

7. Buerkle, "Marks & Spencer Plans to Brighten Its Image."

8. "Case Study: Stevensons Garment Dyers," *Industry Forum*. Retrieved October 12, 2004, from www.industryforum.net/assets/pdfs/stevesons.pdf

9. P. Dapiran, "Benetton—Global Logistics in Action," *International Journal of Physical Distribution & Logistics Management* 22, 1992 no. 6: 7–13.

10. Hau Lee, Corey Billington, and Brent Carter, "Hewlett-Packard Gains Control of Inventory and Service through Design for Localization," *Interfaces* 23 (July/August 1993): 1–11.

11. Corey Billington and Blake Johnson, "Creating and Leveraging Options in the High Technology Supply Chain," *Journal of Applied Corporate Finance*, 2000.

12. The number of options was retrieved from the Dell site on May 6, 2004: www1.us.dell.com/content/products/features.aspx/featured_desktop3?c=us&cs=19&l=en&s=dhs

13. Dell has no parts inventory since that inventory is carried by its suppliers and Dell does not pay for it until it is delivered to its plants.

14. To increase customer satisfaction, Sherwin Williams actually manufactures some of the most popular colors at its factory and stocks them in the retail stores. These fast-moving colors allow customers who want them to buy immediately, without waiting for the mixing operation in the store. This does not increase significantly either the inventory costs or the forecasting challenge since these are the few colors that sell in high volume.

15. UPS press release, August 9, 2004. Retrieved October 20, 2004, from: www.ec.ups.com/ecommerce/clicks/trade_direct.html

Chapter Thirteen

1. "Sony to Cut Number of Suppliers," *Taipei Times*, August 19, 2003, p. 11.

2. James Rice and Richard Hoppe, "Supply Chain vs. Supply Chain: The Hype and the Reality," *Supply Chain Management Review*, September–October 2001.

3. The structure and nature of the chaebols and keiretsu groups is described in many references. See, for example, Rafael La Porta, Florencio Lopez-de-Silane, and Andrei Shleifer, "Corporate Ownership around the World," *Harvard Institute of Economic Research Paper* no. 1840, August 1998. See also Stephen Ferris, Kenneth Kim, and Pattanaporn Kitsabunnarat, "The Costs (and Benefits?) of Diversified Business Groups: The Case of Korean Chaebols," *Journal of Banking & Finance* 27 (2003): 251–273.

4. Toshihiro Nishiguchi and Alexandre Beaudet, "The Toyota Group and the Aisin Fire," *Sloan Management Review* 40, no. 1 (1998): 49–59.

5. Ibid.

6. Chris Koepfer, "A 'Just-In-Case' Case." *Modern Machine Shop Online*, September 11, 2001. Retrieved October 12, 2004, from www.mmsonline.com/columns/0497et.html.

7. Nishiguchi and Beaudet, "The Toyota Group and the Aisin Fire."

8. Valerie Reitman, "Toyota Motor Shows Its Mettle after Fire Destroys Parts Plant," *Wall Street Journal*, May 8, 1997. p A1.

9. Ibid.

10. Nishiguchi and Beaudet, "The Toyota Group and the Aisin Fire."

11. Ibid.

12. "Mitch: The Deadliest Atlantic Hurricane Since 1780," *National Oceanic and Atmospheric Administration*, January 25, 1999. Retrieved October 12, 2004, from lwf.ncdc.noaa.gov/oa/reports/mitch/mitch.html

13. Ibid.

14. The original quote is usually attributed to Andrew Carnegie.

15. Christopher B. Pickett, "Strategies for Maximizing Supply Chain Resilience: Learning from the Past to Prepare for the Future," Master of Engineering in Logistics thesis, June 2003, Massachusetts Institute of Technology, Cambridge, Mass.

16. Jim Stanton, "Land Rover Jobs at Risk after Bust Up," *Scotsman. Business.Com*, January 14, 2002. Retrieved February 27, 2005, from business. Scotsman.com/topics.ctm?tid=1036Aid-50952002

17. From the U.K. Parliament records. See www.parliament.the-stationery-office.co.uk/pa/cm200102/cmhansrd/vo020124/debtext/20124–08.htm

18. Cranfield University School of Management, "Creating Resilient Supply Chains: A Practical Guide," U.K. Department of Transport report, 2003.

19. Pickett, "Strategies for Maximizing Supply Chain Resilience."

20. P. Hoult, "Land Rover's Rough Ride," *Legal Week*, September 12, 2002.

21. J. Martha and S. Subbakrishna, "Targeting a Just-in-Case Supply Chain for the Inevitable Next Disaster," *Supply Chain Management Review*, September/ October 2002, pp. 18–23.

22. Another well-known example is the oil market. When a pipe in Iraq is blown up the price of crude climbs around the world.

23. Jack Neff, "Wal-Mart Weans Suppliers: Retail Behemoth Doesn't Want to Be 'Sole Source of Survival' for Vendors," *Advertising Age* 74, no. 48 (December 1, 2003): 1.

24. The CDC site contains information about the flu in the United States. See www.cdc.gov/flu/

25. Shawn Rhea, "Warning Signs Could have Predicted Flu Shot Crisis," Courier Post Online, November 7, 2004. www.courierpostonline.com/columnists/cxrh110704a.htm

26. Associated Press, "Officials Found Earlier Contamination at Flu Vaccine Plant," *New York Times*, November 18, 2004, p. 24.

27. Shawn Rhea, "Warning Signs Could Have Predicted Flu Shot Crisis."

28. Jim Rice and Federico Caniato, "Supply Chain Response to Terrorism: Creating Resilient and Secure Supply Chains," *Interim Report of Progress and Learnings*, Supply Chain Response to Terrorism Project, MIT Center for Transportation and Logistics, Cambridge, Mass., August 8, 2003.

29. Author's interview with Shlomo Sherf, managing director of Electra Ltd. Rishon Le-Zion, Israel, July 13, 2003.

30. As the performance of 64-bit AMD server processors started to best Intel's products, several analysts' reports suggested that Dell may start using AMD as a second processor manufacturer, despite its long-term relationships with Intel. Dell CEO disclosed such intentions during an interview with Infoworld. Retrieved December 20 from www.infoworld.com/article/04/11/11/HNdelltouseamd_1.html.

Chapter Fourteen

1. "Taiwan Quake Starts to Hit Chip Supply," *Electronics Weekly*, October 6, 1999. p. 2.

2. Jerry Ascierto, "Supply-Chain Blues Hit Apple," *Electronic News* 45, no. 42 (October 18, 1991): 4.

3. Tom Quinlan, "PC Prices Taking an Unusual Turn: Up," *San Jose Mercury News*, October 20, 1999, p. A1(2).

4. "PC Makers Feel the Pinch," *Electronics Times*, October 25, 1999, p. 4. Retrieved October, 16, 2004, from www.findarticles.com/p/articles/mi_m0WVI/is_1999_Oct_25/ai_57482917

5. J. Martha, and S. Subbakrishna, "Targeting a Just-in-Case Supply Chain for the Inevitable Next Disaster," *Supply Chain Management Review*, September/October 2002, pp. 18–23.

6. Quinlan, "PC Prices Taking an Unusual Turn."

7. Dell does not view demand as an exogenous force. Rather, it sees demand as something that the company can and should manage. The forecast is set by the salesperson, and the salesperson is accountable to sell everything in the plan. This prevents wildly optimistic sales plans leading to purchase of excess inventory. And accountability is reinforced because salespeople are compensated on selling their plan. Changing prices and configurations in near-real-time, Dell can then steer demand to fit available supply.

8. Stuart Smith, "Building the Culture and Systems to Manage Uncertainty at Dell," conference presentation in *The New Frontier for Managing Supply Network Uncertainty*, The Stanford GSM Forum and MIT Center for Transportation and Logistics joint conference, Cambridge, Mass., December 3–4, 2003.

9. "PC Makers Feel the Pinch."

10. Christopher B. Pickett, "Strategies for Maximizing Supply Chain Resilience: Learning from the Past to Prepare for the Future," Master of Engineering in Logistics thesis, June 2003, Massachusetts Institute of Technology, Cambridge, Mass.

11. Tom Andel, "I Need It Now!" *Material Handling Engineering* 54, no. 8 (August 1999).

12. Krich Srinivasan, "Service Parts Logistics at Caterpillar: What Works: Both Old and New," Caterpillar Logistics Services, Inc. Presentation in the seminar: *Service Parts Inventory Management*, MIT Center for Transportation and Logistics, Cambridge, Mass., March 19–20, 2002.

13. Andel, "I Need It Now!"

14. Srinivasan, "Service Parts Logistics at Caterpillar."

15. Andel, "I Need It Now!"

16. "TSMC Global Earthquake Response," Fleishman Hillard Crisis Communications: Business, Taiwan Semiconductor Manufacturing Company. 2000. Retrieved October 12, 2004, from www.fleishman.com/overview/reputation/silver_anvil/kvo.html

17. Ibid.

18. SSB stands for "single side band." A sideband is a band of frequencies higher than or lower than the carrier frequency, containing energy as a result of the modulation process. Transmission in which only one sideband is transmitted is called single-sideband transmission. It is used mainly in amateur radio. Its use significantly reduces the amount of electrical power used (by up to 12 times), while still leaving the audio or other information present in the sideband. See, for example, www.wordiq.com/definition/Single_Side_Band

19. Norman Augustine, "Managing the Crisis You Tried to Prevent," *Harvard Business Review*, November-December 1995, pp. 146–158.

20. Other car companies, who were also accused of sudden acceleration, quietly instituted a switch which requires pressing the brake while engaging the gear in reverse, a mechanism that is still prevalent today.

21. The nature of the mathematical issue is described, for example, in www.willamette.edu/~mjaneba/pentprob.html.

22. Ibid.

23. To see Intel's announcement of the chip replacement program and its many rules, refer to support.intel.com/support/processors/pentium/sb/CS-012748.htm. The document was clearly written by an engineer or a lawyer and not a marketing executive. It meant that even while replacing the chips Intel looked at the program as a necessary evil, not as a brand enhancing opportunity.

24. Howard Lutnick, "Where Were You When . . . September 11, One Year On," *BBC News*. Retrieved October 12, 2004, from news.bbc.co.uk/1/shared/spl/hi/world/02/september_11/where_were_you_when/html/2.stm

25. Jaikumar Vijayan, "IT Redundancy Helps Bond Trader Rebound From Attacks," *Computerworld*, December 10, 2001.

26. Meryl Gordon, "Howard Lutnick's Second Life," *New York Magazine*, December 10, 2001. Retrieved October 12, 2004, from www.newyorkmetro.com/nymetro/news/sept11/features/5486/

27. "Cantor CEO Pledges Profits to Victims' Families," *CNN*, September 20, 2001. Retrieved October 12, 2004, from www.cnn.com/2001/U.S./09/20/vic.ceo.victims.families/

28. Andrew Clark, "Missing 700 Taken off Cantor Payroll, Families Upset by Decision," *Guardian*, September 27, 2001. Retrieved October 12, 2004, from www.guardian.co.uk/wtccrash/story/0,1300,558816,00.html

29. Joseph Martha and Eric Vratimos, "Creating a Just-in-Case Supply Chain for the Inevitable Disaster," *Mercer Management Journal*, no. 14, November 2002. Retrieved October 12, 2004, from www.mercermc.com/defaultFlash.asp?section=Perspectives

30. Greg Ip, "Companies Are Seeing Efficiencies Erode as Security Worries Drag on Productivity," *Wall Street Journal*, October 24, 2001.

31. Gale Morrison, "Taiwan Continues to Rattle Supply Chain," *Electronic News*, no. 45 (November 8, 1999).

32. Pickett, "Strategies for Maximizing Supply Chain Resilience."

33. D. Armstrong, V. Hua, and P. Sarker, "Idling Time: The West Coast Shutdown Is Beginning to Hurt Workers and Industries Dependent on Imports," *San Francisco Chronicle*, October 3, 2002. Retrieved October 12, 2004, from lists.iww.org/pipermail/iww-news/2002-October/000351.html.

34. U.S. Centers for Disease Control, *Interim Influenza Vaccination Recommendations—2004–05 Influenza Season*. Retrieved October 12, 2004, from www.cdc.gov/flu/protect/whoshouldget.htm

Chapter Fifteen

1. Chapter 8 brought up some aspects of a security culture. The focus in chapter 15 is on flexibility culture that contributes to resilience.

2. This definition is based on H. Schwarz and S. M. Davis, "Matching Corporate Culture and Business Strategy," *Organisational Dynamics* 14 (Summer 1981): 30–37. Other definitions are described in Abby Benson, "The Role of Organizational Culture in Creating Secure and Resilient Supply Chains," Master of Engineering in Logistics thesis, June 2005, Massachusetts Institute of Technology, Cambridge, Mass.

3. These definitions follow the work of Edgar H. Schein, *Organizational Culture and Leadership,* 2nd ed. (San Francisco: Jossey-Bass, 1992).

4. Google uses a similar philosophy, allowing its software developers to spend up to 20 percent of their time on their own projects. One such project led in 2004 to the Google News feature (news.google.com).

5. This view of Toyota was suggested by my colleague, Professor Charley Fine of the MIT Sloan School of Management.

6. This section is based, in part, on Blaine Paxton, "The Dell Operating Model," master's thesis at the Leaders for Manufacturing Program, Massachusetts Institute of Technology, Cambridge, Mass., May 2004.

7. See comment 12 in chapter 10.

8. Based on presentation given by Chris Holt, vice president of UPS Consulting in San Jose on October 14, 2004. Chris is a graduate of the Master of Engineering in Logistics program at MIT.

9. "I.T. as an Aircraft Carrier," *MoreBusiness.com.* Retrieved October 15, 2004, from www.morebusiness.com/running_your_business/management/d924553790.brc

10. Gene I. Rochlin, Todd R. La Porte, and Karlene H. Roberts, "The Self-Designing High Reliability Organization: Aircraft Carrier Flight Operations at Sea," *Naval War College Review*, Autumn 1987.

11. Herb Kelleher, "A Culture of Commitment," *Leader to Leader*, 4 (Spring 1997): 20–24. The article was retrieved October 15, 2004, from the Leader to Leader Institute Web site, leadertoleader.org/leaderbooks/L2L/spring97/kelleher.html.

12. Interview with Rear Adm. Mark P. Fitzgerald, Commander of U.S.S. Theodore Roosevelt Battle Group. Retrieved December 15, 2004, from www.navyleague.org/seapower_mag/sept2001/ready_gameday.htm

13. When leaders ask employees to sacrifice without showing personal example, the result is low morale and bad service. As U.S. Air was pressuring its workers for another round of salary cuts in December 2004, many employees called in sick, in a show of defiance not organized by their union, creating havoc with the Christmas 2004 holiday travel season. Many sited the fact that CEO Bruce Lakefield kept his generous compensation package while asking for employees' sacrifices as a reason for calling in sick.

14. Marshall L. Fisher, Anna McClellan, and Ananth Raman, "Supply Chain Management at World Co. Ltd.," *Harvard Business Case Study 9-601-072*, April 4, 2001.

15. Kelleher, "A Culture of Commitment."

16. Stephen Ambrose, *Citizen Soldiers: The U.S. Army from the Normandy Beaches to the Bulge to the Surrender of Germany, June 7, 1944–May 7, 1945*, reprint ed. (New York: Simon & Schuster, September 24, 1998).

17. The term *mindfulness* is used to describe high-reliability organizations (such as aircraft carriers, nuclear power plants and firefighting crews) by Karl Weick and Kathleen Sutcliff, *Managing the Unexpected: Assuring High Performance in the Age of Complexity*, University of Michigan Business School Management Series (San Francisco: Jossey-Bass, 2001).

18. "Auxillium West—The HR Manager—Corporate Culture." Retrieved October 16 from www.auxillium.com/culture.shtml.

19. Kelleher Part 3: Great Employees Lay the Foundation for Great Business, Business Week Online, December 24, 2003. Retrieved December 15, 2004, from www.businessweek.com/bwdaily/dnflash/dec2003/nf20031224_2773_db062.htm

20. See Maslow's hierarchy of needs in Abraham Maslow, *Motivation and Personality*, 2nd ed. (New York: Harper & Row, 1970).

21. Benson, "The Role of Organizational Culture in Greating Secure and Resilient Supply Chains."

22. Geoffrey Mika and Kaizen Sensei, "Eliminate All Muda," *Manufacturing Engineering: Quality Scan* 126, no. 4 (April 2001). Retrieved in October 2004 from www.sme.org/manufacturingengineering.

23. Weick and Sutcliff, *Managing the Unexpected: Assuring High Performance in the Age of Complexity*.

24. Janice Lord, "Really MADD: Looking Back at 20 Years," *Driven Magazine*, Spring 2000. Retrieved October 16, 2004, from www.madd.org/aboutus/0,1056,1686,00.html

25. Gordon Bethune, *From Worst to First: Behind the Scenes of Continental's Remarkable Comeback*, new ed. (Hoboken, N.J.: Wiley, 1999).

26. See, for example a CNN-Money report retrieved October 16 from money.cnn.com/2004/02/25/technology/business2_culture/

Chapter Sixteen

1. Amit Mukherjee, "Planning for an Ambiguous World," A Forrester Case Study, Forrester Research, March 2003.

2. There are numerous books and other sources regarding the use of EVA. See, for example, J. L. Grant, *Foundation of Economic Value Added*, 2nd ed. (Wiley, September 2002).

3. The level of risk is not reflected in standard financial report and therefore will rarely be reflected in the firm's stock price.

4. Perversely, the 2002 Sarbanes-Oxley act, which was put in place in the United States to increase the accountability of senior management, may have created incentives not to perform proper risk analysis. Given the litigious environment in the United States, senior officers and board members will forever be faced with the allegation that not enough was done to avoid and mitigate risks if a disruption, whose risk was identified, were to take place. Some senior executives and board members may feel that if the risks are not identified, they will not be subject to personal responsibility for failing to avoid them. Good business practices, however, demand risk assessment and a proper investment to mitigate risks. If the risks and the costs of risk mitigation are diligently assessed and the business judgment well-reasoned, counsel will, no doubt, find a way to properly document the process to minimize unwarranted liability.

5. While safety stock can also be used to smooth out day-to-day operations, recall that the thesis of this book (set forth in chapter 10) is that if extra safety stock is used, it should not be allowed to create "slop" but rather managed in a SOSO (Sell One Stock One) fashion and used only in severe emergencies.

6. In some cases, insurance premiums may be lowered for resilient organizations. But most insurers do not have the tools to assess whether their insured's actions will so reduce the likelihood of an intentional attack that the insurer would offer proper discounts. An exception was relayed to the author by Nissim Malchi, chief financial officer of El Al. While negotiating their new insurance rate in London with a group of insurance companies, a note was delivered to El Al's chief negotiator, Yoram Golan, saying that a bomb has just been found on an El Al plane. It was discovered and dismantled without an incident by El Al security. After a moment of hesitation, Golan showed the insurance executives the note. They were all stunned and asked for a a few minutes to confer privately. After many long minutes the El Al team was called in and was told that this was a proof, for the insurance team, that El Al has strong security measures and their rates would not be affected by the incident.

7. CBP officials have stated publicly that C-TPAT certified companies are six time less likely to be selected for an enforcement examination than non members, and three times less likely to be selected for a commercial examination. CBP Commissioner Robert Bonner described the "green lane" in October 2003 as "C-TPAT shippers sending their goods through CSI ports, via C-TPAT carriers, to C-TPAT importers in the United States. If all of those pieces line up, those shipments should and will get the green lane through the border and into American commerce. If all those pieces line up, we know that those shipments are low risk, and our officers ordinarily won't need to waste their time inspecting them."

8. A different taxonomy of the collateral benefits of security is catalogued by Jim Rice and Philip Spayd, "Collateral Benefits of Security," MIT Center for Transportation and Logistics Report, Cambridge, Mass., (expected) May 2005.

9. Interview with the MIT project team, October 1, 2004.

10. Interview with the MIT project team, November 17, 2004.

Index